D0721685

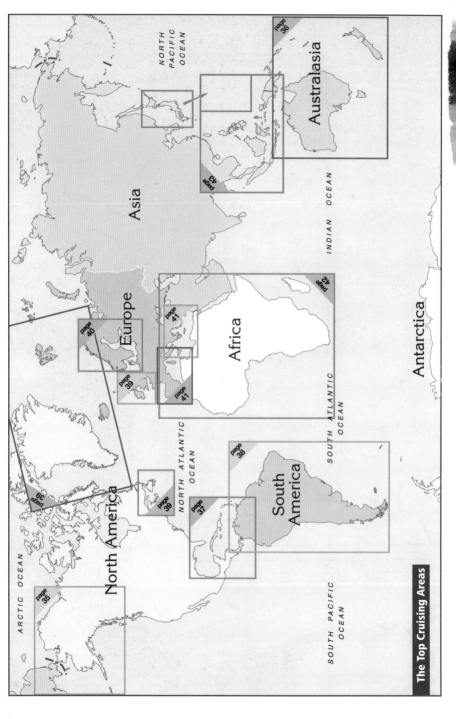

The Top Cruising Areas

✷ INSIGHT GUIDES

CRUISING
ALL QUESTIONS ANSWERED

DOUGLAS WARD
THE WORLD'S FOREMOST AUTHORITY ON CRUISING

APA PUBLICATIONS | L |

Part of the Langenscheidt Publishing Group

2

☀ INSIGHT GUIDES

CRUISING
ALL QUESTIONS ANSWERED

Written by
Douglas Ward
Managing Editor
Brian Bell

Distribution

United States
Langenscheidt Publishers, Inc.
36–36 33rd Street 4th Floor
Long Island City, NY 11106
Fax: (1) 718 784-0640

Worldwide
**Apa Publications GmbH & Co.
Verlag KG (Singapore branch)**
38 Joo Koon Road, Singapore 628990
Tel: (65) 6865-1600.
Fax: (65) 6861-6438

Printing

Insight Print Services (Pte) Ltd
38 Joo Koon Road, Singapore 628990
Tel: (65) 6865-1600.
Fax: (65) 6861-6438

©2008 Apa Publications GmbH & Co.
Verlag KG (Singapore branch)
All Rights Reserved

First Edition 2008

The UK edition of this book is
published as a Berlitz title, *The
First-Time Cruise Guide*

CONTACTING THE EDITORS

We would appreciate it if readers
would alert us to errors or outdated
information by writing to:

**Apa Publications, P.O. Box 7910,
London SE1 1WE, England.
Fax: (44) 20 7403-0290.
insight@apaguide.co.uk**

THE RIGHT CHOICE FOR YOU
Douglas Ward explains how this book helps you find it

Cruising has become one of the travel industry's fastest growing sectors. That's not surprising: cruises cover a wide range of destinations and offer notably good value for money.

But, with about 80 companies catering for more than 16 million passengers a year, the variety can initially be baffling. Pick a ship or destination that doesn't satisfy your taste and a cruise will disappoint every bit as much as an ill-chosen land-based vacation.

That's where this book comes in. It will help you define what you are looking for in a cruise vacation and advises you on how to find it. It provides a wealth of information, including a look at life aboard ship and how to get the best from it. More than 350 ships, from large resort vessels to luxury boutique ships, are rated. Specialist cruises are discussed, too, culminating with that ultimate travel experience: the around-the-world cruise. Lavish photography aims to convey the cruise experience, and practical advice is given on how to prepare for it. What's more, the book is totally independent and is not subsidized by advertising or sponsorship of any kind.

Defining what's good

Having spent over 5,400 days at sea participating in more than 970 cruises, I can promise you that my advice is born of experience and not hear-say.

My first job at sea was as leader of a small jazz and dance band aboard Cunard Line's *Queen Elizabeth*, then the

Cruise ship congestion in the US Virgin Islands.

Ward inspects a ship's deck.

world's largest passenger ship. Over 17 years, I worked for eight cruise companies, lastly as cruise director. Then, in 1984, I wrote the first edition of what has become the annual 700-page *Berlitz Complete Guide to Ocean Cruising and Cruise Ships*, from which the present book draws some material.

For the *Complete Guide*, I devised a ratings system which has long been accepted within the industry. I allocate each ship a maximum possible score of 2,000 points, systematically based on its general profile and condition, its food, accommodation, service, and quality of the cruise operation. This system, relying on rigorous measurement and observation over many years, forms the basis for the rankings given to the 350-plus ships in the comprehensive chart at the back of this book.

I hope that this book will help you find the right ship and destination for your requirements. Please be aware that, although sample prices are provided for such things as extra-cost restaurants, spa treatments and other items, prices may have changed since this book went to press.

CONTENTS

Pictured: Disney Cruise Lines show.

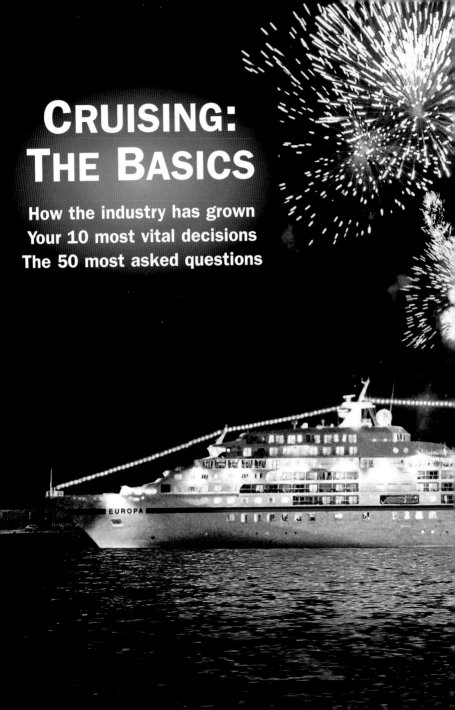

CRUISING:
THE BASICS

How the industry has grown
Your 10 most vital decisions
The 50 most asked questions

EUROPA

WHY CRUISE VACATIONS ARE POWERING AHEAD

Douglas Ward, veteran of almost 1,000 cruises, explains why ocean-going ships have shaken off their old elitist image and are attracting more than 16 million passengers a year worldwide

Compared to most land vacations, cruises offer great value for money. For a start, the initial fare includes your accommodation, main meals and in-between snacks, entertainment, lectures, social functions, participation events, movies, and use of the ship's facilities, including the fitness centre, casino, and perhaps air tickets and transfers to get to and from your cruise ship. You can be as active, or as relaxed and pampered as you like – and you have to pack and unpack only once.

You can choose whether to begin your cruise at a US or Canadian port or to save time by flying to a foreign port to join the cruise ship there. If you're planning a Euro-pean cruise, of course, you'll have to fly, unless you have the time and funds to treat yourself to an old-style transatlantic crossing on the *Queen Mary 2*.

Cruising from US/Canadian ports

This is often dubbed "Homeland Cruising" – a term introduced by Norwegian Cruise Line in 2002 – and, with a choice of more than 4,000 cruises to choose from, there should be one to suit your needs. You can simply drive or take the train to a local port city, or take a domestic flight to get to it.

Honolulu and San Juan are considered domestic flights for Americans, while Canadian embarkation ports are designated international flights. Likewise, American ports are considered as international destinations if you fly from Canada. Some cruise lines provide bus transportation to many of the ports.

There are about 20 such ports, including: Baltimore, Bayonne (Cape Liberty), Boston, Charleston, Ft. Lauderdale (Port Everglades), Galveston, Gulfport, Honolulu, Houston, Jacksonville, Los Angeles (Long Beach or San Pedro), Miami, New Orleans, New York City, New York (Red Hook Point, Brooklyn), Norfolk, Philadelphia, Port Canaveral, St. Thomas, San Diego, San

> *More than 350 ocean-going cruise ships, each carrying from 50 to more than 5,000 passengers, visit almost 2,000 destinations around the world each year.*

Carnival Victory cruises out of Miami, Florida.

Francisco, San Juan, Seattle, Tampa, and Wilmington; and from the Canadian ports of Montreal and Vancouver. Many smaller ports cater for the very small ships that cruise along the coastal areas and inland waterways of the Continental United States and Canada.

Most ports also have car parking facilities for cruise passengers at reduced fees, and these can be reserved and confirmed when you make your cruise booking.

While some, like Miami and Fort Lauderdale, have good facilities for checking in, many do not, and long lines are the result, particularly when 50 motorcoaches arrive at almost the same time. For a rating of North American ports, see the table on page 11.

One downside of "Homeland Cruising" – for some people, anyway – is that a ship sailing out of, say, Philadelphia, will attract many other people from the surrounding area, and that could mean you'll bump into any of your neighbors who've had the same idea as you. It also makes for particularly strong regional dialects aboard any given ship, and can even change the ways that passengers act and dress.

New York ports

Note that different cruise lines use different ports for cruises starting from New York. Cunard Line and Princess Cruises use Red

12 REASONS TO TAKE A CRUISE

❶ **Value.** The package includes accommodation, food and travel – though you have to watch out for extras.

❷ **Convenience.** You may be able to drive to your port of embarkation. If not, the cruise line can arrange flights, baggage handling, and transfers to and from the ship. And you only have to unpack once.

❸ **Choice.** There are over 30,000 cruises to choose from, covering virtually the entire globe.

❹ **See new places.** The ship will change the destination for you, and shore excursions add local flavor.

❺ **Comfort.** A suite or cabin – your home from home – can be as small as a tent (at about 60 sq. ft) or as large as a villa (at 3,000 sq. ft).

❻ **Good Food.** All meals are included, from breakfast through to midnight snacks.

❼ **Family Togetherness.** Many ships have supervised activities for children. Cruising is also a great way for groups of friends to vacation together.

❽ **Make new friends.** The relaxed environment encourages you to meet like-minded people.

❾ **Learning Experience.** Most cruise ships have lecturers, covering a wide range of subjects.

❿ **Adventure.** A cruise can take you places impossible to reach by almost any other means, such as the Antarctic Peninsula, the Arctic, or to remote islands.

⓫ **Staying Healthy.** You can pamper yourself in a spa (though usually at extra cost).

⓬ **Entertainment.** Professional entertainment ranges from spectacular Vegas-style production shows to intimate piano bars. Some ships have rock faces to climb and electronic golf simulators.

A whalewatching trip along Alaska's Inside Passage.

Hook Point Terminal, Brooklyn. Norwegian Cruise Line uses the recently refurbished Passenger Ship Terminal, Manhattan (Pier 90, 12th Avenue/48th Street). Celebrity Cruises and Royal Caribbean International use Cape Liberty, Bayonne, New Jersey, which is almost impossible to get to by public transportation.

Cruising from non-US ports

To join cruises that sail from ports not on the North American continent, you'll need to fly to get to and from the embarkation and disembarkation ports. When the embarkation port is a long way from home – for example, in Europe, Southeast Asia, Australia or New Zealand – it's a good idea to fly a few days before the cruise begins. This gives you time to get used to the new time zone, see a few sights – and perhaps, if an airline is having a bad day, to allow baggage to catch up with you.

Early booking means greater savings. Also, many lines let you extend your vacation and have special pre- and post-cruise hotel/resort or safari game-park extra stay packages available at appealing rates.

To Alaska via Canada

The US Passenger Services Act of 1886 requires that only US flag and US-built vessels can be used to carry passengers between two US ports, but it allows foreign-flag vessel to pick up or drop off passengers while calling at a single US port.

Since most large cruise ships are registered not in the United States but with a foreign-flag nation (such as the Bahamas, Bermuda, Liberia, Malta, Panama, and the United Kingdom), most cruises to Alaska start and end in Vancouver, British Columbia. This meets the Act's requirements, but it does have the effect of keeping business away from ports such as Seattle, San Francisco and Los Angeles.

Passports

If you don't have one, apply in plenty of time. If you have one that's valid for less than six months, you'll need to replace it. Remember to check passports of all family members, including children.

Apply in good time for all visas required for a trip. Some countries impose a time limit for a visit starting from the visa's date of issue. Your passport should have at least two pages blank because some countries need both a left- and right-hand page to accommodate their imposing visa. Some countries may also require you to supply an International Vaccination Certificate with a visa application. In case you lose your passport while traveling, make a copy of its details and carry them with you separately.

Terminal ambitions

While no cruise line has yet acquired its own port, cruise companies such as P&O and Star Cruises own and operate some cruise terminals. However, more cruise lines are now building and managing passenger terminals in conjunction with local port authorities. Costa Cruises, for example, has built – and manages – a terminal in Barcelona. It began operating in 2006 and has berthing priority for all ships in the Carnival Corporation portfolio of cruise companies.

Familiar and unfamiliar food

Most cruise lines feature mainly American-style cuisine, or cuisine that is often described as international, while more European-style cuisine is typically provided

Large resort ships put on Las Vegas-style shows.

THE BEST AND THE WORST NORTH AMERICAN (HOMELAND) PORTS

After the terrorist attacks of September 11, 2001, many American passengers simply didn't want to fly overseas, and so the main US-based cruise lines decided to start sending more ships cruising from US and Canadian ports. This resulted in "Homeland Cruising ports." The half a dozen ports that ships regularly sailed from grew almost overnight to around 25.

One of the unfortunate results of the "fear of terror" mentality was that overnight the welcoming by personnel in embarkation ports – called the "hospitality factor" – decreased dramatically, as all passengers were treated as potential terrorists.

Sadly, the "hospitality factor" has turned into the "hostility factor," with many overenthusiastic security personnel at ports having undergone a hospitality by-pass. After so many complaints, the Maritime Evaluations Group has built a detailed picture of ports and the user-friendliness and hospitality factors during both embarkation and disembarkation, with a possible total score of 100.

As a benchmark, the terminal facilities, luggage handling, user-friendliness and hospitality factor of personnel at the Port of Yokohama in Japan would score an excellent 94 out of 100. The comparisons are telling.

● Included in this chart: terminals and appearance and cleanliness, security personnel, attitude, check-in, security control, luggage handling by porters (often seeking tips), ease of disembarkation, immigration and customs, security personnel, luggage storage and identification system, porters, and ease of access to transportation and car parks.

FACILITIES RATED OUT OF 100

Port	Total
Baltimore	63
Boston	44
Cape Liberty, Bayonne, New Jersey	57
Charleston	53
Fort Lauderdale (Port Everglades)	45
Galveston	45
Gulfport	44
Honolulu	54
Houston	42
Jacksonville	44
Los Angeles (Long Beach)	48
Los Angeles (San Pedro)	52
Miami	38
Montreal	53
New Orleans	50
New York (Brooklyn)	54
New York (Manhattan)	47
Norfolk	52
Philadelphia	49
Port Canaveral	54
St. Thomas	51
San Diego	55
San Francisco	49
San Juan	46
Seattle	59
Tampa	53
Vancouver	71

Disney Cruise Line creates that theme park feel.

aboard the ships of European cruise lines (examples: Cunard Line, Fred Olsen Cruise Lines, Hebridean International Cruises, and P&O Cruises).

Note that beef, lamb and pork cuts are different on both sides of the Atlantic, so what you ordered may not be quite the cut, shape or size you thought it was going to be.

For example, there are 15 British cuts of beef, 17 American cuts, and 24 French cuts. There are 6 American cuts of lamb, 8 British cuts, and 9 French cuts. There are 8 American cuts of pork, 10 British cuts, and 17 French cuts.

While American passengers typically like iced water, or a jug of iced tea at lunch, most European passengers don't like ice in their water, and few drink iced tea.

If you care about cutlery, note that only a few cruise lines with large resort ships provide the correct, specially shaped fish knives, or the correct soup spoons (oval for thin bouillon-style soups and round for creamy soups).

The way ahead

The trend toward large resort ships is continuing. Some 33 ships over 100,000 tons are already in service and are due to be joined by 15 more by the end of 2012. Royal Caribbean International's next ship is designed to carry up to 6,400 passengers.

But some lines will highlight small ship cruising to appeal to those who don't like crowds. One advantage of these smaller ships is that they can dock at many delightful ports around the world which can't accommodate the large resort ships.

Another trend is toward expedition and nature cruises, which are fully covered in this book. Adventurous shore excursions, from dog sledding in Alaska to elephant riding in Thailand, are also on the increase. ❏

10 Myths About Cruises

❶ Cruising's not for me
Singles, families, couples, honeymooners, second honeymooners and groups of friends enjoy cruises. That covers most people.

❷ I'm going to get seasick
Technology makes today's cruise ships very stable, and fewer than 3 percent of all cruise passengers ever feel seasick. If you *are* concerned, choose a cabin in the center of the ship, on a lower deck, where there would be minimal movement.

❸ Cruise ships are too confining
The scenery constantly changes and you can visit many ports. Itineraries are planned so that most days are spent on shore and you cruise through the night to wake up in a new destination (possibly even a new country).

❹ Cruises are expensive
Compared to land-based holidays, where so many incidentals soon add up, a cruise is a bargain. Remember: most essential items are pre-paid. Things get expensive only when you succumb to the blandishments of the bars, casino, spa, premium dining rooms, art auctions and organized shore excursions.

❺ There's nothing to do
Activities range from fencing, bowling and bungee-jumping to enjoying hot-stone massages, steambaths, saunas and facials in the ship's spa. Specialist lecturers cater for a wide range of interests. Evening entertainment aboard the large resort ships includes ice-skating shows, Broadway-style stage productions, nightclubs, lounges, and casinos. Whether you want to relax by the pool, go parasailing over coral reefs, or ziplining over rain forests, there is no lack of options.

❻ It's too formal
Today's ships have few formal evenings in the dining room, and these are optional. Many cruise lines offer casual, alternative dining options. And, if even that's too much effort, there is always room service – perhaps on your own balcony.

❼ I will have to be seated for dinner with people I don't know
Although many cruise ships have assigned seating for dinner, some have "eat when you want, where you want, and with whom you want" dining. Most also have casual eateries that can provide a change from assigned tables and fixed dining times.

❽ There's too much food
The array of food is tempting, but eating doesn't have to be an all-day activity. Simply take small portions, and have balanced meals; many ships have low-cal, low-fat, heart-healthy or spa meals.

Choose a large resort ship and you can walk for miles – literally. Use the stairs instead of taking the lift, and you'll stay fit. There are wellness/health spas, technogyms filled with weapons of mass reduction, and steam rooms and saunas.

Children have easy access to computers.

❾ The children will be bored
They can not only be creative with arts and crafts activities, but can also discover new friends, and learn about many things. On many ships, teenagers have their own lounges and clubs.

❿ I'll be out of touch
Most ships today have internet connectivity 24/7, at a comfortable price (about 50 cents a minute). Some have ship-wide wi-fi connectivity, and satellite telephone communications, and you can call home if necessary – though this can be pricey. ❑

THE 10 DECISIONS FIRST-TIME CRUISEGOERS SHOULD MAKE

Word-of-mouth recommendations are useful but reflect personal likes and dislikes. It's important to decide at an early stage what your own priorities are. Here's how...

❶ Find a specialist

While the internet will tell you what's on offer, almost all internet cruise sites are supported by advertising, suggesting bias towards preferred cruise suppliers or last-minute booking consolidators. It pays to *find a specialist cruise agent* at an early stage. Be wary of internet-only "agencies" with slick websites – some have been known to disappear suddenly without trace.

A good agent will talk you through all the important details, such as choice of cabin, dining seating, ships and cruise lines best suites to your needs. Their advice is free, and they also should be able to recommend pre- and post-cruise programs, and travel and hotel arrangements to suit you.

They also know that for you to become a *repeat* client, they must find the ship, cruise line, and cruise that's right for you, for the right reasons. They are able to consider many lines and cruise products in order to point you in the best direction, as well as find the most attractive fares available.

It's important to define what you are looking for in a first cruise – adventure, activity, fun, relaxation, visiting specific destinations – and this book is designed to help you clarify your preferences.

❷ Where and when?

Choose where you want to go from the wide variety of destinations described on pages 32–6. And decide when you want to cruise. Alaska cruises operate only in summer, when the Caribbean may be too hot for some tastes. Northern Europe is best in summer, while South America and Southeast Asia are best in winter. If a special theme appeals, choose your season accordingly – for example, Carnival in Venice, Carnival in Rio, Formula One racing in Monte Carlo.

❸ How long?

Decide on the length of cruise you can afford. If your embarkation port isn't close to home, allow for the extra journey time. The standard length of a Caribbean cruise is seven

LEFT: a Costa cruise ship heads into Dubai.

days – although three- or four-day cruises from US ports to the Bahamas or Mexican Riviera are popular, too. In Northern Europe most cruises last 12–14 days. To go around South America, allow 30 days or more. For the Antarctic Peninsula, allow 21 days. An around-the-world cruise lasts 90–120 days.

❹ Choose the right ship

Size does matter. Do you want to spend your vacation in the company of 100, 200, 500, 1,000 or 4,000-plus other people? Would you prefer a ship with non-stop entertainment and fun activities for the family? Or are spas and body-pampering treatments important? Your choice of ship will be more limited if you would like to experience cruising under sail, or with specialist lecturers, or a coastal and inland waterways cruise, or an adventure/ expedition cruise. For more about all these options, see pages 180–207.

❺ Accommodations

For a first cruise, choose an outside-view cabin. An interior (no-view) cabin means you'll have no idea what the weather is like when you wake up. If you are concerned about motion sickness, it's best to choose a cabin in the mid-section of the ship.

The average size of a large resort ship cabin is 180–200 sq ft (16.5–18.5 sq meters). Anything less and you may feel a bit cramped – closet space is limited, but you'll need fewer clothes than you might think. Many passengers like a private balcony.

❻ Dining

If the ship has two dinner seatings, as many large resort ships do, choose the later seating (usually 8.30pm) so that you have enough time ashore on the days the ship is in port without having to rush back to shower and change for a 6.30pm first seating. Some ships have several dining venues, and you to eat when and with whom you wish.

❼ Health and fitness

If you need to exercise, check that your chosen ship has adequate facilities, space and equipment. Aboard some large ships, you'll need to book as there may be a 30-minute time limit to use the treadmill or video bike. It's also best to book early to guarantee spa treatments such as massages and facials.

❽ Families

If you have a family, choose a family-friendly ship. The large resort ships have the most comprehensive facilities, while some small ships have none at all. Most children love cruising – it's an educational, fun, learning, entertaining and social experience.

If you prefer to avoid children, steer clear of the main school vacation periods. Several ships are child-free *(see page 18)*.

❾ Dress codes

Dress codes today are informal, if not downright casual, so you don't have to buy a tux. Aboard most large resort ships, particularly on Caribbean cruises, few people dress in formal wear, unless they're aboard one of the smaller, more luxurious ships or on a transatlantic crossing aboard Cunard Line's *Queen Mary 2*. Do remember that ships move, so flat (or half-height heel) shoes are strongly recommended for women.

❿ Extra costs

Budget for extra-cost items such as shore excursions, drinks (unless they are included), meals in an "alternative" dining venue, spa treatments, gaming, and other items of personal expenditure. Allow for buying souvenirs and other items ashore. Last, but not least, make sure you have full insurance cover (from door to door is advisable).   ❑

Much space is being devoted to onboard spas.

THE 50 MOST FREQUENTLY ASKED QUESTIONS

There are many things the brochures don't tell you. Here are frank answers to the questions about ocean cruising most often asked by those contemplating a vacation afloat

WHO GOES CRUISING

Isn't cruising just for old people?

The average age of passengers gets younger each year, with the average age of first-timers now well under 40. But retirees find cruising a safe and comfortable way to travel and many have plenty of get-up-and-go.

On a typical cruise you'll meet singles, couples, families with children of all ages (including single parents and grandparents), honeymooners, second- or third-time honey-

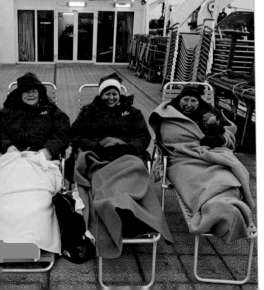

Staying comfortable on an Arctic expedition cruise.

mooners, groups of friends, and college buddies. In fact, today's passengers are likely to be your next-door neighbors.

Won't I get bored?

Usually, it's the men who ask this question, but get them aboard and often there's not enough time in the day to try all the things they want to do – as long as you choose the right ship, for the right reasons. There are more things to do aboard today's ships than there is on almost any Caribbean island. So, whether you want to lie back and be pampered, or be active nonstop, you can do it on a cruise holiday, and you will only have to pack and unpack once.

Just being at sea provides an intoxicating sense of freedom that few places on dry land can offer. And, in case you think you may feel cut off without contact, almost all large resort ships (those carrying over 1,600 passengers) offer internet access, pay-per-view movies, digital music libraries, and ship-wide wi-fi access.

Are there facilities for singles?

Yes. A cruise holiday is good for those traveling alone (over 25 percent of all passengers are solo travelers – worldwide, that's over 4 million a year), because it is easy to meet other people in a non-competitive environment. Many ships have dedicated cabins for singles and special add-on rates for single occupancy of double cabins. Some

ABOVE: in Mexico on an American Safari Cruise.
RIGHT: the wheel turns in a Carnival casino.
BELOW: seeking serenity and self-awareness at sea.

cruise lines will even find a cabin mate for you to share with, if you so desire.

However, in cabins with three or four berths (two beds plus upper berths), personal privacy doesn't exist. Also, some companies sell two-bed cabins at a special single rate, but don't bother to remember that many people who cruise solo do so because their spouse or partner has died, and the last thing they want is to be in a cabin with two beds.

DO CRUISES SUIT HONEYMOONERS?

Absolutely. A cruise is the ideal setting for romance, for shipboard weddings aboard ships with the right registry (they can also be arranged in some ports, depending on local regulations), receptions, and honeymoons. Most decisions are already made for you, so all you have to do is show up. Many ships have double, queen- or king-sized beds, too. And for those on a second honeymoon, many ships can perform a "renewal of vows" ceremony; some will make a charge for this service.

Why is it so expensive for singles?

Because it's a couples world. Almost all cruise lines base their rates on double occupancy, as do hotels. Thus, when you travel alone, the cabin portion of your fare reflects an additional supplement. While almost all new ships are built with cabins for double occupancy, older ships have more single occupancy cabins.

And what about children?

A cruise provides families with more quality time than any other type of vacation, and family cruising is the industry's largest growth segment. Activities are tailored to various age groups – even Disney has cruise ships for families. A cruise is also educational, allows children to interact in a crime-free environment, and takes them to destinations in comfortable, familiar surroundings. In fact, children have such a good time aboard ship and ashore, you may have difficulty getting them home after the cruise – as long as you have chosen the right ship. And you as parents, or as a single parent, will get time to enjoy life, too. While children don't like organized clubs, they will probably find they make new friends quickly.

If you cruise aboard one of the 10 major cruise lines, you may find gratuities for your children automatically added to your onboard account. NCL, for example, requests $5 per day from each child of 3–12 years, while those over 13 pay the adult rate of $10 per day.

Are there child-free ships?

If you don't like crowds, noise, and long lines, try a small ship – a sail-cruise vessel or a river or barge cruise could also provide the right escape. Companies that operate child-free ships include P&O Cruises (*Arcadia, Artemis*), Saga Cruises (*Spirit of Adventure, Saga Rose, Saga Ruby*) and Thomson Cruises (*The Calypso*).

Can I go cruising if I'm pregnant?

Yes, but most cruise lines will not allow a mother-to-be to cruise past her 28th week of pregnancy. You may need to produce a doctor's certificate.

Is having hay fever a problem?

Actually, people who suffer from hay fever and pollen allergies benefit greatly from a cruise. Most sufferers I have talked to say that their problems simply disappear on a cruise – particularly when the ship is at sea.

Disney Cruise Line's ships always have mice aboard.

Are hygiene standards high enough?

News reports often focus on hygiene and sanitation aboard cruise ships. In the 1980s, the North American cruise industry agreed with the Centers for Disease Control (CDC) that hygiene and sanitation inspections should be carried out once or twice yearly aboard all cruise ships carrying American passengers, and the Vessel Sanitation Program (VSP) was born. The original intention of the VSP was to achieve and maintain a level of sanitation that would lower the risk of gastro-intestinal disease outbreaks and assist the cruise industry to provide a healthy environment for passengers and crew.

It is a voluntary inspection, and cruise lines pay handsomely for each inspection. However, the 42 inspection points are judged to be a good system that all should adhere to. The inspections cover two main areas:

● Water sanitation, including free chlorine residuals in the potable water system, swimming pool and hot tub filters.

● Food sanitation: food storage, preparation and serving areas, including bars and passenger service pantries.

The ships score extremely well – the ones that undergo inspections, that is. Some ships that don't call on US ports would possibly not pass the inspections every time. Older ships with outdated galley equipment and poor food storage facilities would have a harder time com-

A Nintendo Wii game for kids aboard *Norwegian Pearl*.

CAN I BRING MY PETS ?

Pet animals are not allowed aboard cruise ships, with one exception: the regular transatlantic crossings aboard Cunard Line's ocean liner *Queen Mary 2*. It continues the tradition of the now-withdrawn *QE2* by providing air-conditioned kennels, plus a genuine British lamppost and New York fire hydrant for dogs' convenience, and cat containers.

plying with the USPH inspection standards. Some other countries also have strict health inspection standards.

However, if the same USPH inspection standards were applied to restaurants and hotels ashore, it is estimated that at least 90 percent or more would fail, consistently.

Anyone concerned about personal hygiene should note that some ships have fixed shower heads. A removable shower and hose are better for reaching those parts that fixed head showers can't. Check with your cruise provider *before* you book.

What about the Norwalk virus?

This temporary but highly contagious condition occurs worldwide. Humans are the only known hosts, and only the common cold is reported more frequently than viral gastro-enteritis as a cause of illness in the USA. About 23 million Americans each year are

diagnosed with the effects of the Norwalk-like virus (NLV gastroenteritis, sometimes known as winter vomiting virus). It is more prevalent in adults and older children than in the very young.

Norwalk is part of the "calicivirus" family. The name derives from the chalice or calyx, meaning cuplike; this refers to the indentations of the surface of the virus. The disease itself is self-limiting, is mild, and is characterized by nausea, vomiting, diarrhoea, and abdominal pain. Although it can be transmitted by person-to-person contact, it is more likely to arrive via contaminated foods and water, so make sure you wash your hands thoroughly after using the toilet.

Shellfish (most notably clams and oysters), salad ingredients (particular salad dressings) and fruits are the foods most often implicated in Norwalk outbreaks.

Water can also be a common source of outbreaks – water aboard cruise ships stored in tanks, etc. A mild and brief illness typically occurs 24 to 48 hours after contaminated food or water has been consumed, and lasts for 24 to 72 hours. The virus can also be brought on board when passengers are ashore in foreign ports with poor hygiene standards.

Note that only cruise ships are required to report every incidence of gastrointestinal illness. Nowhere else in the health system of the US are such viruses a reportable illness.

Crowded pools need good hygiene standards.

Where is smoking allowed?

Some cruise lines allow smoking in cabins, while some permit it only in cabins with balconies. Almost all cruise lines prohibit smoking in restaurants and food service areas; very few ships have smoking sections in dining rooms. If you are concerned, check with the cruise line or a travel agent before booking.

Non-smokers will be pleased to know that most ships now have totally non-smoking dining rooms and show lounges, and many ships now allow smoking only on the open decks. However, you could be sunbathing on an open deck and the person next to you can light up – not a healthy situation.

Cigar smoking is still in vogue, and several ships have cigar bars and lounges. Examples: *Adventure of the Seas, Amadea, Asuka II, Brilliance of the Seas, Crystal Serenity, Crystal Symphony, Europa, Explorer of the Seas, Freedom of the Seas, Grand Mistral, Independence of the Seas, Liberty of the Seas, Mariner of the Seas, MSC Armonia, MSC Fantasia, MSC Lirica, MSC Musica, MSC Opera, MSC Orchestra, MSC Poesia, MSC Sinfonia, Navigator of the Seas, Norwegian Dawn, Norwegian Gem, Norwegian Jewel,*

Norwegian Pearl, Norwegian Star, Norwegian Sun, Queen Mary 2, Queen Victoria, Radiance of the Seas, Serenade of the Seas, Seven Seas Mariner, Seven Seas Voyager, Silver Shadow, Silver Whisper, SuperStar Virgo, and *Voyager of the Seas.* Note, however, that ships starting or ending their cruises in a US port are not permitted to carry genuine Cuban cigars. Instead, most cigars will be made in the Dominican Republic.

What are the chances of being seasick?

Today's ships have stabilizers – large underwater "fins" on each side of the hull – to counteract any rolling motion, and most cruises are in warm, calm waters. As a result, fewer than 3 percent of passengers become seasick. Yet it's possible to develop some symptoms – anything from slight nausea to vomiting.

Both old-time sailors and modern physicians have their own remedies, and you can take your choice or try them all (but not at the same time):

● When you notice the first movement of a ship, walk back and forth on the deck. You will find that your knees, which are our own form of stabilizer, will start getting their feel of balance and counteraction. This is known as "getting your sea legs."

● Get the fresh sea breeze into your face (arguably the best anti-

dote of all), and if nauseated, suck an orange or a lemon.

● When on deck, focus on a steady point, such as the horizon.

● Eat lightly. Do not make the mistake of thinking a heavy meal will keep your stomach well anchored. It will not.

Drugs. *Dramamine* (dimenhydrinate, an anti-histamine and sedative introduced just after World War II) will be available aboard in tablet (chewable) form.

Ciba-Geigy's *Scopoderm* (or Transderm Scop), known as "The Patch," contains scopolamine and has proven effective. Possible side effects are dry mouth, blurred vision, drowsiness and problems with urinating.

If you are really distressed, the ship's doctor can give you an injection to alleviate discomfort. It may make you drowsy, but the last thing on your mind will be

staying awake during the movie.

A natural preventive is ginger in powder form. Mix half a teaspoon in a glass of warm water or milk, and drink it before sailing. This is said to settle any stomach for up to eight hours.

"Sea Bands" (or "Aquastraps") are a drug-free method of controlling motion sickness. These are slim bands (in varying colors) that are wrapped around the wrist, with a circular "button" that presses against the acupressure point Pericardium 6 (nei kuan) on the lower arm. Attach them a few minutes before you step aboard and wear on both wrists throughout the cruise.

Another drug-free remedy can be found in ReliefBand, a watch-like device worn on the wrist. It is said to "emit gentle electrical signals that interfere with nerves that cause nausea."

Viewing the Midnight Sun during an Arctic cruise.

Haven't people been murdered during a cruise?

Violent crime is much less common on a cruise than during land-based vacations, but there have been a few suspicious deaths, and a number of passengers have gone missing, mainly in the Caribbean and on Mexican Riviera cruises. A small number have been thrown over a balcony by another passenger, typically after an alcohol-fueled argument.

Murder is hard to prove if no body is found (did he jump or was he pushed?). Another headache is that, if the alleged crime happens at sea, the jurisdiction responsible for investigating it will depend on the ship's registry, perhaps in Panama, Liberia or Malta.

WHAT CRUISING COSTS

Isn't cruising expensive?

Compare what it would cost on land to have all your meals and entertainment provided, as well as transportation, fitness and sports facilities, social activities, educational talks, parties, and other functions, and you can see the remarkable value of a cruise.

Also, a ship is a destination in itself, which moves to other destinations. No land-based resort can provide that variety. The choice ranges from basic to luxury, so give yourself a budget, and ask your professional travel supplier how to make the best use of it.

A seven-day cruise is advertised at a very cheap price. Is there a catch?

As a rule, yes. If the price is a fraction of what you might pay for a decent hotel room in London or New York without meals or entertainment, something is not quite as it seems. Before booking, read the fine print.

Look at all the extra costs such as tips to cabin and dining room stewards, shore excursions, drinks, plus getting to and from the ship. The price per person advertised could well be for a four-berth cabin adjacent to the ship's laundry or above the disco, but in any event, not in a desirable location – just like a dirt-cheap hotel room in London or New York.

Should I pay the brochure price?

Not without checking around. A cruise's brochure price is set by the sales and marketing departments of cruise lines, rather like the "recommended retail price" of a new car is set by the manufacturer. It's the price they would like to achieve to cover themselves against currency fluctuations, international bonding schemes and the like. But, in the real world, discounts attract business, and so there is always some leeway. Also, travel

A beach snack at the expensive end of the market.

WHAT ARE PORT CHARGES?

These are levied by the various ports visited by cruise ships, rather like city taxes imposed on hotel guests. They help pay for the infrastructure required to provide facilities including docks, linesmen, security and operations personnel, and porters at embarkation and disembarkation ports.

agents receive a commission (typically 10–15%, plus special overrides for volume bookings). So, as a consumer, always ask for the "best price" and watch out for special offers in newspapers and magazines.

European cruises cost more than in the Caribbean. Why?

There are several reasons. Almost all aspects of operations, including fuel costs, port charges, air transportation, supplying food to the ships, are higher. European-sourced food has more taste – eggs with real yellow yolks, and food free from chemical additives, coloring and flavoring – than is found in the processed foods that cruise lines often purchase from US-based suppliers.

Companies can make more money than in the cut-price Caribbean, where sun, sea, and sand are the main attractions, whereas sightseeing, architecture, culture, and other things are part of a more enriching cruise experience.

The price of shore excursions in Europe is high. A couple of years ago, for example, admission prices to the Acropolis in Greece more than doubled.

How inclusive is "all-inclusive"?

That's like asking how much sand is on the beach. It usually means that transportation (often including flights), accommodation, food, and entertainment are wrapped up in one neat package. Today on land, however, "super clubs" offer everything "all-in" including drinks, although mostly low-quality brands are provided, with a much smaller selection than aboard most cruise ships.

While that concept works better aboard small ships (those carrying fewer than 500 passengers), large cruise ships (those carrying more than 1,200 passengers) provide more facilities and more reasons for you to spend money on board. So "mostly inclusive" might be a better term to use, particularly as spa treatments and medical services are definitely *not* included.

Do ships have different classes?

Yes and no. Gone are the class distinctions and the pretensions of formality of the past. Differences are now found mainly in the type of accommodation chosen, in the price you pay for a larger cabin (or suite), the location of your cabin (or suite), and whether or not you have butler service.

Some cruise lines, including Holland America Line and Royal Caribbean International (*Freedom*-class ships only), provide a "concierge lounge" which can be used only by occupants of accommodation designated as suites (thus re-creating a two-class system). Private areas have been created by MSC Cruises (Yacht Club) and Norwegian Cruise Line (The Courtyard) for occupants of the top suites, in an effort to provide exclusivity – and insulation from the masses. In effect, this is like devising a "ship within a ship."

Celebrity Cruises has, in essence, cre-

The Caribbean beats Europe for prices – and weather.

ABOVE: open-air eating aboard *SeaDream I.*
LEFT: why private balconies are worth having.

What is a category guarantee?

It means you have purchased a specific grade of accommodation (just as in a hotel), although the actual cabin may not have been assigned to your booking yet. Your cabin may be assigned before you go, or when you arrive for embarkation.

FACILITIES ABOARD

Can I eat when I want to?

Yes, you can – well, almost. Several major cruise lines offer "flexible dining" which allows you to choose (with some limitations) when you want to eat, and with whom you dine. Just like going out to restaurants ashore, reservations may be required, you may also have to wait in line at busy periods, and occupants of the most expensive suites get priority.

Aboard large resort ships (1,600-plus passengers) the big evening entertainment shows typically are staged twice each evening, so you end up with the equivalent of two-seating dining anyway.

What is "alternative" dining?

Some ships now have alternative dining spots other than the main restaurant. These usually cost extra – typically between $15 and $50 a person, but the food quality, preparation and presentation are decidedly better, as is service

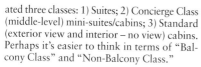

ated three classes: 1) Suites; 2) Concierge Class (middle-level) mini-suites/cabins; 3) Standard (exterior view and interior – no view) cabins. Perhaps it's easier to think in terms of "Balcony Class" and "Non-Balcony Class."

Cabins advertised in newspapers aren't always available. Why not?

Newspaper advertisements are provided way ahead of publication. Meanwhile, some cabin price grades may have sold out. Often, the cheapest "lead-in" price is for a cabin that is small, or has obstructed views, or is in an "inconvenient" or "noisy" location.

Deck games counter the effects of all that eating.

and ambience. Most alternative dining spots are also typically more intimate, and much quieter than the main dining rooms.

What's the difference between an "outside" and an "interior" cabin?

An "outside" (or "exterior") cabin doesn't mean it's outside the ship; it simply means that it has a window (or porthole) with a view of the outside, or there is a private balcony for you to physically be (or look) outside. An "interior" cabin means that it does not have a view of the outside, but it will have artwork or curtains on one wall instead of a window or patio-like (balcony) door.

Should I tip for room service?

No. It's part of the normal onboard duties that the hotel staff are paid to carry out. For more on tipping other staff, see page 155.

CAN I BRING MY GOLF CLUBS?

Yes, you can. However, although cruise lines do not charge for carrying them, some airlines do – worth checking if you have to fly to join your cruise. Some ships cater for golfers with mini-golf courses on deck and electronically monitored practice areas.

Is it hard to find one's way around large resort ships?

Well, it can take at least a few hours, so wear good walking shoes. However, in general, remember that decks are horizontal, while stairs are vertical. The rest comes naturally, with practice. If you're arranging to meet someone, you need to be very specific indeed about the place.

Doesn't it get very noisy aboard these huge ships?

They can be, because of the constant activities and music, and many announcements. Anyone who is allergic to noise should consider taking earplugs, just in case!

ABOVE: the bridge of HAL's *Noordam*.
RIGHT: dining in style on Orient Lines.
BELOW: *Europa* lays on bicycles for free.

CAN I TAKE MY BICYCLE ?

Most cruise lines will let you take your bike (preferably the folding variety due to lack of storage space). If you use a flight case, however, it may not be easy to find storage space for it. Airlines will also charge you to transport your bike. Ask your travel provider to contact the cruise line for its rules. Note that very few ships provide bicycles for free. Those that do include Hapag-Lloyd's *Europa* and *Hanseatic*.

Can I visit the bridge?

Not any more. For insurance and security reasons, almost all cruise ships prohibit bridge visits. However, a Behind the Scenes video on how the ship is run may be shown on the cabin television system.

Are there any ships with walk-in pools (instead of ladders)?

Not many, due to space considerations, although they are useful for older passengers. Examples: *Aurora, Crystal Serenity, Crystal Symphony, Ocean Village, Oriana.*

Do cellular phones work on board?

Cruise passengers use cellular phones on open decks, in cabins, and, sadly, even in restaurants. Most cruise lines have contracts with land-based phone service companies – rates for usage vary, but you will typically pay international roaming rates. Mobile phone signals piggyback off systems that transmit internet data via satellite. When your ship is in port, the ship's network may be switched off and you will pay the going local (country-specific) rate for mobile calls.

If you're desperate to escape the cellular-phone cruise crowd, try an Arctic, Greenland, Antarctic, or a South Pacific cruise. You might just be lucky.

Can I send and receive emails?

Aboard most ships, email facilities have now been added to some degree or other. Many ships have wi-fi, for a fee, allowing you to connect your own laptop. Several ships have an internet café, or internet-connect center, where you can log on for about 50¢ per minute. Note that connections and downloads are often slow compared to land-based services (shipboard emails link through satellite systems, and are therefore more expensive than land-based connections). For many cruise companies, email has now become an important revenue generator.

A choice of movies keeps teens happy.

Where can you see movies?

Some – but not many – ships have a dedicated movie theater. The movies are provided by a licensed film distribution/leasing service. Many newer ships have replaced or supplemented the movie theater with TV sets and DVD players in cabins, or with giant poolside screens for after-dark viewing.

DESTINATIONS

Where can I go on a cruise?

As the saying goes: The world is your oyster! There are over 30,000 different cruises to choose from each year, and about 2,000 cruise destinations in the world. A cruise can also take you to places inaccessible by almost any other means, such as Antarctica, the North Cape, the South Sea islands, and so on. In fact, if you close your eyes and think of almost anywhere in the world where there's water, there's probably a cruise ship or river vessel to take you there. To get an idea of the choice available, see pages 32–6 and 180–207.

What is expedition cruising?

Expedition cruises are operated by small ships that have ice-strengthened hulls or with specially constructed ice-breakers that enable them to reach areas totally inaccessible to "normal" cruise ships. The ships are typically converted to carry passengers in some degree of basic comfort, with comfortable accommodation and a relaxed, informal atmosphere, with expert lecturers and expedition leaders accompanying every cruise.

These cruises really are for small groups, and much care and attention is placed on minimizing the impact on the environment. For more information, see pages 180–5.

Is there a cruise that skips ports?

Yes, but it isn't really a cruise. It's a transatlantic crossing, from New York to Southampton, England (or vice versa), aboard Cunard Line's *Queen Mary 2*.

WHAT IS A PANAMAX SHIP?

This is one that conforms to the maximum dimensions possible for passage through the Panama Canal – useful particularly for around-the-world voyages. These dimensions are: 294 meters (964.56 ft) long, with a beam of 32.3 meters (105.97 ft); or below approximately 90,000 gross tons. The ship pictured above is preparing to enter a lock on the canal.

Can I shop in ports of call?

Yes, you can. Many passengers embrace retail therapy when visiting ports of call such as Dubai, Hong Kong, Singapore, St. Maarten, and St. Thomas, among many others. However, it's prudent to exercise self-control. Remember that you'll have to carry all those purchases home at the end of your cruise; duty-free liquor – a favourite, for example – is heavy.

Do I have to go ashore in each port?

Absolutely not. In fact, many repeat passengers enjoy being aboard "their" ships when there are virtually no other passengers aboard. Also, if you have a spa treatment, it could be less expensive during this period than when the ship is at sea; some ships have price differentials for sea days/port days – *Queen Mary 2* is one example.

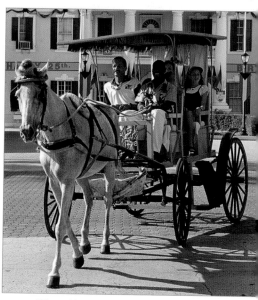

Riding out in style in Nassau, the Bahamas.

MAKING BOOKINGS

Can I fly in the day before or stay an extra day after the cruise?

Cruise lines often offer pre- and post-cruise stay packages at an additional cost. The advantage is that you don't have to do anything else. All will be taken care of, as they say. If you book a hotel on your own, however, you may have to pay an "air deviation" fee, payable if you do not take the cruise line's air arrangements or you want to change them.

Can I pre-book seats on flights?

With packaged holidays such as cruises, it is normally not possible to reserve airline seats prior to check-in, and, although the cruise line will typically forward your requests for preferred seating, these may not be guaranteed. However, some airlines allow you to check-in online, access the seating plan and select your favourite seat.

Should I book early?

The further you book ahead, the greater will be any discount applied by the cruise line. You'll also get the cabin you want, in the location you want, and you may even be upgraded. When you book late (close to the sailing date), you may get a low price, but you typically won't get the cabin or location you might like, or – worse still – in ships with two seatings for dinner, you won't be able to choose early or late seating.

AND FINALLY...

What are cruising's downsides?

The meet and greet staff at airports in general are a weak link in the chain. Much anticipated ports of call can be aborted or changed due to poor weather or other conditions. Some popular ports (particularly in the Caribbean) can become extremely crowded – there can be up to 12 ships in St. Thomas, or six in St. Maarten at the same time. It's as if you've invited 20,000 other people to join your vacation.

Onboard expenses can mount up rapidly aboard the large resort ships, as can the cost of shore excursions – especially those involving flightseeing tours.

Fellow passengers, and those lacking social

manners and etiquette can also be irritating, notably in the dining room where you may have to share a table with strangers.

Where did all the money go?

Apart from the cruise fare itself, there could be other incidentals such as government taxes, port charges, air ticket tax, and fuel surcharges. On board, extra costs may include drinks, mini-bar items, cappuccino and espresso coffees, shore excursions, internet access, sending or receiving email, beauty treatments, casino gaming, photographs, laundry and dry-cleaning, babysitting services, wine tasting, bottled water placed in your cabin, and medical services.

A cruise aboard a ship belonging to a major cruise line could be compared to buying a car, whereby motor manufacturers offer a basic model at a set price, and then tempt you with optional extras to inflate the price.

Cruise lines say income generated on board helps to keep the basic cost of a cruise reasonable. In the end, it's up to your self-restraint to stop those little extras mounting up to an unacceptably large sum.

What rights do passengers have?

Very few. After reading a cruise line's Passenger Ticket Contract, you'll see why. A 189-

Where did all the money go? Perhaps here.

word sentence in one contract begins "The Carrier shall not be liable for…" and goes on to cover the legal waterfront.

Where do old cruise ships go when they're scrapped?

They go to the beach. Actually, they are driven at speed onto a not very nice beach at Alang in India, or to Chittagong in Bangladesh, or to Pan Yo in China – the principal shipbreaking places. Greenpeace has claimed that workers, including children, at some of these sites work under primitive conditions without adequate protective equipment. ❑

Showlounge entertainment, Carnival-style.

Cruising's Eventful History

The voyage from England to Egypt made in 1844 by the novelist William Makepeace Thackeray and the trip from New York to the Holy Land described by Mark Twain in his 1869 book *The Innocents Abroad* were precursors of modern cruising's combination of leisure and exploration. In the 1920s "booze cruises" out of New York were an escape from Prohibition, and in the 1930s American and European shipping lines competed to see which could offer the most luxurious transatlantic travel.

Then, in June 1958, the first commercial jet aircraft flew across the Atlantic and turned the economics of transatlantic travel upside down. Even the famous "Queens," noted for their regular weekly transatlantic service, were not immune. Cunard White Star Line's *Queen Mary* was withdrawn in September 1967. *Queen Elizabeth* made its final crossing in October 1968.

Shipping lines that survived tried to mix transatlantic crossings with voyages south to the sun, and a new industry was born. Smaller ships were built, capable of getting into the tiny ports of developing Caribbean islands, and Florida's proximity encouraged their owners to set up their headquarters there. California became the base for cruises to the Mexican Riviera, and Vancouver, in Canada, became the focus for summer cruises to Alaska.

Air/sea and "sail and stay" packages were invented – joint cruise and hotel vacations with inclusive pricing. Some old liners were redesigned and refitted for warm-weather cruising operations.

Cruising today

Today cruising is no longer a shipping business but part of the hospitality industry. New ships have become larger, yet cabin size has been "standardized" to provide more space for entertainment and other public facilities, and to accommodate group bookings. Today's ships boast air conditioning to keep out heat and humidity; stabilizers to keep the ship on an even keel; a high level of mainte-nance, safety, and hygiene; and more emphasis on health and fitness facilities.

Cruise ship design has moved from the traditional, classic, rounded profiles of the past (e.g. *Queen Elizabeth 2*) to functional boxy shapes with squared-off sterns and towering superstructures (e.g. *Celebrity Constellation*). You can squeeze more into a square box than a round one.

Building a modern cruise ship

Ships used to be constructed from the keel (backbone) up. Today they are built in huge sections – not necessarily in a ship-

A cruising poster dating from around 1898.

yard – and joined together in the yard. A large resort ship such as *Carnival Freedom* can have as many as 100 sections. Computer-based design enables a ship to be built in just two years.

The cruise industry, a $60 billion business worldwide, directly employs more than 100,000 shipboard officers, staff and crew, plus around 20,000 employees in onshore offices, and provides business for a host of international suppliers. ❏

MAKING THE BEST CHOICES

Deciding where to go
The right ship and cabin for you
The major lines compared
The best shore excursions

WHERE TO GO

Cruise lines visit around 2,000 destinations around the world, so the first thing to decide is which places you most want to see

Itineraries vary widely, so make as many comparisons as you can by reading the cruise brochures for descriptions of the ports of call. Several ships may offer the same or similar itineraries simply because these have been tried and tested. Narrow the choice by noting the time spent at each port, and whether the ship actually docks or lies at anchor.

The Caribbean

There are more than 7,000 islands in the Caribbean Sea, although many are small or uninhabited. Caribbean cruises are usually destination-intensive, cramming between four and eight ports into one week, depending on whether you sail from a Florida port or from a port already in the Caribbean, such as Barbados or San Juan. This means you could be visiting at least one port a day, with little time at sea for relaxation. This kind of island-hopping leaves little time to explore a destination – but you'd probably get bored after a few days on one island. Although you see a lot of places in a week, by the end of the cruise you may need another week to unwind. Note that June 10 to November 10 is the official hurricane season in the Caribbean, including the Bahamas and Florida.

● **Eastern Caribbean** cruises include ports such as Antigua, Barbados, Dominica, Martinique, Puerto Rico, St. Croix, St. Kitts, St. Maarten, St. Lucia and St. Thomas.

● **Western Caribbean** cruises typically include ports such as Calica, Cozumel, Grand Cayman, Grand Turk, Playa del Carmen, Ocho Rios, Roatan Island.

● **Southern Caribbean** cruises typically include ports such as Antigua, Aruba, Barbados, La Guaira (Venezuela), Tortola, San Juan.

Europe/Mediterranean

Traveling within Europe (including the Aegean, Baltic, Black Sea, Mediterranean, and Norwegian fjord areas) by cruise ship makes economic sense. Consider these benefits:

● Although no single cruise covers

PRECEDING PAGES: P&O's *Artemis* visits Stockholm, Sweden.
BELOW: Antigua is a popular Caribbean port of call.

Connoisseurus

Veg.

com

ABOVE: Joan Miró paving in Barcelona.
RIGHT: gondolas on the Grand Canal, Venice.

every port, cruise ships offer a comfortable way of exploring the area's rich mix of destinations, cultures, history, traditions, architecture, lifestyles and cuisines – all within one cruise – and without having to pack and unpack each day.

● So many of Europe's major cosmopolitan cities – Amsterdam, Athens, Barcelona, Copenhagen, Genoa, Helsinki, Lisbon, London, Monte Carlo, Nice, Oslo, St. Petersburg, Stockholm, and Venice – are on the water. It is far less expensive to take a cruise than to fly and stay in decent hotels, and have to pay for food and transport in addition.

● You will not have to try to speak or understand different languages when you are aboard ship as you would ashore – if you choose the right ship.

● The chances of having a crime-free vacation are much greater aboard a ship.

● Aboard ship you use a single currency, typically US dollars, British pounds or euros.

● Interesting shore excursions are offered.

● Lecture programs provide insights before

THE PROS AND CONS OF CRUISING'S PRIVATE ISLANDS

Several cruise lines offering Bahamas/Caribbean itineraries feature a "private island." This is a small island close to Nassau in the Bahamas controlled by the cruise line and outfitted with all the ingredients to host an all-day beach party. Also available are water sports, scuba, snorkeling, crystal-clear waters, warm sands, even a hammock or two, and, possibly, massage in a beach cabana.

There are no reservations to make, no tickets to buy, and no hassles with taxis. But be aware that you may be sharing your private island with more than 3,000 others from a large ship anchored for a "beach barbecue."

One bonus is that a "private

Half Moon Cay, the Bahamas.

island" won't be cluttered with hawkers and hustlers, as are so many Caribbean beaches. And security is very tight, so there's no

fear of passengers being mugged.

Private island beach days are not all-inclusive. You pay premium prices for snorkel gear and mandatory swim vest, rental pleasure craft, and "banana" boat fun rides. Examples: Sunfish sailboat rental, $40 per hour; snorkel gear rental, $10 per hour; floating foam mattress, $6; bottle of water, $2.50–$4; ice cream, $1.50–$3; water bicycle, $5–$10 per 15 minutes; use of hammock, $2.50–$5.

Just another revenue raiser? Cruise lines argue they need to recoup their investment – for instance, Disney Cruise Line spent $25 million developing and outfitting Castaway Cay (formerly Gorda Cay), and Holland America Line spent $16 million on Half Moon Cay.

LEFT: Alaska cruise train with domed railcars.
ABOVE: getting up close to Alaska's glaciers.

you step ashore. Small ships are arguably better than large resort ships, as they can obtain berthing space; the large resort ships may have to anchor in more of the smaller ports, so it can take time to get to and from shore, and you'll probably have to wait for shore tender tickets. Many Greek islands are accessible only by shore tender.

Some companies allow more time ashore than others, so compare itineraries in the brochures; it's probably best to choose a

Donkeys await passengers at Hydra, Greece.

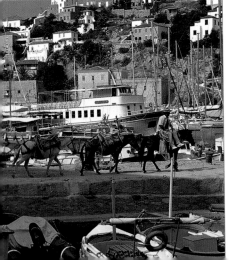

regional cruise line, such as Louis Hellenic Cruises *(see page 115)*, for these destination-intensive cruises, for example.

Alaska

These are especially popular because:
● They offer the best way to see the state's magnificent shoreline and glaciers.
● Alaska is vast, and relatively unexplored. There is a wide range of shore excursions, including floatplane and helicopter tours. Other excursions include "dome car" rail journeys to Denali National Park to see North America's highest peak, Mt. McKinley.
● Pre- and post-cruise journeys to Banff and Jasper National Parks can conveniently be made from Vancouver.

There are two popular cruise routes:
❶ **The Inside Passage Route**, a 1,000-mile (1,600-km) stretch of protected waterways carved a million years ago by Ice Age glaciers. This usually includes visits to tidewater glaciers, such as those in Glacier Bay's Hubbard Glacier or Tracy Arm (just two of the 15 active glaciers along the 60-mile/100-km Glacier Bay coastline). Typical ports of call are Juneau, Ketchikan, Skagway, and Haines.
❷ **The Glacier Route**, which usually includes the Gulf of Alaska during a one-way cruise between Vancouver and Anchorage. Ports of call might include Seward, Sitka, and Valdez.

Holland America Line and Princess Cruises

own many facilities in Alaska (hotels, tour buses, even trains) and between them have invested more than $300 million in the state. Indeed, Holland America Line–Westours is Alaska's largest private employer. Both companies take 250,000-plus people to Alaska each year. Other lines depend on what's left of local transportation for their land tours.

In ports where docking space is limited, some ships anchor rather than dock. Many cruise brochures do not indicate clearly which ports are known to be anchor ports, where tenders are needed to reach land.

With around 1 million cruise passengers a year visiting Alaska and several large resort ships likely to be in port on any given day, there's so much congestion in many of the small ports that avoiding crowded streets can

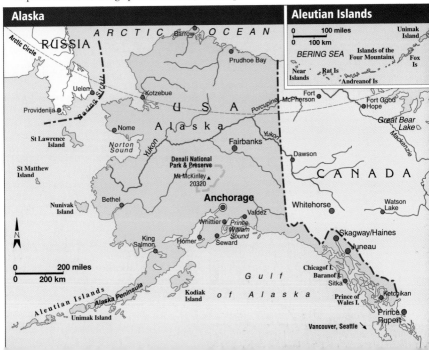

be difficult. Even nature is retreating; with more people around, wildlife is harder to spot. And many of the same shops are now found in Alaska as well as in the Caribbean. The more adventurous might consider one of the more unusual Alaska cruises to the far north, around the Pribilof Islands (superb for bird watching) and into the Bering Sea.

Finally, remember that Alaska isn't always good weather cruising – it can be very wet and windy and excursions may be canceled or changed at the last moment.

Mexican Riviera

These cruises typically sail from Los Angeles or San Diego, along Mexico's west coast, calling at ports such as Cabo San Lucas, Mazatlan, Puerto Vallarta, Manzanillo, Ixtapa/Zihuatanejo, and Acapulco.

Australasia

If you live in Europe or North America, the flight to your port of embarkation will be a long one. It's advisable to arrive at least two days before the cruise, as the effects of time changes and jet lag can be severe. This will also give you time to explore a local city.

Harnessing camel power on an Australian beach.

Distance aside, the region has so much to offer that it's worth taking a cruise of at least 14 days. Australia, New Zealand, the islands of the South Pacific, Hong Kong, China, Japan, Indonesia, Malaysia, Singapore, Thailand, and Vietnam are all fascinating and rapidly developing destinations. ❏

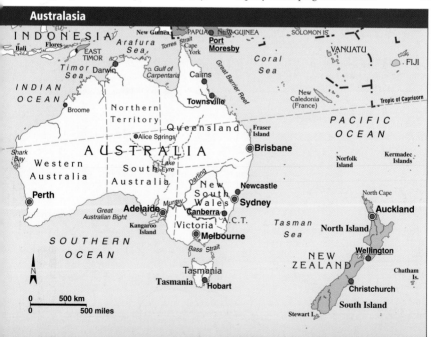

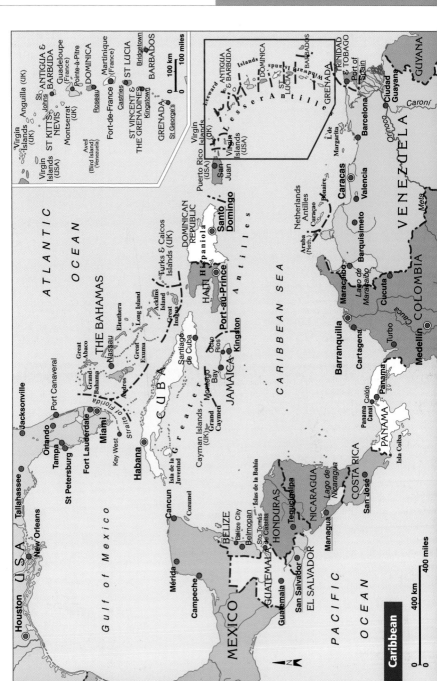

Caribbean

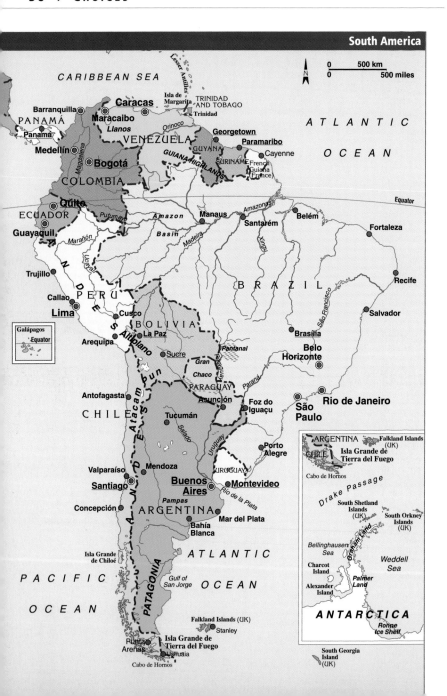

The Arctic

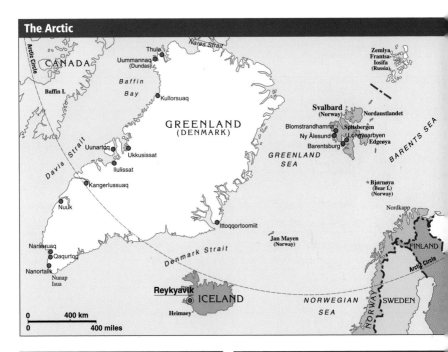

Canada, New England and Bermuda

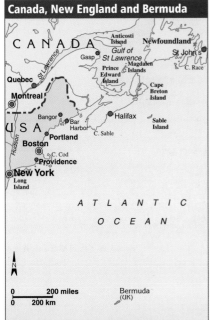

United Kingdom

The Baltic and Northern Europe

Western Mediterranean

Eastern Mediterranean

Africa

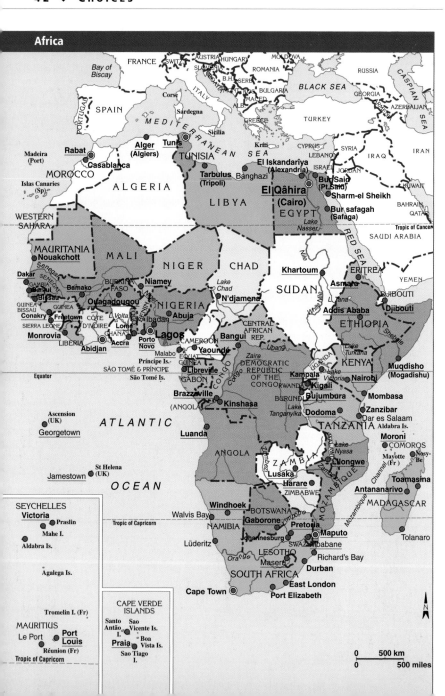

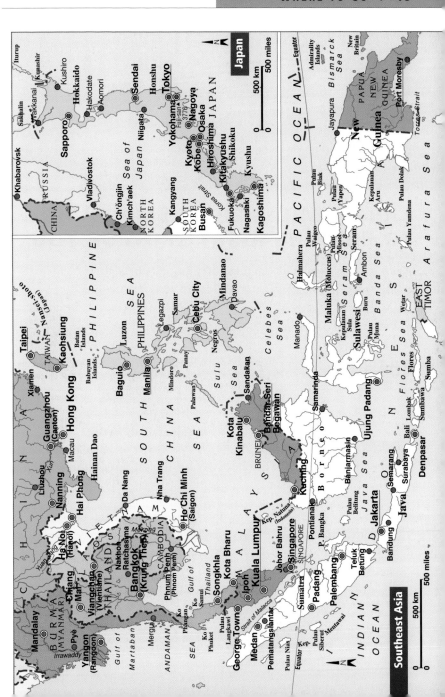

Japan

N

500 km
500 miles

Southeast Asia

500 km
500 miles

LARGE, MID-SIZE OR SMALL? HOW TO PICK THE RIGHT SHIP FOR YOU

The biggest cruise ships can now carry more than 6,000 passengers. The smallest cater for just 50. Here's what you need to know to choose between the various options

Which ship? The picture above, showing the *Wind Star* (148 passengers) alongside the *Zuiderdam* (2,387), highlights the choice now available. There's something to suit virtually everyone, so take into account your own personality and tastes.

Whatever the physical dimensions, all cruise ships provide the same basic ingredients: accommodation, activities, food, service, and ports of call, although some have higher standards than others – and charge more.

Is bigger really better?

The trend has been towards ever larger ships *(see list on page 46),* and in 2009 a new "largest cruise ship in the world" will debut. At 220,000 tons, 1,181 ft (360 meters) long and carrying up to 6,400 passengers, Royal Caribbean International's codenamed *Project Genesis* will be innovative and exciting – as opposed to quiet and relaxing.

Being aboard a large resort ship can be like being in a large shopping mall rather than a neighborhood store. Waiting for an elevator can be frustrating. What if 5,000 passengers all wanted room service at the same time? And disembarkation can be like getting out of a major sports stadium after a game.

The introduction of new ships continues at a frenetic pace, with more than 30 new ships scheduled for delivery by the end of 2012,

THE FOUR SIZE CATEGORIES

Ships are measured in gross tons – an indication of volume of revenue-producing interior spaces, not a weight – and come in four principal size categories:

Large resort ships
50,000–220,000 tons
1,600–6,000+ passengers

Mid-size ships
25,000–50,000 tons;
600–1,600 passengers

Small ships
5,000–25,000 tons
200–600 passengers

Boutique ships
1,000–5,000 tons
50–200 passengers

fueled by an increase in demand for high-value cruise vacations, and ever larger ships with more facilities and options.

LARGE RESORT SHIPS

Here the ship rather than the destination is the main attraction. Providing a "Las Vegas at sea" experience, with high-tech facilities, lots of dining options, "big show" entertainment and casino gaming, these ships are good for night owls – and great for singles.

For families, these fun ships offer the greatest choice of facilities, sports and organized activities for both adults and children. There's often a walk-around promenade deck outdoors, and accommodation varies from large villas and "penthouse suites" complete with butler service to tiny interior (no-view) cabins. Almost all have state-of-the-art electronic in-cabin interactive entertainment facilities.

Large resort ships are highly programmed. It is difficult, for example, to go swimming in the late evening or after dinner – decks are cleaned and pools are often netted over by 6pm. Having champagne delivered to outdoor hot tubs late at night is virtually impossible. There can be a feeling of "conveyor-belt" cruising, and, because the basic cruise price is low, you'll find lots of onboard revenue centers.

Pay more, get more

Exclusivity costs more. Their sheer size means that these ships can include more spaces for "privacy" – exclusive areas such as concierge lounges, sanctuaries and courtyards with relaxation areas and other facilities that are out of bounds for the masses. You may feel it's worth paying an extra daily charge to spend a little quiet time in "The Sanctuary" aboard some ships of P&O Cruises and Princess Cruises. More money will buy your own private box in the showlounge (Royal Court Theatre, *Queen Victoria*), a spa suite with all its extra perks (*Costa Concordia, Costa Serena*), or a villa with private garden (examples: *Norwegian Dawn, Norwegian Gem, Norwegian Pearl, Norwegian Star*).

In the future, exclusivity will

mean having your own private sunbathing space, private tailor-made excursions, and more. But you'll still have to be with the "lower classes" when you go through security.

Large Resort Ships: Disadvantages

● Trying to find your way around the ship can prove frustrating. If you meet someone on the first day and want to meet them again, you'll need to set a specific place and time or you'll probably never locate them again.
● Lines to wait in: for embarkation, the information desk, elevators, informal buffet meals, fast food grills, shore tenders, shore excursions, security checkpoint (when returning to the ship), immigration, and disembarkation.
● The itineraries may be limited by ship size,

Carnival ships can dominate the harbor in a destination.

and there are too many tender ports where you need to take a number, sit in a lounge, and wait, and wait…

● There are constant announcements, perhaps in several languages.

● Signage can be confusing; there will be a lack of elevators at peak times.

● Dining room staff provide fast service, so it's hard to dine in a leisurely fashion.

● The food may well be unmemorable. Cooking for 4,000-plus is on an industrial scale.

● Telephoning room service can be frustrating, particularly in ships with telephone answering systems that put you on hold.

● Room service breakfast is not generally available on the day of disembarkation.

● In early evening, the deck chairs are taken away, or strapped up so they can't be used.

● The in-cabin music aboard the latest ships

is supplied through the television set, and it may be impossible to turn off the picture (so much for romantic darkened cabins).

● You will probably have to use a sign-up sheet to use gym equipment such as treadmills or exercise bicycles.

● The larger the ship, the more impersonal the service – except for "butler" service in penthouse suites.

MID-SIZE SHIPS

Choose a mid-size ship (600–1,600 passengers) for a small-town – as opposed to big-city – atmosphere, with some low-key entertainment and fewer facilities. It will suit you if you are more of an individual and don't like or need constant organized participation activities.

It is easy to find one's way around a mid-sized ship, and they are well suited to the smaller ports of the Aegean and Mediterranean, being more maneuvrable than large resort ships. Several operate around-the-world cruises and other long-distance itineraries to exotic destinations not really feasible aboard many large resort ships or small ships.

Accommodation varies from large "penthouse suites" with butler service to tiny interior (no-view) cabins. These ships will generally be more stable at sea than small ships, due to their increased size and draft. They provide more facilities, more entertainment, and more dining options. But they don't offer as wide a range of public

CRUISE SHIPS OVER 100,000 TONS

Ship	Tonnage
Freedom of the Seas	158,000
Independence of the Seas	158,000
Liberty of the Seas	158,000
Queen Mary 2	148,528
Explorer of the Seas	137,308
Voyager of the Seas	137,280
Adventure of the Seas	137,276
Mariner of the Seas	137,276
Navigator of the Seas	137,276
MSC Fantasia	133,000
Celebrity Solstice	122,000
Crown Princess	116,000
Emerald Princess	116,000
Ventura	116,000
Diamond Princess	113,000
Sapphire Princess	113,000
Caribbean Princess	112,894
Carnival Splendor	112,000
Costa Concordia	112,000
Costa Serena	112,000
Carnival Conquest	110,319
Carnival Freedom	110,000
Carnival Glory	110,000
Carnival Liberty	110,000
Carnival Valor	110,000
Star Princess	108,977
Golden Princess	108,865
Grand Princess	108,806
Costa Fortuna	105,000
Costa Magica	105,000
Carnival Triumph	101,509
Carnival Victory	101,509
Carnival Destiny	101,353

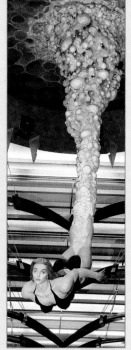

Ceiling art, *Freedom of the Seas*.

ABOVE: the pool aboard a large Carnival ship.
RIGHT: hot tub in *Hanseatic*, a luxury small ship.

rooms and facilities as the large resort ships. Few have large show lounges for large-scale production shows, so entertainment tends to be more of the cabaret variety.

SMALL SHIPS

Choose a small ship (200–600 passengers) if you are seeking a quiet, serene holiday with more personalized service, probably without children, and don't need much entertainment – just good food and relaxation. These ships are more like small inns than mega-resorts. They can access ports that large resort ships can't. Cruises are often longer, with a reasonable balance between port and sea days.

Some of the world's most exclusive cruise ships belong in this group – but so do most of the coastal vessels with basic, unpretentious amenities, sail-cruise ships, and the expedition-style cruise vessels that take passengers to see nature. If you want to swim in the late evening, or have champagne in the hot tub at midnight, it is easier aboard boutique or small ships than aboard the inflexible larger ships.

However, small ships do not have the bulk, length, or beam to sail well in open seas in bad weather conditions, or the range of public rooms or open spaces that the large resort ships can offer. Options for entertainment, therefore, are limited.

BOUTIQUE SHIPS

Choose a boutique-size ship (50–200 passengers) for a relaxing, exclusive, private and unstructured yacht-style holiday, with fine personal service, outstanding cuisine, and attention to detail. There will be little entertainment other than a cocktail pianist or a few DVDs, but there will be plenty of high-luxe. Most allow you to sit where you wish in the dining room. Nightlife is mainly after-dinner conversation, or reading.

Some small ships have a hydraulic marina water sports platform located at the stern and carry equipment such as jet skis, windsurfers, a water ski powerboat, and scuba and snorkeling gear. When the ship is at anchor, going ashore is speedy, with a continuous tender service and no lines.

This type of ship is for those who would like their own private motor yacht, but would prefer not to sustain the crew or maintenance costs. ❏

Boutique exclusivity aboard the 108-passenger *SeaDream I.*

HOW TO CHOOSE THE RIGHT CABIN

What is the smallest acceptable size? What's the best location? Is a suite worth the extra money? How important is it to have a balcony?

Y ou should feel at home when at sea, so it is important to choose the right accommodation, even if most of your time in it is spent with your eyes shut. You can have everything from a spacious villa with private garden to a cabin smaller than a prison cell. Choose carefully, for if you find your cabin – wrongly called a "stateroom" by some companies – is too small when you reach the ship, it may be too late to change or upgrade it.

Carnival adds a smile to its cabin service.

Cruise lines assign cabins only when deposits have been received, although they may guarantee the grade and rate requested. If this is not done, or if you find a disclaimer such as "All cabin assignments are confirmed upon embarkation of the vessel," get a guarantee in writing that your cabin will not be changed on embarkation.

Types of accommodation

There are three main types, but with many variations in each category:
● **Suites:** the largest living spaces, almost always typically with a large private balcony; and "junior" suites, with or without private balcony. Villas really are the largest of suites, with a number of different rooms, plus a courtyard or small garden.
● **Outside-view cabins:** a large picture window or one or more portholes, with or without private balcony.
● **Interior (no-view) cabins:** so called because there is no window or porthole.

Cabin sizes

Cabins provide more or less the same facilities as hotel rooms, except space. Viewed by most owners as little more than a convenient place for passengers to sleep, shower, and change, cabin space is often compromised in favor of large public rooms. In some smaller interior (no-view) and outside cabins, changing clothes is a challenge.

The latest ships have more standardized cabin sizes because they are built in modular form. I consider 180 sq ft (16.7 sq meters) to

ABOVE: underwater exploration in a Celebrity suite.
RIGHT: Owner's Suite aboard *SeaDream I*.
BELOW: ending the day aboard *Sun Princess*.

be the minimum acceptable size for a modern "standard" cabin. All have integrated bathrooms (mostly made from non-combustible phenolic glass-reinforced plastic). Ask your travel agent for the dimensions of the cabin you have selected.

The best locations

An "outside-view" cabin is recommended for first-time passengers: an "interior (no-view)" cabin has no portholes or windows,

making it more difficult to orient yourself or to gauge the weather or time.

When at sea, ships pass on the left side, so if you would like to see them, book a suite/cabin on the port (left) side of the ship – particularly if you book a cabin with a private balcony.

Take into account personal habits when choosing the cabin location. If you like to go to bed early, avoid a cabin close to the disco. If you have trouble walking, choose a cabin close to the elevator and preferably in the centre of a ship – particularly a large resort ship carrying over 1,600 passengers.

Generally, the higher the deck, the higher the cabin price, and the better the service. This is an inheritance from transoceanic times, when upper-deck cabins and suites were sunnier and warmer.

Cabins in the center of a ship are more stable and tend to be noise- and vibration-free. Ships powered by diesel engines (which means most modern vessels) create and transmit some vibration, especially at the stern, during maneuvering.

Cabins at the front of a ship are slightly crescent-shaped, given that the outer wall follows the curvature of the ship's hull. But they can be exposed to early-morning noises such as the anchor being dropped at ports where the ship is too big to dock.

Many brochures indicate cabins with "obstructed views." Cabins on lower decks are closer to engine noise and heat, especially at the aft of the vessel and around the engine casing. In many older ships, elevators may not operate to the lowermost decks.

Cabins with interconnecting doors are good for families or close friends, but the dividing wall is usually so thin you can hear the conversation next door.

Ask what personal toiletries are provided in the cabin grade you have booked. There is little standardization and some ships don't provide such things as a shower cap, or separate shampoo and conditioner.

Private balconies

Continuing the trend started by Romeo and Juliet, balconies are all the rage – in hotels, apartments, and aboard cruise ships. Once you've had one, you'll be hooked. A private balcony (sometimes called a "veranda," or "terrace") is just that. It adjoins your cabin and you can use it to sit, enjoy the view, dine, or even have a massage.

The value of a private balcony, for which you pay a premium, comes into its own in warm weather areas. Balconies are like cruises: they're addictive, and allow floor-to-ceiling light to flood the cabin.

Some private balconies are not so private, however. Balconies not separated by full floor-to-ceiling partitions (examples: Carnival Destiny, Carnival Triumph, Carnival Victory, Maasdam, Oriana, Queen Mary 2, Ryndam, Seven Seas Mariner, Seven Seas Voy-

ager, Statendam, and Veendam) don't quite cut it. You could get noise or smoke from your neighbor. Some ships have balconies with full floor-to-ceiling privacy partitions and an outside light (examples: Celebrity Century, Celebrity Galaxy, Celebrity Mercury). Some partitions in Celebrity Century, Celebrity Galaxy, and Celebrity Mercury are

THE 20 LARGEST SUITES AFLOAT

Ship	Total (sq. ft)	Total (sq. m)
Norwegian Dawn *	4,390.0	407.8
Norwegian Gem *	4,390.0	407.8
Norwegian Jade *	4,390.0	407.8
Norwegian Jewel *	4,390.0	407.8
Norwegian Pearl *	4,390.0	407.8
Norwegian Star *	4,390.0	407.8
Celebrity Constellation	2,530.0	235.0
Celebrity Infinity	2,530.0	235.0
Celebrity Millennium	2,530.0	235.0
Celebrity Summit	2,530.0	235.0
Queen Mary 2	2,249.7	209.0
Freedom of the Seas	2,025.0	188.0
Independence of the Seas	2,025.0	188.0
Liberty of the Seas	2,025.0	188.0
Seven Seas Mariner	2,002.0	186.0
Celebrity Century	1,514.5	140.7
Celebrity Galaxy	1,514.5	140.7
Celebrity Mercury	1,514.5	140.7
Silver Shadow	1,435.0	133.3
Silver Whisper	1,435.0	133.3

Note: The sizes shown include balconies.
* = also includes a large garden area.

LEFT: a balcony has become a must-have.

of the full type, while some are partial. Another downside of private balconies is that you may not be able to escape loud music being played on the open swimming pool deck atop the ship – annoying when the noise goes on until the early hours. Also, some ships have balconies too small to accommodate even two reclining chairs.

Some suites with forward-facing private balconies may not be so good, as the wind speed can make them all but unusable. And when the ship drops anchor in ports of call, the noise pollution can be awful for a while.

A "French balcony" has doors open to fresh air, but there's no balcony for you to step onto unless your feet are less than six inches long.

All private balconies except French balconies have railings to lean on atop glass panels or solid steel plates, so you can't look out to sea when seated (examples: *Costa Classica, Costa Romantica, Dawn Princess, Oceana, Sea Princess,* and *Sun Princess*). Better are ships with balconies that have clear glass (examples: *Aurora, Brilliance of the Seas, Celebrity Century, Celebrity Galaxy, Celebrity Mercury, Empress, Radiance of the Seas,* and *Serenade of the Seas*) or horizontal bars.

Facilities

These vary tremendously, but in general cabins provide some, or all, of the following:

● Two beds or a lower and upper berth (possibly, another one or two upper berths) or a double-, queen- or king-size bed. In some ships, twin beds can be pushed together to form a double.

● Depending on cabin size, a chair, or chair and table, or sofa and table, or even, in higher accommodation grades, a separate lounge or sitting area.

● Vanity/desk unit with chair or stool.

● Closet space, some drawer space, plus storage room under beds for suitcases.

● Bedside night stand/table unit.

● Private bathroom (generally small) with shower, washbasin, and toilet. Higher-grade cabins and suites may have full-size bathtubs. Some have a whirlpool bath and/or bidet, a hairdryer, and more space.

● Towels, soap, shower cap, shampoo, and conditioner. Upscale ships provide a greater selection of items.

● Electrical outlets for personal appliances, usually 110 and/or 220 volts.

● Multi-channel radio, TV (regular satellite channels or closed circuit), and DVD player.

● Telephone, for inter-cabin or ship-to-shore communication.

● A refrigerator and bar (higher grades).

● A personal safe.

Many first-cruise passengers are surprised

Penthouse Suite bedroom, *Norwegian Spirit.*

ABOVE: a suite aboard *Celebrity Constellation*.

to find their cabin has twin beds that cannot be placed together. Aboard some ships you will find upper and lower berths (a "berth" is a nautical term for a bed held in a wooden or metal frame).

A "Pullman berth" is one that tucks away out of sight during the day, usually into the bulkhead or ceiling. You have to be agile enough to climb up a short ladder at night to get into an upper berth.

WHAT A BUTLER DOES

A butler is more a personal valet than a waiter. Some of the things that a well-trained butler will do for you:

- Unpack and pack for you
- Clean your shoes
- Bring you hors d'oeuvres each evening
- Make tea and coffee
- Mix you a cocktail
- Serve dinner in your suite
- Make restaurant and spa reservations
- Have your clothes washed, pressed or dry-cleaned
- Lay out your night clothes (if you wish)
- Provide a personal wake-up call
- Bring you board games, or DVDs and CDs
- Deliver letters and messages to other passengers
- Handle requests for private parties, welcome your guests and serve them

The Suite Life

Suites are the most luxurious and spacious of all shipboard accommodation, and typically come with butler service. A suite (traditionally short for a "suite of rooms") should measure at least 400 sq ft (37 sq meters), and comprise a lounge or sitting room separated from a bedroom by a solid door – not just a curtain; a bedroom with a large bed; one or more bathrooms; and an abundance of closet, drawer, and other storage space. The best suites are usually located in the most desirable position, and both privacy and good views should be standard.

Many cruise lines inaccurately describe some accommodation as suites, when they are nothing more than a large cabin with a curtain that divides sitting and sleeping areas.

Suites come into their own on long voyages with several days spent wholly at sea. Be aware that in the large resort ships, a whole deck or two may be devoted to penthouses and suites, but occupants will have to share the rest of the ship's facilities with those in lower-priced accommodation.

That means there is no preferential seating in the showroom, the dining rooms, or on sunbathing decks. You may, however, get separate check-in facilities and preferential treatment upon disembarkation, but your luggage will be lumped together with everyone else's.

Typical Cabin Layouts

These rates are typical of those you can expect to pay for ⓐ a seven-day and ⓑ a 10-day Caribbean cruise aboard a modern cruise ship. The rates are per person and include free roundtrip airfare or low-cost air add-ons from principal North American gateways

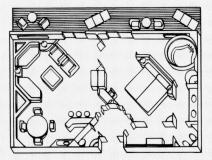

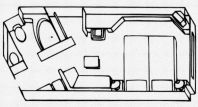

Large outside-view double with bed and convertible daytime sofabed, bathroom with shower, and good closet and drawer space.

ⓐ **$1,500** ⓑ **$2,250**

Luxury outside-view suite with private verandah, separate lounge area, vanity area, extra-large double or queen-sized bed, bathroom with tub, shower, and extensive closet and storage space.

ⓐ **$2,000** ⓑ **$3,500**

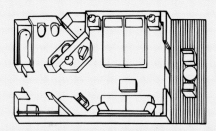

Junior suite with twin beds, lounge area, bathroom with shower, large walk-in closet, and private balcony.

ⓐ **$1,750** ⓑ **$2,500**

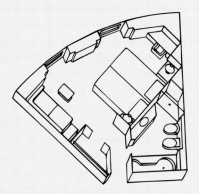

Deluxe outside-view cabin with lounge area, double or queen-size beds, bathroom with tub, shower, and ample closet and storage space.

ⓐ **$1,750** ⓑ **$2,500**

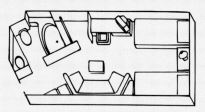

■ *Note that in some ships, third- and fourth-person upper berths are available for families or friends wishing to share. The upper Pullman berths, not shown on these cabin layouts, are recessed into the wall or ceiling above the lower beds.*

Interior no-view cabin with two lower beds convertible to queen-size bed (plus a possible upper third/fourth berth), bathroom with shower, and some closet space.

ⓐ **$800** ⓑ **$1,000**

THE MAJOR CRUISE LINES

Is big necessarily better? We compare what the world's largest cruise companies have to offer when it comes to cuisine, service and ambience

The mainstream cruise industry may appear diverse, but it is dominated by a few major players: Carnival Cruise Lines, Celebrity Cruises, Costa Cruises, Cunard Line, Holland America Line, MSC Cruises, Norwegian Cruise Line, P&O Cruises, Princess Cruises, Royal Caribbean International, and Star Cruises. In fact, the consolidation of power is even greater: eight of these 11 lines are owned by just three corporations:

Same old ocean, viewed from a brand-new elevator.

● *Carnival Corporation* (head office: Miami, Florida) owns major brands such as Carnival Cruise Lines, Costa Cruises, Cunard Line, Holland America, and Princess Cruises. It also owns Aida Cruises, Ocean Village, P&O Cruises, P&O Cruises (Australia), and Seabourn Cruise Line, as well as 75 percent of Spain-based Iberocruceros.
● *Royal Caribbean Cruises* (head office: Miami, Florida) owns Azamara Cruises, CDF Croisières de France, Celebrity Cruises, and Royal Caribbean International.
● *Star Cruises Group* (head office: Kuala Lumpur, Malaysia) owns Star Cruises, Norwegian Cruise Line and NCL America.

Between them, Holland America Line and Princess Cruises virtually control Alaska large resort ship cruising, and own hotels, lodges, tour companies and much land-based transportation (other operators have to buy their services). This virtual monopoly came about in 2002–3 when Princess Cruises' parent company, P&O Group, sold its cruising division to the Carnival Corporation.

It sounds monopolistic, but it is not really more so than some tour operators in Europe that own travel agency chains, hotels, an airline, and cruise ships.

What makes them different

So how does one choose between the companies? The marketing tags they use in television advertising provide a clue: Carnival Cruise Lines (*Ain't We Got Fun*); Celebrity Cruises (*Starring You*); Costa Cruises (*Cruising Italian Style*); Holland America Line (*Signature*

ABOVE: a sculpture enlivens the deck of a Costa ship.
RIGHT: cruise ships such as *Carnival Pride* carry thousands of people and are like floating cities.

of Excellence); Norwegian Cruise Line (*Freestyle Cruising*); Princess Cruises (*Escape Completely*); and Royal Caribbean International (*Way More than a Cruise*). Cunard Line, MSC Cruises and Star Cruises do not advertise on television.

What they have in common

All offer one thing: a well-packaged cruise vacation (generally of seven days), typically with a mix of days at sea and days in port, plenty of food, reasonable service, large-scale production shows and trendy cabaret acts, plus large casinos, shopping malls, and extensive spa and fitness facilities. Nine offer a variety of "drive to" embarkation ports within the US ("homeland cruising").

The major lines' ships have a lot in common, too. They all have art auctions (except MSC Cruises and Star Cruises), bingo, horse racing, shopping talks for ports of call (pushing "recommended" stores), programs for children and teens, wedding vows renewal programs, and wi-fi or internet connect centers (costing, typically, about 50 cents per minute). All (except MSC Cruises) still feature the "Peppermill

---

THE MAJORS UNDER THE MICROSCOPE: WHO DOES WHAT BEST

- **Carnival Cruise Lines** is known for all-round fun, activities and casinos for the lively, no-sleep needed youth market – although many passengers are over 45.

- **Celebrity Cruises** has the best food, the most elegant ships and spas, and is really underpriced.

- **Costa Cruises** has the edge on European style and lively ambience, with multi-nationality passengers, but the swimming pools are full of noisy children in peak holiday periods.

- **Cunard Line** has ocean liners and runs a regularly scheduled transatlantic service.

- **Holland America Line** has all the

right touches to appeal especially to seniors and retirees: smiling service staff, lots of flowers, traditions, good cooking demonstrations and alternative grill rooms.

- **MSC Cruises** tailors its onboard product to European passengers, and displays fine Italian flair together and a high level of service and hospitality.

- **Norwegian Cruise Line** is good for a first cruise for families with children, with a great choice of restaurants and eateries, and good entertainment, and friendly service staff.

- **P&O Cruises** operates both family-friendly and child-free ships,

with British traditions, food and entertainment.

- **Princess Cruises** has consistent product delivery, although the ships have rather bland decor, and passengers tend to be older.

- **Royal Caribbean International** is good for the Caribbean (naturally), for first-time cruisers and families, with a variety of entertainment, and interesting programs for families with children.

- **Star Cruises** has ships that are based in Southeast Asia and specializes in cruises for Asians, Australians, and British passengers, with a good choice of restaurants and ethnic cuisine.

Carnival Freedom dominates an old harbor.

Routine" (the waiter brings a huge peppermill to your table before you've even tasted the food), but none offer tableside carving or flambée items.

Extra costs include port taxes, insurance, gratuities to staff, and use of washer/ dryers in self-serve launderettes. Some lines offer their own credit cards, with points useable for upgrades, discounts, and "free" cruises.

Standing in line for embarkation, disembarkation, shore tenders and for self-serve buffet meals is inevitable aboard all large resort ships. The ships do, however, differ in their characters, facilities, maintenance, space, crew-to-passenger ratio, food and service, crew training, and other aspects.

CARNIVAL CRUISE LINES

Ships

Fantasy-class ships: *Carnival Ecstasy* (1991), *Carnival Elation* (1998), *Carnival Fantasy* (1990), *Carnival Fascination* (1994), *Carnival Imagination* (1995), *Carnival Inspiration* (1996), *Carnival Paradise* (1998), *Carnival Sensation* (1993)

Destiny-class ships: *Carnival Conquest* (2002), *Carnival Destiny* (1996), *Carnival Dream* (2009), *Carnival Freedom* (2007), *Carnival Glory* (2003), *Carnival Liberty* (2005), *Carnival Splendor* (2008), *Carnival Triumph* (1999), *Carnival Valor* (2004), *Carnival Victory* (2000)

Spirit-class ships: *Carnival Legend* (2002), *Carnival Miracle* (2004), *Carnival Pride* (2002), *Carnival Spirit* (2001)

Odd ship out: *Holiday* (1985)

About the company

Carnival Cruise Lines, the world's largest and most successful single cruise line, is a brilliantly organized company whose large resort ships provide opportunities for active fun. More than 20 new ships have been introduced since the line was founded in 1972.

Carnival does not sell itself as a "luxury" or "premium" cruise line. It consistently delivers exactly the well-packaged cruise vacation its brochures promise, for which there is a huge and growing first-time cruise market. Its smart ships have the latest high-tech entertainment facilities and features, and some include extra-cost alternative dining spots.

The line has upgraded some aspects of its operation and product (it needed to). The *Carnival Fantasy*-class ships are receiving an overdue multi-million dollar make-over,

ABOVE: Carnival projects an image of fun cruising.
RIGHT: a dazzling dining room aboard the 85,920-ton *Carnival Legend*, which carries 2,680 passengers.

including an adults-only sunbathing area, pool decks (a thatched roof over one of two hot tubs and the addition of palm trees and new mid-deck stairways), the creation of a new lobby bar, expanded children's and teens areas, and more inter-connecting cabins.

So what's it really like?

It's an all-American experience: cruising for those with a low boredom threshold – exciting, noisy, challenging, but blood pressure-raising, organized fun, slickly packaged with about 60 different itineraries. So forget relaxation – save that for when you get home.

Carnival's "fun" cruising really is for families with children and teens (anyone under 21 must be accompanied by a parent, relative or guardian) and youthful adults. Carnival ships are also good for whole-ship charters and incentive groups, for multi-generational passengers and for family reunions. Typically, about half of Carnival's passengers are taking their first cruise. About 30 percent are under the age of 35, 30 percent are over 55, the other 40 percent are between 35 and 55.

The dress code is decidedly casual – indeed, most waiters are better dressed than most passengers – particularly during youth-heavy holiday seasons and spring breaks, when clothes appear almost optional. Although Carnival is all about "happy," it's an impersonal cruise experience, overseen by young cruise directors who deliver the same jokes and banter on every trip. Perhaps it doesn't matter so much because this will be the first cruise for most passengers. Repeat customers, however, have a distinct sense of déjà vu, but carry a Gold Card for better recognition from hotel staff (Platinum for those who have cruised with Carnival more than 10 times).

The ships are clean and well maintained – if you don't peer too closely. Open deck space may look adequate when you board, but on days at sea you can expect your plastic deck chair, if you can find one that's free, to be kissing its neighbor – it's probably tied to it. There are no cushioned pads for the deck lounge chairs, which are hard to sit on (if you use just a towel) for any length of time.

You may well encounter lots of smokers,

GLITZ, GLAMOUR AND GAMBLING

Carnival's ships are floating playgrounds for young, energetic adults who need constant stimulation, close contact with lots of others, as well as the three Gs – glitz, glamour and gambling – a real "life on the ocean rave." Every night reminds you of New Year's Eve. Like life in the fast lane, this is cruising in theme-park fantasyland, with constant upbeat music, and participation games typically found in summer camp. While the fastidious might view some participation events as degrading, they are well liked by those who associate such activities with "fun" – the cruise line's theme. Typical are participation games such as Water Wars – a pool-based attraction aboard all Carnival ships, with two "battle stations" from which participants catapult each other with water balloons.

and masses of fellow passengers walking around in unharmonious clothing – passengers dress better on longer cruises such as Panama Canal sailings – clutching plastic sport drinks bottles at any time of the day or night. The decibel level is high: it is difficult to escape from noise and loud music, and "background" music is played even in cabin hallways and elevators 24 hours a day. Huge poolside movie screens are being fitted aboard Carnival's ships.

Expect to be subjected to a stream of flyers advertising daily art auctions, "designer" watches, "inch of gold/silver" and other promotions, while "artworks" for auction are strewn throughout the ships. Also, expect intrusive announcements (particularly for activities that bring revenue), and waiters hustling you to have drinks. *Carnival Capers*, the ship's daily program, is among the industry's poorest information sheets, in terms of layout and print quality, and most of it is devoted to persuading you to spend money.

There are libraries but few or no books, and bookshelves are always locked by 6pm, because you are expected to be out in the (revenue-earning) public areas each evening. If you enjoy casino gaming at sea, you could join Carnival's Ocean Players Club, which brings benefits to frequent players, depending on your level of skill.

● **Accommodation:** The balconies in many of

HOW THE MAJOR CRUISE LINES SCORE ON CUISINE AND SERVICE

Scores out of maximum 10. Note that these ratings do not reflect extra-cost "alternative" restaurants

Food	Carnival Cruise Lines	Celebrity Cruises	Costa Cruises	Cunard Line	Holland America Line	MSC Cruises	Norwegian Cruise Line	P&O Cruises	Princess Cruises	Royal Caribbean Int.	Star Cruises
Dining Room/Cuisine	6.1	7.6	6.4	8.1	7.4	7.8	6.2	7.1	7.3	6.0	6.5
Buffets/Informal Dining	5.9	7.1	5.8	7.4	6.5	6.8	6.3	6.0	6.7	6.1	6.1
Quality of Ingredients	6.0	8.0	6.2	8.0	6.9	7.5	6.3	7.1	6.7	6.3	7.7
Afternoon Tea/Snacks	4.2	6.9	5.1	7.8	5.7	6.8	4.8	6.6	5.9	5.0	6.4
Wine List	5.8	8.2	5.6	8.0	6.2	7.3	6.5	7.2	6.5	6.0	6.0
Overall Food Score	**5.60**	**7.56**	**5.82**	**7.86**	**6.54**	**7.24**	**6.02**	**6.80**	**6.62**	**5.88**	**6.54**
Service											
Dining Rooms	6.2	8.2	6.2	8.0	7.4	7.6	6.8	7.0	7.3	6.1	7.3
Bars	6.3	7.7	6.5	7.8	7.1	7.5	6.9	7.1	7.4	6.3	6.7
Cabins	6.4	7.7	6.8	7.9	7.5	7.6	6.5	7.6	7.2	6.2	6.6
Open Decks	6.0	7.5	5.8	7.6	6.6	7.5	6.2	6.4	6.8	6.1	6.4
Wines	5.0	7.7	5.3	8.0	6.1	7.6	6.4	6.0	6.2	5.2	6.0
Overall Service Score	**5.98**	**7.76**	**6.12**	**7.86**	**6.94**	**7.56**	**6.56**	**6.82**	**6.98**	**5.98**	**6.60**
Combined food/service	**5.79**	**7.66**	**5.97**	**7.86**	**6.74**	**7.40**	**6.29**	**6.81**	**6.80**	**5.93**	**6.57**

ABOVE: the balcony-rich *Carnival Triumph*.
RIGHT: it's possible to escape from all the activities.

the cabins with "private" balconies aren't so private – most can be overlooked from other cabins located on the deck above and from various public locations. You may have to carry a credit card to operate the personal safes – inconvenient. New mattresses and bed linen, also available for sale, have been fitted to all beds.

● **Passenger niggles:** The most consistent complaints include the fact that most activities are geared around trying to sell you something. Free-to-enter onboard games have pint-sized "prizes," while the cost of playing bingo keeps rising. Many people object to the heavy sales pitches for products in spas. The intrusive photographers are almost impossible to escape. The recorded poolside music is repetitious. And then there's disembarkation...

● **Embarkation and disembarkation:** This can be a bothersome procedure, depending on the port. When you do finally walk across the gangway after check-in, the few staff members on duty will merely point you in the direction of your deck or to the ship's elevators instead of escorting you to your cabin. There is little finesse and not enough attention to individuals.

Carnival operates from many "drive to" embarkation ports within the United States, and the company promotes a "vacation guarantee program" that is almost useless (check the Carnival brochure for details).

Decor

The decor is stunningly creative, although you probably wouldn't want to let the ships' interior designer loose in your home. But there's no denying that Joe Farcus, the "neon-lithic" genius behind the decor, creates a dramatic impact, from the carpets to the ceiling, mixing more colors than a rainbow could aspire to. Strangely, the sensory overload works. It's pure magic, whimsical, and very entertaining.

So, if you love color, you'll be fine. If you prefer monochrome, take sunglasses. Excepted from the dazzle are the clinical public toilets, which could do with cheering up – the designer clearly hasn't been in one lately.

Gratuities

Added to your onboard account will be $9.75 per person per day (the amount charged when this book went to press). You can have this amount adjusted, although this will mean visiting the information desk. Additionally, 15% is added to your account for all bar, wine and spa charges. The onboard currency is the US dollar – and this applies even when the ship is operating in European waters.

Cuisine/Dining

All Carnival ships have one or two main dining rooms, and dinner has four seating times (except aboard *Carnival Legend, Carnival Miracle, Carnival Pride* and *Carnival Spirit,* which have two main restaurants, each with two seating times). Menus are standardized across the fleet, and all dining venues are non-smoking.

Don't even think about a quiet table for two, or a candlelight dinner on deck – it's not Carnival's style (unless you pay extra to go to an "alternative" restaurant). Dining aboard a Carnival ship is all about table mates, social chat, lively meals, and fast eating. Tables are, however, nicely set with white tablecloths, plenty of silverware, and iced water/iced tea whenever you want it. Oh, and the tired old peppermill routine (where the waiter brings a huge peppermill to your table before you've even tasted the food) is all part of the show – delivered with friendly service that lacks polish but invites extra gratuities.

The main dining rooms marry food and show business. Waiters sing and dance, and there are constant waiter parades with flashing lights to create some excitement.

Taste-filled food is not the company's strong point, but quantity, not quality, is – although consultant chef Georges Blanc has created daily "Georges Blanc Signature" menu items. The company does strive to improve its cuisine and menu choices look good, but the actual food delivered is simply banquet-style catering, with its attendant standardization and production cooking.

While meats are of a decent quality, poultry, fish, seafood and desserts are disappointing. Sauces and gravies are used well as disguises, and there are few garnishes. The selection of fresh green vegetables, breads, rolls, cheese and ripe fruit is limited, and there is much use of canned fruit and jellied desserts, not to mention packets of jam, marmalade, butter, sugar – the same stuff you'd find in the average family eatery in the USA.

It is virtually impossible to obtain anything remotely unusual or off-menu, and the "always available" items appear to have disappeared from the menus. Vegetarian menus and children's menus are available at all meals, although they wouldn't get a generous

---

Inspirational restaurant surroundings aboard *Carnival Inspiration,* whose decor has an art nouveau look.

ABOVE: Carnival caters well for kids' tastes.
RIGHT: the entertainment is high in razzle-dazzle.

score for their nutritional content. Spa Carnival Fare has been introduced to provide healthy dining options.

The wine list, however, is good and quite varied – it even includes some fine Bordeaux reds of good vintage – but there are no wine waiters or decent-sized wine glasses. Carnival has also initiated a really good "wines by the glass" program, with state-of-the-art storage and presentation facilities that enable wines to be served properly in several locations and not just in the restaurants aboard each ship.

● **Alternative Dining Spots**
Carnival Conquest, Carnival Destiny, Carnival Freedom, Carnival Glory, Carnival Liberty, Carnival Miracle, Carnival Splendor, Carnival Triumph, Carnival Valor
These extra-cost restaurants feature fine table settings, china and silverware, and leather-bound menus. Menu favorites include prime American steaks such as filet mignon (9 ounces), porterhouse steak (24 ounces) and New York strip loin (be prepared for huge cuts of meat – shown to you at your table before you order), and broiled lobster tail, as

Waiters on Carnival ships serve both food and wine, which doesn't work at all well. They pour wine like soft drinks – too fast.

well as stone crab claws from Joe's Stone Crabs of South Miami Beach.

Reservations are necessary, and a cover charge of $30 per person for service and gratuity is payable.

A connoisseur's wine list is impressive – it includes such names as Opus One and Château Lafite-Rothschild. The food is very good, and the ambience is reasonably quiet. But if you are a couple and you have just two glasses of wine each (Grgich Hills Chardonnay or Merlot, for example, at $12.50 a glass), and pay the cover charge, that's over $100 for dinner. Caviar would cost an extra $29 for a 1-ounce serving.

Are alternative dining spots worth the extra money? Yes, I believe they are.

● **Casual Eateries**
All ships also have large food court-style spaces for casual food, fast-food items, grilled meats, pizzas (each ship serves over 800 pizzas in a typical day), stir fry, deli and salad items. There are self-help beverage stands, coffee that looks like rusty water, and tea provided in paper cups with a teabag (tea dust, as far as I'm concerned), plastic or wooden stirrers (no teaspoons and no saucers), and

ABOVE: geometric seating for sun lovers.
LEFT: afternoon tea and a view of the ocean.
BELOW: the scale of the atrium is astonishing.

Best ships for children: *Carnival Conquest, Carnival Destiny, Carnival Freedom, Carnival Glory, Carnival Legend, Carnival Liberty, Carnival Miracle, Carnival Pride, Carnival Spirit, Carnival Splendor, Carnival Triumph, Carnival Valor, Carnival Victory.* **Ships with fewer facilities:** *Carnival Ecstasy, Carnival Elation, Carnival Fantasy, Carnival Fascination, Carnival Imagination, Carnival Inspiration, Carnival Paradise, Carnival Sensation* (note: *Holiday* has almost no facilities).

packets of chemical "milk" or "creamer."

But some people are happy to have it that way, and it's actually better than what's offered aboard the ships of its competitor, Royal Caribbean International.

● **The Coffee/Tea Factor**

Regular coffee is weak and poor, scoring 1 out of 10 (paper/foam cups in buffet areas). Espresso and cappuccino coffees score 2 out of 10 (paper/foam cups, in buffet areas).

For Children:

Carnival is a fine family-friendly cruise line, carrying more than 575,000 children a year, and "Camp Carnival," the line's extensive child/youth program, is well organized and extensive. There are five age groups: Toddlers (ages 2–5); Juniors (6–8); Intermediate (9–11); Tweens (12–14, Circle C) and late Teens (15–17, with Club O2). Even the under-twos are now being catered to, with special programs aboard each ship. Meanwhile, Family Fun Nights are all about reconnecting parents to their children – something many can do only on vacation. Soft-drinks packages can be bought for children (adults, too). Note that a babysitting service is not available after 10pm.

Entertainment

The ships have big showlounges, all non-smoking, and large-scale flesh-and-feather production shows. On a typical cruise, there will be one or two large-scale shows, with male and female lead singers and a clutch of dancers backed by a 10-piece live orchestra and supported by pre-recorded backing tracks.

These are loud, ritzy-glitzy, razzle-dazzle, Las Vegas-style revues with little or no story line or flow – lots of running around on stage and stepping in place, but little real dancing. The skimpy costumes are very colorful, as is the lighting, with extensive use of "color mover" lights. Stage "smoke" is much

ABOVE: cooling off in the outdoor pool.
RIGHT: keeping the muscles toned.
BELOW: the deck can be an outdoor gym.

overused – to the irritation of anyone seated in the front few rows.

Carnival rotates entertainers aboard its ships, so that passengers see different acts each night, and specialty acts take center stage on nights when there is no production show. There's also live music in just about every bar and lounge – although there appears to be a trend to replace live music with more DJs – and smutty late-night adults-only comedy.

Cabaret acts include vocalists, magic acts, ventriloquists, and comedy jugglers. Each cruise has karaoke nights, a passenger talent show, and a discotheque with ear-splitting volumes and megaphones to enable you to converse with your partner.

Spa/Fitness Facilities

Spa/Fitness facilities are operated by Steiner Leisure, a specialist concession, whose young, revenue-conscious staff will try to sell you Steiner's own-brand beauty products. Some fitness classes are free; others, such as yoga and kick-boxing, cost extra (typically $10 per class), and you'll need to sign up to join.
Examples of treatments: Swedish Massage ($116 for 50 minutes); Aroma Stone Massage

($175 for 75 minutes); Couples Massage ($242 for 50 minutes); Facial ($109 for 50 minutes); Seaweed Body Wrap, with half-body massage ($176 for 90 minutes). It's prudent to book appointments early.

The Spa Carnival layout spaces and facilities are identical to other ships in the same "class," as follows:

● *Carnival Legend, Carnival Miracle, Carnival Pride, Carnival Spirit*
SpaCarnival spans two decks, is located directly above the navigation bridge in the forward part of the ship and has 13,700 sq ft (1,272 sq meters) of space. Facilities on the lower level include a solarium, eight treatment rooms, lecture rooms, sauna and steam rooms for men and women, and a beauty parlor; the upper level consists of a large gymnasium with floor-to-ceiling windows on three sides, including forward-facing ocean views (with a large array of the latest in muscle-pumping electronic machines), and an aerobics room with instructor-led classes (the aerobics room and gymnasium together measure almost 6,000 sq ft/560 sq meters).
● *Carnival Conquest, Carnival Destiny, Carnival Freedom, Carnival Glory, Carnival*

The funnel's "X" identifies a Celebrity ship.

Miracle, Carnival Splendor, Carnival Triumph, Carnival Valor

SpaCarnival spans two decks (with a total area of 13,700 sq ft/1,272 sq meters), and is located directly above the navigation bridge in the forward part of the ship (accessible from the forward stairway). Facilities on the lower level include a solarium, eight treatment rooms, lecture rooms, sauna and steam rooms for men and women, and a beauty parlor; the upper level consists of a large gymnasium with floor-to-ceiling windows on three sides, including forward-facing ocean views. It has the latest in muscle-pumping electronic machines, and an aerobics room with instructor-led classes, some of which cost extra.

● *Carnival Ecstasy, Carnival Elation, Carnival Fantasy, Carnival Fascination, Carnival Imagination, Carnival Inspiration, Carnival Paradise, Carnival Sensation*

SpaCarnival is located on Sports Deck, forward of the ship's mast, and accessed from the forward stairway. It consists of a gymnasium with ocean-view windows that look out over the ship's bow – you could "cycle" your way to the next port of call if you so wish – complete with a good array of the latest in muscle-pumping electronic machines, an aerobics exercise room, men's and women's changing rooms (towels are provided), sauna and steam rooms, and beauty salon.

Ships

Century-class ships: *Celebrity Century* (1995), *Celebrity Galaxy* (1996), *Celebrity Mercury* (1997)

Millennium-class ships: *Celebrity Constellation* (2002), *Celebrity Infinity* (2001), *Celebrity Millennium* (2000), *Celebrity Summit* (2001)

Solstice-class ships: *Celebrity Equinox* (2009), *Celebrity Solstice* (2008)

Other ships: *Celebrity Xpedition* (2001)

About the company

In the 1990s, its formative years, Celebrity Cruises established an outstanding reputation for its cuisine, particularly in the main dining rooms, with a formal presentation and service. It advertises itself as a premium line with a taste of luxury, and that, in a nutshell, sums it up nicely because the product delivery on board is superior to that of its parent company, Royal Caribbean International.

The ship are instantly recognizable, thanks to the "X" on the funnel denoting the third letter of the Greek alphabet, the Greek "chi" or "C" in English, for Chandris, the family that founded Celebrity Cruises in 1989.

In 2007 Celebrity Cruises created a new company, **Azamara Cruises**, with mid-size ships, including *Azamara Journey* (2000) and

Azamara Quest (2000). The idea is to focus on lesser-visited destinations around the world, and offer in-depth shore experiences. All hotel services and cruise operations are, however, operated by Celebrity Cruises.

So what's it really like?

The ships are spotlessly clean and extremely well maintained. There are always lots of flowers and flower displays – some ships have flower shops, where you can buy fresh blooms for special occasions.

There is a lot of fine artwork aboard Celebrity's ships; it may not be to everybody's taste, but it is probably the most remarkable collection of contemporary art in the cruise industry. The company provides a lot of the niceties that other lines have long forgotten, although some are now playing "catch up": being escorted to your cabin on arrival by a steward; waiters who carry your trays when you obtain food from buffets or casual eateries; water spritzes on the pool deck. On days at sea in warm weather areas, if you are sunbathing on deck, someone will bring you a cold towel, and a sorbet, ice water or iced tea.

Regardless of the accommodation grade, Celebrity Cruises delivers a well-defined North American cruise experience at a modest price. Book a suite-category cabin for the extra benefits it brings – it's worth it. Strong points include the many European staff and the high

A shore excursion on the Galápagos Islands

level of service, fine spas with a good range of facilities and treatments, taste-filled food served in fine European dining tradition, a "zero announcement policy" (which means little intrusion), cloth towels in public restrooms instead of the paper towels found aboard most major companies. Such touches differentiate Celebrity Cruises from its competitors.

Its ships have significantly more staff than other ships of comparable size and capacity. This is especially noticeable in the housekeeping and food and beverage departments, and results in a superior product.

Celebrity's ships are best suited to well-educated, more sophisticated adult couples (both young and not so young), families with older children and teenagers, and singles who like to mingle in a large ship setting with stylish surroundings, reasonably decent entertainment, and food and service that are extremely good, at a price that represents excellent value for money.

Even so, such things as topless

CELEBRITY'S CLASS CONSCIOUSNESS

There really are three different "classes" aboard Celebrity ships: those in accommodation designated as suites; those in standard exterior-view and interior (no view) cabins; and a third that comes between the two, known as "Concierge Class."

Concierge Class adds another dimension and items that bring added value to passengers. Enhanced facilities include priority embarkation, disembarkation, tender tickets, alternative dining and spa reservations; European duvet; double bed overlay (no more falling "between the cracks" for couples); choice of four pillows (goose down pillow, isotonic pillow, body pillow, conformance pillow); eight-vial flower vase on vanity desk; throw pillows on sofa; fruit basket; binoculars; golf umbrella; leather telephone notepad; larger beach towels; hand-held hairdryer. Balconies get better furniture. In the bathrooms: plusher Frette bathrobe; larger towels in sea green and pink (alternating days); flower in silver vase in bathroom. It all adds up to more value for your money, and better recognition from staff.

sunbathing spaces are now available aboard all ships (except *Azamara Journey, Azamara Quest, Celebrity Xpedition*). Meanwhile, what were formerly cigar smoking lounges have been turned into cozy jazz/piano lounges. Some cruises aboard some ships are designated as child-free.

Sadly, background music is now played almost everywhere, and any lounge designated as "music-free" is typically full of activities and participation events, so it's hard to find a quiet corner to sit and read.

Embarkation: When you first embark, a member of staff, dressed in a crisp white uniform (or black butler's uniform if you are in one of the more expensive suites) will escort you and carry your hand luggage to your cabin, with white glove service and a smile.

So, what's the difference between Celebrity Cruises and its parent, Royal Caribbean International? Here are a few examples relating to food items:

● **Royal Caribbean International** (*Brilliance of the Seas*)

Café: Seattle Coffee Company coffee served in paper cups.

Dining Room Food: overcooked, poor quality (think leather briefcase) meat.

Dining Room: no tables for two.

In the Windjammer Café, waiters do not help

The casino aboard *Azamara Journey*.

passengers to tables with trays; plastic plates are used, cutlery is wrapped in paper napkins, melamine mugs for coffee/tea, tea selection disappointing, and poor-quality (Lipton) teas. Public restrooms have paper towels.

● **Celebrity Cruises** (*Celebrity Century*):

Cova Café: Coffees/teas served in china cups/saucers, with doily and chocolate.

Dining Room Food: Good standard of food and presentation.

Dining Room: Tables for two are available.

Lido Cafe: Waiters line up to help passengers with trays to tables. Real china, white cloth napkins, polished cutlery, and a decent selection of teas are provided.

The public restrooms have cloth towels.

Formal dining aboard *Celebrity Millennium*.

Decor

The decor is elegant – Greek, classical, minimalist, although it could be said to be a little antiseptic and cool in places. Celebrity Cruises has some of the most eclectic sculptures and original artwork, from Picasso to Warhol, found at sea. The colors do not jar the senses, and cannot be said to be glitzy – except for the casinos, which are mostly vulgar.

The ships absorb people well, and the flow is, for the most part, good, except for entrances to showlounges and in photo galleries. Each public room subtly invites you to move on to the next.

Gratuities

US$10 per person per day is added to your onboard account. You can have this amount adjusted if you visit the guest relations desk before the end of the cruise. Additionally, 15% is added for all bar, wine purchases, and 10% for spa treatments. The onboard currency is the US dollar.

For Children

Junior passengers are divided into four groups: Shipmates (3–6 years), Cadets (7–9), Ensigns (10–12), Teens (13–17).
● **Best ships for children:** *Celebrity Constellation, Celebrity Infinity, Celebrity Millennium, Celebrity Summit.* Almost as good: *Celebrity Century, Celebrity Galaxy, Celebrity Mercury.*

Cuisine/Dining

The dining rooms aboard all ships are non-smoking areas. There are two seatings for dinner, and open seating for breakfast and lunch. Table settings are excellent, with fine quality linen, china and glassware. Tables for two are available – far more so than most of the other major lines. What sets Celebrity apart is the superior training and supervision of dining room waiters, and the service.

The food represents a wide range of culinary influences; it is based on classical French cuisine, modified to appeal to North Americans and European alike. Menus are standardized across the fleet. The variety of cuisine in the main dining rooms is good, the food has taste, and it is very attractively presented and served in a well orchestrated oper-

The library aboard *Celebrity Xpedition.*

ation that displays fine European traditions. Full service in-cabin dining is also available for all meals, including dinner.

The food is made fresh from high-quality ingredients – no pre-made sauces, soups, or croissants here. Take croissants, for example. Those found aboard Celebrity ships are made fresh each morning, while aboard most competitors' ships they are purchased ashore. There's a big difference in their taste and consistency, depending on what kind of dough and butter are used.

Celebrity Cruises also has well-trained sommeliers and wine waiters who know their subject. The four largest ships (*Celebrity Constellation, Celebrity Infinity, Celebrity Millennium, Celebrity Summit*) have special wine rooms in their "alternative" restaurants that you can actually have dinner in, and fine wines that can cost more than $10,000 a bottle – but also wines that start at about $20.
● **Casual Eateries**
There are casual self-serve buffets aboard all Celebrity Cruises' ships. Most are laid out in continuous lines, which causes lines to form at peak times – when morning shore excur-

Celebrity's large-scale shows get mixed reviews.

sions return, for example, by lunchtime. However, Celebrity is trying to be more creative with these buffets, and, like other cruise lines, has stations for pasta, sushi, salads, grilled and rotisserie items, and hot food items. When you have chosen your food, a waiter will take your tray to a table. A bar trolley service for drinks and wines is provided at lunchtime, and wine waiters are always on hand to discuss and take wine orders for dinner. All the ships make great martinis.

● **The Coffee/Tea Factor**
Regular Coffee: Weak and poor. Score: 2 out of 10. Espresso/Cappuccino coffees: Score: 3 out of 10. Note that, if you order espresso/cappuccino coffees in the dining room, there is a charge; they are treated like a bar item.

Cova Cafés cost extra, but are worth it. They are genuine Italian coffee houses, staffed by helpful, uniformed servers.

Cova Café: All ships have a Cova Café, a seagoing version of the original Café di Milano that was located next to La Scala Opera House in Milan. The shipboard cafés are in prominent locations, and display cases show off the extensive range of Cova coffee, chocolates and alcoholic digestives for sale. Cova Cafés provide an agreeable setting for those who like fine Italian coffees, pastries and cakes. Breakfast pastries are superb – favorites include the Italian pane con cioccolata (chocolate pastry). Cova coffee comes in a proper china cup, with a Cova chocolate on the side, and the tables have tablecloths.

Entertainment

The company has little cohesive policy regarding big production shows, and can't seem to get them right. Shows aboard some ships are quite decent, with good costuming and lighting, but others look dated and lack story line, flow or connectivity. Each ship carries its own resident troupe of singers/dancers and audiovisual support staff. Bar service, available throughout shows, disrupts concentration. While some cabaret acts are good, they are the same ones seen aboard many ships. All showlounges are non-smoking venues.

Celebrity vessels have a variety of bands and small musical units, although there is very little music for social dancing, other than disco and pop music.

Then there are the summer camp-style audience participation events, games and talent shows that don't sit well with Celebrity's quality of food and service. It's time for some new ones. There are also the inevitable country line dances and playschool routines.

On days at sea the program is crammed with things to do, though the emphasis is on revenue-enhancing activities such as art auctions, giant jackpot bingo, and horse racing.

Spa/Fitness Facilities

Celebrity Cruises, acknowledging the popularity of spas and fitness facilities, has been improving its offerings. Spa/fitness programs are staffed and operated by Steiner Leisure, a specialist concession, whose staff, who have sales targets as well as enthusiasm, will try to sell you Steiner's own-brand beauty products. Some fitness classes are free; others, such as yoga, and kickboxing, cost $10 per class. Being aboard will give you an opportunity to try some of the more exotic massages.

Massage (including exotic massages such as Aroma Stone massage, Chakra Balancing massage and other well-being massages), facials, pedicures, and beauty salon treatments cost extra. Examples: massage at $120 (50 minutes), facial at $120, seaweed wrap (75 minutes) $190 – to which you need to add a gratuity of 10 percent. Personal training sessions in the gymnasium cost $83 for one hour.

Costa pays tribute to Christopher Columbus.

COSTA CRUISES

Ships

Atlantica-class ships: *Costa Atlantica* (2000), *Costa Mediterranea* (2003)
Fortuna-class ships:*Costa Concordia* (2006), *Costa Fortuna* (2003), *Costa Luminosa* (2009), *Costa Magica* (2004), *Costa Pacifica* (2009), *Costa Serena* (2007)
Classica-class ships: *Costa Classica* (1992), *Costa Romantica* (1993)
Other ships: *Costa Allegra* (1992), *Costa Europa* (1986), *Costa Marina* (1990), *Costa Victoria* (1996)

About the company

Costa Crociere (Italian for Costa Cruises) traces its history back to 1860 when Giacomo Costa started an olive oil business. The first ship, in 1924, transported that oil. Costa's first passenger ship entered service in 1948. The company specializes in cruises for Europeans or passengers with European tastes, and particularly Italians, during the summer. Costa has initiated an aggressive newbuild policy in recent years, in order to modernize the company's previously aging fleet of different sized ships.

Most ships are well maintained, although there are inconsistencies throughout the fleet. The same is true of cleanliness – some ships are very clean, while others are a little dusty around the edges, as are its shore tenders. The ships have a laid-back European "feel" to their decor and manner of product delivery. Carnival Corporation, which owns Costa Cruises, bought part of the company in 1997 (together with Airtours), and the rest in 2000.

So what's it really like?

Costa is noted for its "Italian" ambiance. There are few Italian crew members, however, although many officers are Italian. Nevertheless, Costa's lifestyle is perceived to be Italian – lively, very noisy, yet easygoing. The dress code is casual, even on formal nights.

Costa does a good job of providing first-

ABOVE: the pool aboard *Costa Magica*.
MIDDLE: *Costa Atlantica*'s jazzy decor.
RIGHT: *Costa Allegra*'s statuesque atrium.

time cruise passengers with a packaged holiday that is a mix of sophistication and basic fare, albeit accompanied by loud music. Most passengers are Italian, with a generous sprinkling of other Europeans. One night at the end of each cruise is reserved for a "Roman Bacchanal," when passengers dress up toga-style for dinner and beyond. This is a cruise line for those who like to party. If you want quiet, take earplugs – good ones.

On European and Mediterranean cruises, English will be the language least spoken, as most passengers will be Italian, Spanish, French and German. On Caribbean itineraries, a high percentage of passengers will speak Spanish, as the ships carry passengers from several Latin American countries in addition to passengers from North America.

Expect to cruise with a lot of children of all

> At embarkation, few staff members are on duty at the gangway when you arrive, and they will merely point you in the direction of your deck, or to the ship's elevators instead of escorting you to your cabin.

ages if you book for peak holiday cruises – and remember that in Europe schoolchildren at certain times such as Easter have longer vacations. On some European itineraries, passengers embark and disembark in almost every port along the way, which makes for a rather disjointed cruise experience, because there is almost no start or end to the cruise.

There is extensive smoking on board. No-smoking zones and signs are often ignored to the frustration of non-smoking passengers, and ashtrays are moved at whim; many of the officers and crew also smoke, even when moving through public rooms, so they don't bother to enforce the no-smoking zones.

The cabins tend to be on the mean side in size, but the decor is fresh and upbeat, and the bathrooms are very practical units. Some ships have cabin bathrooms with sliding doors – an excellent alternative to those that open inward, using up space.

Decor

Older Ships: *Costa Allegra, Costa Classica, Costa Europa, Costa Marina, Costa Romantica, Costa Victoria* have a distinctively European feel. They are lively without being brash, or pastel-toned without being boring, depending on the ship you choose.

Newer, larger ships – *Costa Atlantica, Costa Concordia, Costa Fortuna, Costa Magica, Costa Mediterranea, Costa Serena* – have an "in-your-face" brashness similar to the ships of Carnival Cruise Lines, with grainy and unflattering digital artwork on walls and panels, and even inside elevators.

The "entertainment architecture," as designer Joe Farcus calls it, can't be ignored. There is an abundance of jazzy colors, fine or grotesque sculptures (depending on your taste) and huge murals that are both impressive and mind-numbing.

Gratuities

The onboard currency is the euro (Europe/Mediterranean cruises), or US dollar (Caribbean cruises). On the former, €32 per 7-day cruise per person is charged to your onboard account, plus 10% to all bar and wine orders. On Caribbean cruises, the figures are $53 per 7-day cruise per person and 15% for bar and wine orders. Many non-Italians would prefer to choose when to tip and how much. To have these amounts adjusted, you need to visit the information desk.

Cuisine/Dining

All ships have two seatings for dinner; dining times on Europe/Mediterranean and South America cruises are usually later than those in the Caribbean because Europeans and Latin passengers eat much later than North Americans. Few tables for two are available, most being for four, six, or eight. All dining rooms are smoke-free – in theory.

The cuisine is best described as continental, with many regional Italian dishes and much emphasis on pasta: 50 pasta dishes per cruise. Except for pasta dishes (made fresh on board) and cream sauces, presentation and food quality are not memorable, and are the subject of many negative comments from passengers. While the quality of meat is adequate, it is often disguised with gravies and rich sauces. Fish and seafood tend to lack taste, and are often over-

COSTA CRUISES: BEST SUITED TO...

Costa ships are best suited to young (and young at heart) couples, singles and families with children who enjoy big-city life, outdoor cafés, constant and noisy activity, eating late, loud entertainment, and food more notable for quantity than quality.

All printed materials (room service folio, menus, etc.) are in six languages (Italian, English, French, German, Portuguese, and Spanish). Announcements are made in at least two languages in the Caribbean and at least four in Europe and the Mediterranean.

cooked. Green vegetables are hard to come by. Breads and bread rolls are usually good, but the desserts are of supermarket quality and lack taste.

There is a wine list but no wine waiters; table waiters are expected to serve both food and wine, which doesn't work well. Almost all wines are young – very young.

● **Alternative Dining**

If you opt for one of the "alternative" restaurants aboard the larger ships, note that a cover charge applies: €20 per person plus 10% service charge (Europe/Mediterranean cruises), or $20 per person plus 15% service charge (Caribbean cruises).

● **Casual Eateries**

All ships have self-serve lido buffets. In most, you have to move along with your tray, but the latest ships have more active stations and individual islands. The items available are quite basic. All ships except *Costa Europa* also have a pizzeria.

● **The Coffee/Tea Factor**

Regular Coffee: Decent and quite strong. Score: 5 out of 10.

Espresso/Cappuccino coffees (Lavazza) are among the best served by the 10 major cruise lines: the main competition is from Celebrity Cruises' Cova Café; Star Cruises also serves

If you might expect to find jovial Italian waiters serving you, you'll be disappointed, although the restaurant managers could be Italian. Service is inconsistent across the Costa fleet.

Lavazza. All Costa ships have coffee machines in most lounges/bars. Score: 8 out of 10.

For children

Junior passengers are in four groups: Kids Club is for 3–6; Junior Club is for 7–12; Teen Club is for 13–17. The program varies by ship, itinerary and season. Group babysitting is available 6.30–11pm. During port days, babysitting is available generally 8.30am–12.30pm and 2.30–6.30pm.

● **Best ships for children:** *Costa Atlantica, Costa Concordia, Costa Fortuna, Costa Magica, Costa Mediterranea, Costa Serena.* But not: *Costa Allegra, Costa Classica, Costa Europa, Costa Marina, Costa Romantica, Costa Victoria.*

Entertainment

Each ship carries its own resident troupe of singers/dancers and audio-visual support staff, but Costa Cruises is not known for the

Costa Cruises offers a wide range of massages.

quality of its entertainment. What it does present tends to be of the "no finesse" variety, with revue-style shows that have little story line, poor choreography and execution, but plenty of fast-moving action – more stepping in place than dancing – and lots of volume. It's entertainment to pass the time rather than remember.

Cabaret acts (typically singers, magicians, comedy jugglers, ventriloquists, and so on) are entertaining but rather ho-hum.

Most of the passenger participation activities include poolside games such as a "Belly Flop" competition, election of the "Ideal Couple," and other juvenile games – but some families love them. There are also dance classes, and the inevitable "Fine Art Auction."

Spa/Fitness Facilities

These vary according to ship and size. The newest and largest ships (*Costa Atlantica, Costa Concordia, Costa Fortuna, Costa Magica, Costa Mediterranea* and *Costa Serena*) have more space and better facilities, while the others (*Costa Allegra, Costa Europa, Costa Marina*) have only basic facilities.

Spa/fitness facilities are staffed and operated by Steiner Leisure, a specialist concession, whose young staff will try to sell you Steiner's own-brand beauty products. Some fitness classes are free, while some, such as yoga, and kick-boxing, cost $10 per class.

However, being aboard will give you an opportunity to try some of the more exotic treatments, particularly some of the massages available. Massage (including exotic massages such as Aroma Stone massage, Chakra Balancing massage and other well-being massages), facials, pedicures, and beauty salon treatments cost extra – massage, for example, costs about $2 per minute, plus gratuity. It's wise to make appointments early.

Aboard *Costa Concordia* and *Costa Serena*, Samsara Spa accommodation grades benefit from Oriental-themed decor and Samsara bathroom amenities, and 12 Samsara Suites have direct access to the Samsara Spa

Costa Marina: good views of where you've been.

facilities and special packages and concessions. To use the sauna/steam and relaxation areas aboard some of the ships, you'll need to buy a day pass, for €35 per person.

CUNARD LINE

Ships:

Queen Mary 2 (2004), *Queen Victoria* (2007).

About the company

Cunard Line was established in 1839, as the British and North American Steam Packet Company, to carry the Royal Mail and passengers from the Old World to the New. Its first ship, *Britannia*, sailed on its maiden voyage on American Independence Day in 1840, and the author Charles Dickens crossed the Atlantic aboard the ship in 1842.

Since 1840, Cunard Line has always had ships built to sail across the North Atlantic. From 1850 until the arrival of *QE2* in 1969, all of the line's ships and those of White Star

QM2 at San Francisco's Golden Gate Bridge.

Line (with which Cunard merged in 1934) had several classes. Your luggage label, therefore, declared not only your name but also what you could afford. Today, there's no class distinction, other than by the grade of accommodation you choose. In other words, you get what you pay for, as on any cruise ship.

So what's it really like?

Sailing aboard a Cunard Line ship is quite different to being aboard a standard cruise ship. The vessels incorporate a lot of maritime history and the grand traditions of ocean liners – as opposed to the average cruise ship, with its tendency to tacky high-street trappings. Assuming your sea legs can cope with sometimes less than calm waters, a transatlantic crossing is supremely civilized, particularly if you are able to enjoy being cosseted in accommodation that allows you to dine in the "grill"-class restaurants with their fine cuisine and presentation.

Cunard Line's ships have well-stocked libraries, run by professional librarians, not cruise staff, as well as bookshops in which ship buffs can buy Cunard memorabilia.

Cunard Line ships are best suited to a wide range of seasoned and well-traveled couples and single passengers who enjoy the cosmopolitan setting of an ocean liner, with their extensive array of facilities, public rooms, dining rooms, and lecture programs. A wide range of joint travel programs, tour configurations and pre-post stays is integrated into the marketing of all Cunard Line ships

Male social hosts – typically 10 on an around-the-world cruise – serve as dancing partners for women traveling alone. This is a popular program started by Cunard Line in the 1970s. The ships also carry lecturers who specialize in several avenues of life enrichment.

Cunard Line is the only cruise line that allows you to take your dog or cat with you (*Queen Mary 2* transatlantic crossings only).

Cuisine/Dining

Cunard Line provides good-quality ingredients (sourced in Europe and the USA). The cuisine is still of a mass market standard – you'll find butter in packets in some venues. However, at the self-serve buffets, salt and pepper are usually provided on each table. Espressos and cappuccinos are available in the dining rooms, and at extra cost in many bars. Cunard uses Colombian coffee.

Both Cunard Line ships have "grill rooms" as well as traditional large restaurants, and casual self-service dining venues. Grill rooms are more exclusive and some have à la carte menus, while the main restaurants have fixed menus. The grill rooms have seating dining at assigned tables, when you wish, while the main Britannia Restaurants (the same name is used in both ships) have two seatings.

The cuisine includes many traditional British favorites, together with extensive French dishes as well as regional specialties from around the world, nicely presented on Wedgwood china.

For Children

Children's facilities are quite good aboard both *Queen Mary 2* and *Queen Victoria*, though they aren't as extensive as aboard the former *Queen Elizabeth 2*. Youngsters are supervised by real English nannies.

Gratuities

The onboard currencies are the British pound and the US dollar, depending on the operating area. Gratuities are automatically charged to your onboard account – you will need to visit the information desk to make any changes necessary.

The present amount is $13 per person per day (Grill Class accommodation, including children) or $11 per person per day (all other accommodation). In addition, 15% is auto-

ABOVE: traditional dining, Cunard-style.
BELOW: Beef Wellington aboard *Queen Mary II*.

matically added to all bar and wine, and health spa/salon bills.

Entertainment

The main production shows are colourful and visual. All production shows are performed to pre-recorded backing tracks to supplement the showband. Other shows consist of cabaret acts – typically singers, magicians, mime artistes, comedy jugglers, and, occasionally, comedians – doing the cruise ship circuit. A number of bands and small musical units provide live music for dancing and listening.

Spa/Fitness Facilities

The spa/fitness centers are operated by Canyon Ranch (*QM2*) and Harding Brothers/Multitrax Maritime under the brand name "The onboard Spa Company (*Queen Victoria*), with prices that generally match those of land-based health resorts.

Romantic cruising: *Queen Victoria*'s Grand Lobby.

HOLLAND AMERICA LINE

Ships

Amsterdam (2000), *Eurodam* (2008), *Maas-dam* (1993), *Noordam* (2006), *Oosterdam* (2003), *Prinsendam* (1988), *Rotterdam* (1997), *Ryndam* (1994), *Statendam* (1993), *Veendam* (1996), *Volendam* (1999), *Westerdam* (2004), *Zaandam* (2000), *Zuiderdam* (2002).

About the company

Holland America Line, owned by Carnival Corporation, was founded in 1873, and its name is a leftover from the days of transatlantic travel between Holland and the United States. Its newest ships get larger and larger as the line now caters well to multi-generational families with children. It has a private island, Half Moon Cay, in the Bahamas.

So what's it really like?

Fresh management with updated ideas, the line's "Signature of Excellence" program, the food variety and creativity have all made the HAL experience better during the past year. The ships benefit from an abundance of fresh flowers, museum-quality art pieces, and more attention to detail than all the other major lines with the exception of Celebrity Cruises.

ABOVE: horseback excursion, Half Moon Cay.
BELOW: a variety of sports at sea level.

The brand encompasses basically two types of ship. Younger families with children and grandchildren are best suited to the new, larger vessels such as *Eurodam, Noordam, Oosterdam, Westerdam,* and *Zuiderdam,* whereas those of senior years – HAL's traditional audience of repeat passengers from alumni groups – are best suited to ships that

been to sea before. Many crew members have been promoted to supervisory positions due to a host of new ships introduced, but few of those promoted have the formal training, professional or management skills, or experience to do the job well. Internal promotion is fine, but decreased professionalism is not the price that passengers should pay. However, HAL's mainly Indonesian crew members are willing, polite, and smile a lot – particularly if extra tips are forthcoming – which is more than can be said for service staff on land today, particularly in western countries.

HAL is one of only three of the 10 major cruise lines with proper cinemas built into all its ships. It also operates many theme-related cruises, and has an extensive "University at Sea" program of life-enrichment lecturers. The cinemas also have superb full demonstration kitchens built in for a new "Culinary Arts" program that includes celebrity chefs, and interactive cooking demos.

HAL has established smoking and no-smoking areas throughout its ships, but there are many more smokers than you might expect, depending on ship and itinerary.

Holland America Line ships are best suited to older couples and singles (and their grandchildren), who like to mingle in a large ship,

are smaller and less glitzy (*Amsterdam*, *Maasdam*, *Prinsendam*, *Rotterdam*, *Ryndam*, *Statendam*, *Veendam*, and *Zaandam*). All the ships are well maintained, and cleaning takes place constantly. All ships have teakwood outdoors promenade decks, whereas most rivals have artificial grass or some other form of indoor-outdoor carpeting.

Holland America Line has its own training school in Jakarta, Indonesia, and so is able to "pre-train" crew members who have never

The thermal suite aboard *Zuiderdam*.

HAL'S SIGNATURE OF EXCELLENCE

Between 2004 and 2006, "Signature of Excellence" improvements were introduced, at a cost of $225 million. These cover dining, service, accommodation, and activities, and include "Premium-Plus" Euro-Top mattresses, 100 percent cotton bed linens or duvets (top suites only), massage showerheads, fruit baskets, and DVD players. Elemis personal bathroom amenities are provided for all passengers (these are better than Celebrity's present bathroom amenities, for example). Suite occupants also have access to the exclusive

Neptune Lounge (with concierge services), thus in effect creating a two-class system that suite occupants like. Bathrobes and a range of personal toiletries are provided for all passengers, and hot hors d'oeuvres and canapés are always part of the pre-dinner cocktail scene.

Ashore at Half Moon Cay in the Bahamas.

in an unhurried setting with fine-quality surroundings, with plenty of eclectic antique artwork, decent – though not gourmet – food and service from a smiling Indonesian/Filipino crew who don't have the finesse many passengers expect from a "premium" product.

Decor

Aboard *Amsterdam, Maasdam, Prinsendam, Rotterdam, Ryndam, Statendam, Veendam, Volendam, Zaandam*, the decor is rather bland (restful), with eclectic artwork that is focused on Dutch artefacts, mainly from the 16th and 17th centuries.

Aboard the newest ships (*Eurodam, Oosterdam, Westerdam, Zuiderdam*) the decor is more showy, lively and glitzy – acceptable for families with children who like bright things

> When you first embark, a member of staff, in a crisp white uniform (or black butler's uniform if you are in a top suite) will escort you directly to your cabin and carry your hand luggage. Early embarkation and leisurely disembarkation are available.

such as large wall panels with digital "in-your-face" artwork that present an *Alice in Wonderland* look.

You wouldn't go for it in your living room, but aboard these large resort ships it works. It is important, therefore, to choose the right ship for your personality type, and for the facilities that appeal.

Gratuities

$10 per person per day (the amount charged when this book went to press) is added to your onboard account. You can have this amount adjusted, but you'll need to visit the information desk to do so. Additionally, 15% is added to bar and wine accounts. The onboard currency is the US dollar.

Cuisine/Dining

For dinner, Holland America Line features both open seating (on one level) or assigned tables (at fixed times, on the other level) in its dining rooms ; it's called "As You Wish" dining. For breakfast and lunch in the main dining room, an open seating policy applies. All dining venues are non-smoking.

Some tables for two are available, but most are for four, six, eight or 10. The larger tables are ideal for multi-generational families. Fine Rosenthal china and cutlery are used. Live music is provided for dinner. "Lighter option" meals are always available for the nutrition-conscious and the weight-conscious.

Holland America Line food was greatly upgraded when master chef Rudi Sodamin arrived in 2005 as a consultant; he introduced his "Wild About Salmon" and other creative ideas, and the "Culinary Arts Center" (with its own dedicated live interactive demonstration kitchen and guest chef program) has been a success story. In 2008 menus were revamped to include more regional cuisine and more local ingredients.

However, while the USDA beef is very good, poultry and most fish tend to be over-cooked (except when the ships are in Alaska, where halibut and salmon are excellent).

What are not "premium" are the packets of sugar, and packets (instead of glass jars) of supermarket-brand breakfast jams, marmalade and honey, sugar, and butter. Also, coffee and teas are poor-quality, except in the extra-charge Explorations Café. While packets may be suitable for a family diner, they do not belong aboard ships that claim "award-winning cuisine."

Dessert and pastry items are good, suited to American tastes, but canned fruit and jellied desserts are much in evidence. Most of the "international" cheeses are highly colored, processed cheese (cruises in Europe have better access to European cheeses).

HAL also offers complimentary ice cream during certain hours of the day, as well as hot

Cookery lessons are offered on some cruises.

hors d'oeuvres in all bars – something other major lines seem to have dropped, or charge extra for. Cabin service breakfasts are very basic, with only Continental breakfast available and few hot food items.

Holland America Line can provide kosher meals. As the ships do not have kosher kitchens, these are prepared ashore, frozen, and brought to your table sealed in containers.

The wine list relies heavily on wines from California and Washington State, with few decent French or German wines, other than those found in a typical supermarket ashore. A Connoisseur List is available in the Pinnacle Grill.

● **Alternative Dining**

All HAL ships have "alternative dining" spots called "Pinnacle Grill" (or "Pinnacle Grill at the Odyssey Restaurant"), specializing in "Pacific Northwest Cuisine." Items include sesame-crusted halibut with ginger-miso; and an array of premium quality steaks, presented tableside prior to cooking. These are more intimate restaurants with tablecloths, linen napkins and decently sized wine glasses. The food is better than in the main dining rooms. There is a cover charge, and reservations are required.

Checking out the artwork aboard *Zuiderdam*.

LEFT: an aft pool and hot tubs.
ABOVE: entertainment *Noordam*-style.
BELOW: the Greenhouse Spa.

Bulgari china, Frette linens, and Reidel glasses are part of this enhanced dining experience.

● **Casual Eateries**

All ships feature a Lido Deck self-serve buffet. Most are lines you move along with your tray, although the latest ships have more "active" stations (examples: omelets and pasta cooked to order) and individual islands. There are decent salad bars, dessert bars, regional specialties, and grilled fast-food items such as hamburgers, salmon burgers, hot dogs and French fries.

● **The Coffee/Tea Factor**

Regular Coffee: Half decent, but weak (Score: 3 out of 10).

> In the main dining room aboard all HAL ships, espressos and cappuccinos don't cost extra – as they do aboard ships of other major lines – except in the Explorations Café (brand: Seattle's Best Coffee).

Espresso/cappuccino coffees (Dutch) are adequate, served in proper china, but not quite up to the standard of Celebrity or Costa. Score: 6 out of 10.

For Children

Club HAL: Junior passengers are divided into three age-appropriate groups: 3–8, 9–12, and teens. Programming is based on the number of children booked on any given sailing, and children's counsellors are provided accordingly. HAL's children's programs are not as extensive as those of Carnival Cruise Lines, for example, although they are improving with the latest ships.

● **Best ships for children:** *Eurodam, Noordam, Oosterdam, Westerdam, Zaandam, Zuiderdam,* but not: *Amsterdam, Maasdam, Prinsendam, Rotterdam, Ryndam, Statendam, Veendam.*

Entertainment

Holland America Line is not known for lavish entertainment (the budgets aren't high enough). The production shows, while a good attempt, fall short on story line, choreography and performance, while colorful costuming and lighting hide the weak spots. Each ship carries its own resident troupe of singers and dancers and audio-visual support staff. HAL also offers a consistently good, tried and tested array of cabaret acts that constantly pop up on the cruise ship circuit. All showlounges are non-smoking venues.

A number of bands, a string ensemble and solo musicians present live music for dancing and listening in many of the lounges and bars. Each ship has a Crow's Nest Lounge (by day an observation lounge) for social dancing, and there is always serenading string music in the Explorer's Lounge and dining room. Each cruise includes a Crew Show; these vary from poor to very entertaining, depending on your taste. Passengers always seem enthusiastic, because they like connecting staff that they know and have seen during their cruise.

Spa/Fitness Facilities

The Greenhouse Spa, beauty and fitness amenities named after the Texas-based facility, aboard all HAL ships are staffed and operated by Steiner Leisure, a specialist concession, whose young staff will try to sell you Steiner's own-brand Elemis beauty products. Some fitness classes are free; others, such as yoga, kick-boxing or Pilates essentials, cost $11 per class (a special price is offered for unlimited classes).

Massages (including exotic massages such as Aroma Stone massage, Chakra Balancing massage and other well-being massages), facials, pedicures, and beauty treatments cost extra. Examples: well-being massage $109 for 50 minutes; hot stone therapy massage $175 for 75 minutes; reflexology $109 for 50 minutes; Japanese Silk Booster facial 129 for 75 minutes; personal fitness instruction $75 for 60 minutes (course of three for $191).

MSC CRUISES

Ships

Fantasia-class ships: *MSC Fantasia* (2008)
Armonia-class ships: *MSC Armonia* (2001), *MSC Lirica* (2003), *MSC Musica* (2006), *MSC Opera* (2004), *MSC Orchestra* (2007), *MSC Poesia* (2008), *MSC Sinfonia* (2002)
Other ships: *MSC Melody* (1982), *MSC Rhapsody* (1977)

About the company

MSC Cruises is Italy's largest privately owned cruise line. MSC entered the cruise business with the takeover of Star Lauro Cruises (*Achille Lauro* and *Angelina Lauro*) and by buying the cruise ships *Melody* and *Rhapsody*. Its parent company, Mediterranean Shipping Company, is the world's second largest container shipping company.

MSC Cruises has grown extremely fast in a few short years, having benefited from the demise of Festival Cruises by purchasing two of its ships, and by providing a pan-European cruise experience. The company has a number of new ships on order, and could have the world's youngest fleet by 2010.

So what's it really like?

MSC Cruises' ships are best suited to adult couples and singles, and families with children. They are good for those who enjoy big city life, outdoor cafés, constant activity accompanied by plenty of music, late nights, and food ranging from adequate to very good.

The company has evolved quickly as the "new kid on the block." Of all the major

Putting leisure time to good use on an MSC cruise.

cruise lines, it's also the cleanest. It changes bed linen and towels the most; typically, bed linen is changed every second day, towels daily, and bathrobes in suites daily.

The roving band of photographers, taking your picture at every opportunity, can irritate. Particularly intrusive are the tacky photos taken during dinner, when "pirates" and other costumed staff appear behind you when you are smartly dressed.

The ships typically operate in five languages, with embarkation-day announcements in English, French, German, Italian, and Spanish. Mercifully, during the cruise, there are almost no announcements. Given this multilingual emphasis, production shows and other major entertainment displays are more visual than verbal. For the same reason, the ships do not generally carry lecturers.

● **Embarkation:** When you first embark, a member of staff in a crisp white uniform – or black butler's uniform if you are in one of the more expensive suites – will escort you and carry your hand luggage to your suite or cabin, with white-glove service and a smile.

Decor

Except for the two oldest ships, MSC *Melody* and MSC *Rhapsody*, the decor aboard the newer ships is decidedly European, with much understated elegance and high-quality soft furnishings and other materials – although the latest ships have become brighter.

Gratuities

These are charged to your onboard cabin at €6 per person, per day. Drinks prices, however, already include a service charge.

Cuisine/Dining

MSC Cruises provides better-quality ingredients, almost all sourced in Europe, than some other major cruise lines. The cuisine is still mainstream – you'll find butter in packets. However, at the self-serve buffets, salt and pepper are typically provided on each table, not in packets as on most rival cruise lines.

Espresso and cappuccino (Segafredo brand Italian coffee) are available in the dining rooms, at extra cost, and in almost all bars.

Aboard the newest ships, MSC Cruises has

MSC Opera on home territory, visiting Venice.

introduced the Italian "slow food" concept. Always available items include spaghetti, chicken breast, salmon fillet, and vegetables of the day. Refreshingly, the company spotlights regional Italian cuisine and wine, so daily dining room menus feature food from regions such as Calabria, Piedmont, Lazio, Puglia, and Sicily.

All pizza dough is made on board, not brought from ashore, while risotto (featured daily) has become a signature item for MSC Cruises and something the ships make really well. Spaghetti is always available, with a tomato sauce freshly made each day. Many varieties of Italian breads such as bruschetta, focaccia, and panettone, are provided.

● **Room service:** Continental breakfast is complimentary from 7.30 to 10am, while room service snacks can be bought at any other time. A basket of fruit is provided to all cabins at embarkation, and replenished daily for suite-grade accommodation.

For Children

Children are divided into three age groups, with facilities to match: Mini Club for 3 to 9-year-olds; Junior Club for 10–13s; Teenagers Club for those over 14. While the facilities and play areas are not as extensive as those aboard most major cruise lines, a "baby parking" service is useful when parents want to go ashore on excursions. MSC Cruises' mascot is Do-Re-Mi – the von Trapp family of *Sound of Music* fame would be delighted.

Entertainment

The main production shows are colorful and visual, particularly aboard the newest ships. Other shows consist of unknown cabaret acts (typically singers, magicians, mime artistes, comedy jugglers, and others) doing the cruise ship circuit. The ship carries a number of bands and small musical units that provide live music for dancing or listening, but there is no show band, and all production shows are done to pre-recorded backing tracks.

Spa/Fitness Facilities

The spas are operated as a concession by Blue Ocean – except *MSC Musica*, which is operated by Steiner Leisure. Treatments include acupuncture (not aboard *MSC Rhapsody*).

Pause during an MSC latin dance lesson on deck.

NORWEGIAN CRUISE LINE / NCL AMERICA

Ships

NCL: *Norwegian Dawn* (2002), *Norwegian Dream* (1992), *Norwegian Gem* (2007), *Norwegian Jade* (2006), *Norwegian Jewel* (2005), *Norwegian Majesty* (1992), *Norwegian Pearl* (2006), *Norwegian Spirit* (1998), *Norwegian Star* (2002), *Norwegian Sun* (2001)
NCL America: *Pride of America* (2005)

About the company

Norwegian Cruise Line, the originator of contemporary cruising, was founded in 1966 by three Norwegian shipping companies as Norwegian Caribbean Line. The line was bought by Star Cruises in 2000, and has been replacing its older, smaller ships with brand new, larger vessels. NCL also operates NCL America, with mostly American crews and a base

ABOVE: a ten-pin bowling alley aboard *Norwegian Pearl*.
LEFT: NCL's evocation of Hawaii's charms.
BELOW: a game of basketball aboard *Norwegian Jewel*.

in Hawaii. Most comments in this review apply to both brands.

Freestyle Cruising is how NCL describes its operation. Its fleet is diverse, so the cruise experience can vary, although this makes for interesting character variation between the various ship categories. There is more standardization aboard the larger, newer ships. The senior officers are the only thing that's Norwegian – except aboard NCL America vessels, where they are American.

NCL provides a good product for a youthful, active, sports-minded audience. All its ships have sports bars and memorabilia.

Choose this line for a good all-round family cruise with a sporty feel, interesting itineraries, many from "Homeland USA" ports, and lots of dining choices, particularly aboard the newest ships.

Most standard cabins are small, though they have reasonably attractive decor and are functional. Closet and drawer space is very limited aboard the newest ships.

So what's it really like?

If this is your first cruise, you should enjoy a good overall vacation in an upbeat setting. The onboard lifestyle is contemporary, fresh, creative and sporty, with a casualness typical of youthful city dwellers, and with its "eat when you want" philosophy, the shipboard ambiance is casual. So is the dress code – indeed, the waiters may be better dressed than many passengers. The staff is congenial, and you'll find a high percentage of females in cabin and restaurant service departments – more than most major cruise lines. However, revenue centers are everywhere, including "inch of gold," tee shirts, and sunscreen lotion, all sold at tables on the open decks adjacent to swimming pools.

All ships can provide an almost full-size newspaper from a wide choice of US and European titles on the Multicast satellite delivery system (the cost: $3.95 per newspaper, per day). You can also make a special request for your favorite newspaper that's not in the list, although it may cost more.

NCL ships are best suited to first-time young and young-at-heart couples, single passengers, children and teenagers who want upbeat, color-rich surroundings, plenty of entertainment lounges and bars, and high-tech sophistication – all in one programmed but well packaged cruise vacation. There's plenty of lively music, constant activity, entertainment, and food that's mainstream and acceptable but nothing more – unless you pay extra to eat in the "alternative" dining spots. All this is delivered by a smiling, very friendly service staff who lack polish but are willing.

● **Embarkation:** Few staff members are on duty at the gangway when you first arrive, and they merely point you in the direction of your deck, or to the ship's elevators instead of escorting you to your cabin.

● **NCL's Private Island (Great Stirrup Cay):** Only coffee and ice-water are free (there's no iced tea), and all other drinks are charged.

Decor

The newest ships have colorful, eye-catching designs on their hulls, differentiating them from the competition.

Gratuities

A fixed $10 per person per day service charge is added to your onboard account. Children over 13 pay the full adult rate; those aged 3–12 pay $5 per day, and under-3s pay nothing. A 15% gratuity is added to bar, wine and spa charges. Onboard currency: the US dollar.

Cuisine/Dining

NCL has recognized the increasing trend away from formal restaurants (for dining) toward bistros (for eating faster). For cruising, NCL has championed more choices in dining than any other cruise line, except parent company Star Cruises, with its "Freestyle Dining." This allows you to try different types of cuisine, in different settings, when you want. In practice, however, it means that you have to make reservations, which can prove frustrating at times, and getting it just right takes a little planning and, sometimes, waiting.

Freestyle Dining works best aboard the newest ships, which have been specially designed for it: *Norwegian Dawn, Norwegian Gem, Norwegian Jade, Norwegian Jewel, Norwegian Pearl, Norwegian Spirit, Norwegian Star, Norwegian Sun, Pride of America*. The others (*Norwegian Dream, Norwegian*

A Norwegian Cruise Line self-serve buffet.

Majesty) have been modified to accommodate the concept, but you end up with food outlets, not restaurants.

On production show presentation nights, most people want to eat at the same time in order to see the shows, and this causes prime-time congestion, fast service and frustration. However, the ships now have plasma screens in various locations so you can make reservations when you want, and see at a glance the waiting times for a table.

After-dinner espresso/cappuccino coffees are available in the dining rooms without extra charge – a nice feature. Once each cruise, NCL features a Chocoholics Buffet with paper plates and plastic cutlery.

The wine list is quite good, with many excellent wines in the $20–$30 range. But the wine is typically served by table waiters, whose knowledge of wines is minimal.

Cabin service breakfasts are very basic, with only Continental breakfast available and no hot food items – for those, you'll need to go to one of the restaurants or the self-serve buffet. The non-breakfast Room Service menu

Gyrospheric fun aboard *Pride of America*.

has only two hot items available throughout the day: Oriental soup and pizza – the rest is cold (salads and sandwiches).

● **The Coffee/Tea Factor:** Regular Coffee: Weak and poor. Score: 2 out of 10. Espresso/Cappuccino coffees: Score: 4 out of 10. Some bars have espresso/cappuccino machines, which are extra-charge items.

> All NCL ships have self-serve buffet-style eateries. In most, you move along with your tray, although the newest ships have more active stations and individual islands.

For Children

NCL's Junior Cruisers (Kids Crew) program divides children into three groups, according to age: Junior sailors (ages 2–5); First Mates and Navigators (6–12); Teens (13–17). Baby-sitting services are available (group only, not individual) at an extra change. Special packages are available for soft drinks.

● **Best ships for children:** *Norwegian Dawn,* *Norwegian Jewel, Norwegian Star, Norwegian Sun.* But not: *Norwegian Dream* or *Norwegian Majesty.*

Entertainment

NCL has always had consistently good production shows that provide lots of color and spectacle in a predictable – though a little dated – format. Each ship carries its own resident troupe of singers/dancers and audiovisual support staff. There are two or three production shows in a typical 7-day cruise.

They are all very colorful, high-energy, razzle-dazzle shows, with much use of laser and color-mover lights. They're not memorable but, it must be said, they're very entertaining. All showlounges are non-smoking.

Most activities and passenger participation events range from poor to extremely poor. Nintendo wii interactive games are available on large screens.

Spa/Fitness Facilities

The spas are staffed and operated by the Hawaii-based Mandara Spa, owned by Steiner Leisure. Many of the staff are young, and will try to sell you Steiner's own-brand Elemis beauty products. Some fitness classes are free, while others, such as yoga and kick-boxing, cost $10 per class.

However, being aboard will give you an opportunity to try some of the more exotic treatments, particularly the various massages. Massage (including Aroma Stone massage, Chakra Balancing massage and other well-being massages), facials, pedicures, and beauty salon treatments cost extra. Examples: Lomi Lomi Massage ($99 for 50 minutes/$140 for 80 minutes); Mandara Four Hands Massage ($180 for 50 minutes; $280 for 80 minutes).

Aboard some ships, a "Thermal Suite" (sauna, steam room, aromashowers and relaxation area) costs $20 per day, or $75 for a 7-day pass.

NCL America

This "all-American" division of NCL operates *Pride of America*, dedicated to cruising the Hawaiian islands with a year-round base in Honolulu. Having a mostly American crew means that the niceties of food service do not match the standard of European or other international cruise lines.

In general, there's too much of a casual attitude among the unionized staff to guarantee consistent product delivery. However, the ship provides a great way to see the islands of Hawaii in a comfortable, family-oriented way.

Deck shuffleboard keeps the kids amused on a P&O Cruise.

P&O CRUISES

Ships

Child-free ships: *Arcadia* (2005); *Artemis* (1984)
Family-friendly ships: *Aurora* (2000); *Oceana* (2000); *Oriana* (1995); *Ventura* (2008)

About the company

Its full name is the Peninsular and Oriental Steam Navigation Company, though none of its ships is still operated by steam turbines. Based in Southampton, England, it was founded in 1837, just before Samuel Cunard established his company, and was awarded a UK government contract in 1840 to carry the mails from Gibraltar to Alexandria.

P&O Cruises acquired Princess Cruises in 1974, Swan Hellenic in 1982, and Sitmar Cruises in 1988. In 2000 it demerged from its parent to establish itself as P&O Princess plc. It was bought by Carnival Corporation in 2003.

So what's it really like?

P&O Cruises has always been a traditional cruise company, never quite keeping up with the better quality cruise experience provided aboard the Cunard Line ships. However, it has been reinventing itself, and the result is a contemporary onboard cruise product well aimed at the high-street traveler. It specializes in providing all the little things that British passengers have come to expect, including tea/coffee making sets in all cabins, and a wide choice of Indian-cuisine themed food.

Traditionally, P&O Cruises was known for British families who want to go abroad accompanied by their values and food preferences, and sail from a UK port – except for winter Caribbean cruises from Barbados. But

Oceana drops anchor in the Caribbean.

now it's also known for having child-free ships, and so the two products differ widely in their type communal spaces. It also devotes time and effort to providing theme cruises – antiques, art appreciation, classical music, comedy, cricket, gardening, jazz, Scottish dance, etc. The ships typically also carry ballroom dance instructors.

Decor

A mix of British "traditional" (think: comfy, dated armchairs, wood paneling, bistro-style food, non-glitzy). British artists are featured aboard all ships.

Gratuities

For gratuities, you should typically allow £3.50 ($6.80) per person, per day.

Cuisine/Dining

The cuisine is straightforward, no-nonsense British food, reasonably well presented well on nice Wedgwood china. But it tends to be

A quiet corner aboard the 1,975-passenger *Oriana*.

rather bland and uninspiring. It is typical of mass banquet catering with standard fare comparable to that found in a family hotel in an English seaside town like Scarborough.

The ingredients of many meals are disguised by gravies and sauces, as in Indian curries – well liked, of course, by most British passengers. Bread, desserts and cakes are made well, and there is a wide variety. P&O Cruises always carries a decent selection of British, and some French, cheeses.

Most of the dining room staff are from India, and provide service with a warmth that many other nationals find hard to equal. Wine service is amateurish and the lack of knowledge is lamentable.

● **Alternative Dining**

Extra-cost restaurants with menus designed by some of Britain's well-known television celebrity chefs, such as Gary Rhodes and Marco Pierre-White, have been introduced aboard the ships (exception: *Artemis*). They are a mix of trendy bistro-style venues, and restaurants with an Asia-Pacific theme.

● **Casual Eateries**

Self-serve buffets have become popular. However, most of the ships have small, cramped facilities, and passengers complain of having to share them with the countless concession staff who take over tables and congregate in groups. In other words, the buffets are too small to accommodate the needs of most passengers today.

● **The Coffee/Tea Factor:** Regular Coffee: Weak, and poor. Score: 3 out of 10. Tea and coffee-making machines are provided in all cabins.

Self-serve beverage stations are provided at the buffets, but it's often difficult to find proper teaspoons – often only wooden stirrers are available. Espresso/cappuccino coffees in the extra-charge venues are slightly better, but not as good as aboard the ships of Costa Cruises or MSC Cruises, for example.

For Children

P&O Cruises really excels in looking after children. The ships – apart from the child-free ones, of course – have very good facilities and children's counsellors, with lots of activities and participation events that make it a pleasure to take to take the kids on your cruise.

Entertainment

P&O Cruises has always been known for its traditional, "end of pier" entertainment, with lots of pub-like sing-along sessions for the masses. These have been augmented with production shows that provide lots of color and costume changes. All ships carry their own resident troupe of singers and dancers.

P&O Cruises does a good job in providing guest lecturers with varying themes, as well as occasional well-known television personalities and book authors.

Spa/Fitness Facilities

The spa/fitness facilities are operated by the UK concession Harding Brothers, which also provides a wide range of beauty products. Examples of prices: a full body massage is £60 for 50 minutes; an Indian head massage is £42 for 45 minutes; a holistic facial is £45 for 75 minutes. A manicure is £24 for 45 minutes, while a pedicure is £35 for 45 minutes.

PRINCESS CRUISES

Ships

Caribbean Princess (2004), *Coral Princess* (2002), *Crown Princess* (2006), *Dawn Princess* (1997), *Diamond Princess* (2004), *Emerald Princess* (2007), *Golden Princess* (2001), *Grand Princess* (1998), *Island Princess* (2003), *Ocean Princess* (1999), *Pacific Princess* (1999), *Royal Princess*

Movies by moonlight, projected by Princess Cruises.

(2001), *Ruby Princess* (2008), *Sapphire Princess* (2005), *Sea Princess* (1998), *Star Princess* (2002), *Sun Princess* (1995)

About the company

Princess Cruises, founded in 1965, is now part of Carnival Corporation. Its ships are well designed, and passenger flow, particularly aboard the latest ships, is good. Although they are large resort ships, they absorb people well, and there is little sense of crowding – pool decks notwithstanding. But areas around photo galleries are bottlenecks, especially at feeding times when more people are milling about. The ships have a higher-than-average Passenger Space Ratio than competitors Carnival or RCI.

So what's it really like?

Ships in both the mid-size and large categories operated by Princess Cruises are clean and always well maintained, and the promenade decks of some ships have teak deck lounge chairs – others are plastic. Princess Cruises also has a nice balance of officers, staff and crew members, and the line's British connections help it to achieve the feeling of calmness aboard its ships that some other lines lack.

Choose Princess Cruises if you enjoy being with families and fellow passengers of mid-50s and upwards, who want a well-organized cruise experience with unpretentious middle-of-the-road cuisine, a good range of enter-

> *Passenger niggles include the fact that your name is placed outside your cabin adjacent to the "mailbox," and that cabin stewards still knock even when you have placed a "do not disturb" sign on it.*

tainment, and an excellent shore excursion program – arguably the best run of any of the major cruise lines. There are proper cinemas aboard most ships as well as outdoor pool-side mega-screens for showing "movies under the skies" in the evening.

Lines can form at peak times for elevators, the purser's (information) office, and for open-seating breakfast and lunch in the main dining rooms. Lines for shore excursions and shore tenders are also a fact of life aboard large resort ships.

All passengers receive turndown service

and chocolates on pillows each night, as well as bathrobes (on request) and toiletry amenity kits – larger, naturally, for suite/mini-suite occupants – that typically include soap, shampoo, conditioner, and hand/body lotion. A hairdryer is provided in all cabins, sensibly located at a lounge area vanity desk unit.

If you want to keep up with the world, BBC World, CNN, CNBC, ESPN and TNT can be found on the in-cabin color TV system (when available, depending on cruise area).

Countless pieces of questionable "art" are encountered in almost every foyer and public room – an annoying reminder that cruising aboard large resort ships is like living in a bazaar of paintings surrounded by a ship.

The dress code is either formal – usually one formal night per 7-day cruise – or smart casual. The latter seems to be translated by many as jeans or tracksuits and trainers.

The newest ships – *Crown Princess, Emerald Princess, Ruby Princess* – include an adult-only area called The Sanctuary, an extra-cost retreat at the top of the ship, forward of the mast. This provides a "private" place to relax and unwind and includes attendants to provide chilled face towels and deliver light bites. It has thick padded sun-loungers both in the sun and in the shade, a swim-against-the-current pool, and there are also two outdoor cabanas for massages. I par-

The disco aboard the 1,300-cabin *Grand Princess*.

ABOVE: Venice is a popular European port of call.
RIGHT: Princess passengers learn how to sail.

ticularly recommend The Sanctuary in hot weather during Caribbean cruises. It's worth the extra $15 a head per half-day.

Princess's onboard product, especially the food and entertainment, is totally geared to the North American market. But British and other European nationalities should feel at home, as long as they realize that this is all about highly organized, packaged cruising, food and service, with an increasing emphasis on onboard revenue.

Expect to be subjected to a stream of flyers advertising daily art auctions, "designer" watches, specialized classes (Princess Cruises' "ScholarShip@Sea" programs), and the like.

You'll also have to live with many extra-charge items such as ice cream, non-standard coffees and pastry item taken in venues other than the restaurants, $4 per hour for group babysitting services, and $40 for an "introduction to pottery" class. There's a charge for using washers and dryers in self-service launderettes.

Princess Cruises' ships are best suited to couples, families with children and teenagers, and older singles who like to mingle in a large ship setting with pleasing, sophisticated sur-roundings and lifestyle, reasonably good entertainment and fairly decent food and service, all packaged affordably.

The few staff members on duty at the gangway when you first arrive will merely point you in the direction of your deck, or to the ship's elevators instead of escorting you to

HOW TO GET HITCHED AT SEA

Princess Cruises has the most extensive wedding program of any of the major lines, with its "Tie the Knot" wedding packages. The ship's captain can legally marry American couples at sea aboard its ships registered in Bermuda. This is by special dispensation, and should be verified when in the planning stage, and may vary according to where you reside. The basic wedding at sea package costs $1,800, plus $400 for licensing fees. Live music, champagne, a bridal bouquet, a photographer and a wedding cake can all be laid on. Tuxedo rental is available. Harborside or shore-side packages vary according to the port. For the latest rates, see the Princess Cruises website or your travel agent.

Princess stages glamorous shows.

your cabin. An "express check-in" option is available by completing certain documentation 40 days in advance of your cruise.

Decor

If Carnival's ships have the brightest decor imaginable, the decor aboard Princess Cruises' ships is almost the opposite – perhaps a little bland in places, with much use of neu-

> "Personal Choice Dining," a mixture of both traditional (assigned tables and the same waiter each night in one of two seating times) and "your choice" – you choose when you want to eat, and with whom – is provided aboard all Princess ships.

tral tones, calm colors and pastels. This really does suit the passengers who cruise with Princess, and nothing is garish or too bright (we're talking only about the decor here, of course, not the passengers).

Gratuities

Gratuities to staff are added to your account, at $10 per person, per day (gratuities for children are charged at the same rate). If you want to pay less, you'll need to go to the reception desk to have these charges adjusted (that could mean lining up with many other passengers wanting to do the same). Additionally, 15% is added to all bar and wine bills. The onboard currency is the US dollar.

Cuisine/Dining

Although portions are generous, the food and its presentation are disappointing. Fish is often disguised by crumb or batter coating, the selection of fresh green vegetables is limited, and few garnishes are used. However, do remember that this is big-ship banquet catering, with all its attendant standardization and production cooking. Meats are of a decent quality, although often disguised by gravy-based sauces, and pasta dishes are acceptable (though voluminous), and are typically served by section headwaiters who may also make "something special just for you" – in search of favorable comments and gratuities.

If you like desserts, order a sundae at dinner, as most other desserts are just so-so. Ice cream, when ordered in the dining room, is included, but costs extra elsewhere (Häagen Dazs can be found at poolside).

Specially designed dinnerware and good quality linens and silverware are used, such as Dudson of England dinnerware, Frette Egyptian cotton table linens, and silverware by Hepp of Germany. All dining rooms and eateries are smoke-free.

The wine list is reasonable, but not good, and there are no wine waiters – table waiters or section head waiters serve the wine.

Passengers occupying balcony-grade accommodation can enjoy a full-service "Balcony Dinner" for two at $50 per person extra, plus wine.

● **Casual Eateries:** For casual eating, each ship has a Horizon Buffet (open round the clock), and, at night, provides an informal dinner setting with sit-down waiter service. A small, limited bistro menu is also available. The buffet displays are mostly repetitious, but far better than in past years. There is no finesse in presentation, however, as plastic plates are provided, instead of trays. The cabin service menu is quite limited, and the presentation of food items featured is poor.

● **The Coffee/Tea Factor:** Regular Coffee: Weak and poor. Score: 2 out of 10. Espresso/Cappuccino coffees: Score: 3 out of 10. Except for beverage station at the serve-yourself buffets, coffees/teas in bars cost extra.

For Children

Children are divided into three age groups: Princess Pelicans (ages 2–5), Shockwaves (ages 8–12), and Off-Limits or Remix (13–17). The groups are split into age-related activities, and Princess Cruises has good chil-

Children's activities are divided by age group.

dren's counselors and supervised activities.

● **Best ships for children:** *Caribbean Princess, Coral Princess, Crown Princess, Dawn Princess, Diamond Princess, Emerald Princess, Golden Princess, Grand Princess, Island Princess, Ruby Princess, Sapphire Princess, Sea Princess, Star Princess, Sun Princess.* But not: *Ocean Princess, Pacific Princess, Royal Princess*

Entertainment

Princess Cruises' production shows have always been aimed at its slightly older, more elegant passengers. The company prides itself on its glamorous all-American shows, and they should not disappoint. There are typically two or three shows during each 7-day cruise. Each ship has a resident troupe of singers, dancers and audio-visual support staff.

Passenger participation events are put on by members of the cruise staff, who would be well advised to hang on to their day jobs. Most lounges

HOW TO MAKE DINNER ENTERTAINING

Themed dinners are a feature on Princess cruises. On a 7-day cruise, a typical menu cycle will include a Sailaway Dinner, Captain's Welcome Dinner, Captain's Gala Dinner, and Landfall Dinner. A special, extra-cost "Chef's Table Dinner," which takes place in the galley during full dinner operations, is for foodies who like to be involved in the action. It is a "foodertainment" meal (at $75 per person, maximum 10 persons) in which the executive chef interacts with you to make it a memorable occasion; appetizers and cocktails in the galley are followed by multi-course tasting dinner with wines matched to the meal.

and bars have live music. Musical units range from solo pianists to string quartets, from a cappella singers to bands that can provide music for ballroom dancing. Princess Cruises also provides a number of male hosts as dance partners for women traveling alone. All show lounges are non-smoking.

Spa/Fitness Facilities

All Lotus Spa/beauty treatments and fitness facilities are operated and staffed by the Steiner Leisure concession, whose offerings are similar to those already described for Celebrity Cruises and Costa Cruises.

You can now make online reservations for spa treatments before your cruise. But be careful not to clash with shore excursions and other diversions. Days at sea are easiest to book online, and hardest to obtain on board.

ROYAL CARIBBEAN INTERNATIONAL

Ships

Freedom-class ships: *Freedom of the Seas* (2006), *Independence of the Seas* (2008), *Liberty of the Seas* (2007)
Voyager-class ships: *Adventure of the Seas* (2001), *Explorer of the Seas* (2000), *Mariner*

of the Seas (2004), *Navigator of the Seas* (2003), *Voyager of the Seas* (1999)
Radiance-class ships: *Brilliance of the Seas* (2002), *Jewel of the Seas* (2004), *Radiance of the Seas* (2001), *Serenade of the Seas* (2003)
Vision-class ships: *Enchantment of the Seas* (1997), *Grandeur of the Seas* (1996), *Legend of the Seas*(1995), *Rhapsody of the Seas* (1997), *Splendour of the Seas* (1996), *Vision of the Seas* (1998)
Sovereign-class ships: *Majesty of the Seas* (1992), *Monarch of the Seas* (1991)

About the company

Royal Caribbean International, owned and founded in 1969 by Royal Caribbean Cruises, started out as a highly creative cruise line with the advantage of having brand new ships – unlike its main rivals, Carnival Cruise Lines and NCL, which began their operations with pre-owned ships. That advantage has now been eroded. Its onboard product, excellent at first, has now slipped to equal that of Carnival, whose ships, in general, have larger standard cabins.

RCI's ships are shapely, with well-rounded sterns, and interesting design profiles that make them instantly recognizable. They have large, brightly lit casinos, and shopping galleries that passengers have to walk through to

ABOVE: RCI's sports facilities include rock climbing walls.
LEFT: ice skating aboard *Voyager of the Seas*.
BELOW: yoga class aboard *Navigator of the Seas*.

Dolphins greet RCI's *Adventure of the Seas*.

get almost anywhere. All are cleverly designed to extract maximum revenue.

So what's it really like?

RCI provides a cruise experience that is well-integrated, fine-tuned, and comfortable. The product is consistent but homogenous. This is cruising for mainstream America. The ships are all quite pleasing, and some have really comfortable public rooms, lounges, bars, and innovative gimmicks such as ice-skating rinks and rock-climbing walls.

The company competes directly with Carnival Cruise Lines, Norwegian Cruise Lines and Princess Cruises in terms of what's offered on board, as well as the hard sell for onboard revenue (the result of highly discounted pricing in the marketplace). But RCI ships have more glass area and connection with the outdoors and the sea than Carnival's ships, and are are a better bet for families with children.

RCI's largest ships are termed Freedom-class (*Freedom of the Seas, Independence of the Seas, Liberty of the Seas*) and Voyager-class (*Adventure of the Seas, Explorer of the Seas, Mariner of the Seas, Navigator of the Seas, Voyager of the Seas*). They differ from other ships in the fleet – mainly in the internal layout – by having a large mall-like high street – the focal point for most passengers. Many public rooms, lounges and bars are located as adjuncts to the mall. It's rather like a mall with a ship built around it. Unfortunately, in placing so much emphasis on "active" outdoors areas, space has been taken away from the pool areas, leaving little room left just to sit and relax or sunbathe.

The next group of ships (*Brilliance of the Seas, Jewel of the Seas, Radiance of the Seas, Serenade of the Seas*) have lots of balcony cabins, and large expanses of glass, which help to provide more of a connection with the sea. *Enchantment of the Seas, Grandeur of*

There's really nothing "royal" about Royal Caribbean International, except the name. While ships' senior officers are Norwegian or Scandinavian (there is a difference), the service staff are an eclectic mix of many nationalities.

the Seas, *Legend of the Seas, Rhapsody of the Seas, Splendour of the Seas,* and *Vision of the Seas* also have large expanses of glass in the public areas, but not so many balcony cabins.

The oldest ships (*Majesty of the Seas, Monarch of the Seas*), innovative in the late 1980s, now look dated. They have very small, barely adequate cabins, and tiny tub chairs in public rooms, for example, although the average passenger has become larger.

With the introduction of *Freedom of the Seas,* a concierge lounge (available only to suite occupants) was introduced, thus creating a two-class system.

The onboard product is dedicated to those with an active, contemporary lifestyle – rather like Ocean Drive on South Beach, Miami. All ships have a 30-ft (9-meter) high rock-climb-

Standing in line for embarkation, the reception desk, disembarkation, for port visits, shore tenders and for the self-serve buffet stations in the Windjammer Café is inevitable aboard RCI's large resort ships.

ing wall, with five separate climbing tracks. You'll need to plan what you want to take part in wisely as almost everything requires you to sign up in advance.

Passenger niggles:

● There are few quiet places to sit and read – almost everywhere has intrusive background

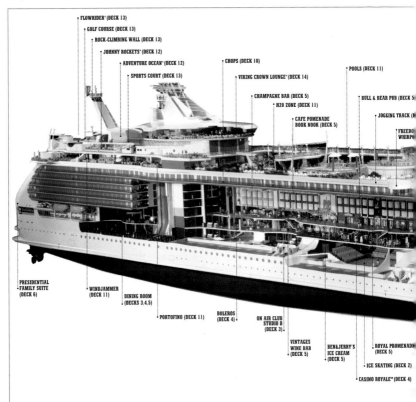

music – even elevators and hallways. Bars also have very loud music.

● There are no cushioned pads for the deck lounge chairs. They have plastic webbing and, even with a towel placed on them, soon become uncomfortable.

● There are frequent announcements for activities that bring revenue, such as art auctions and bingo.

● A stream of flyers advertising daily art auctions, "designer" watches, "inch of gold/silver" and other promotions, while "artworks" for auction are strewn throughout the ship, and frosted drinks in "souvenir" glasses are pushed to the hilt.

● It's often hard to escape the ship's photographers – they're everywhere.

But these are niggles. RCI ships are liked by active, young-minded couples and singles of all ages, families with toddlers, children, and teenagers who enjoy mingling in a large ship setting with plenty of life and high-energy entertainment. The food is more notable for quantity than quality – unless you pay extra for dining in the "alternative" restaurant (not all ships have them). Note that smoking is not allowed in cabins that don't have a balcony.

Service personnel are friendly, but not many offer a greeting when passing you in the corridors, so the hospitality factor could be improved. However, the elevators talk to you – "going up/going down" is informative but monotonous, of course, but the illuminated picture displays of decks are good.

● **Embarkation:** There are few staff members on duty at the gangway when you first arrive,

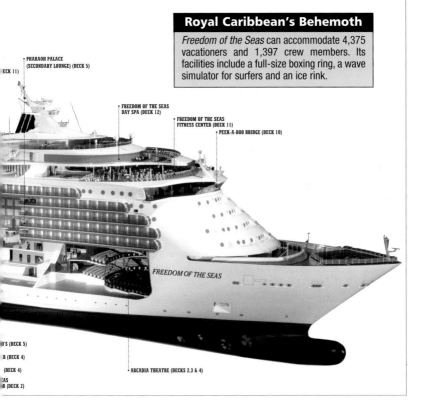

Royal Caribbean's Behemoth

Freedom of the Seas can accommodate 4,375 vacationers and 1,397 crew members. Its facilities include a full-size boxing ring, a wave simulator for surfers and an ice rink.

PHARAOH PALACE
(SECONDARY LOUNGE) (DECK 5)

ECK 11)

FREEDOM OF THE SEAS
DAY SPA (DECK 12)

FREEDOM OF THE SEAS
FITNESS CENTER (DECK 11)

PEEK-A-BOO BRIDGE (DECK 10)

FREEDOM OF THE SEAS

O'S (DECK 5)

R (DECK 4)

(DECK 4)

AS
R (DECK 2)

ARCADIA THEATRE (DECKS 2,3 & 4)

and they will merely point you in the direction of your deck, or to the ship's elevators, instead of escorting you to your cabin. Lines for check-in, embarkation and disembarkation are a bit daunting, but the company does well in making it all flow as smoothly as possible. If you are a non-US resident and stay at an RCI-booked hotel, all formalities can be completed there and then you'll simply walk

> *Crown and Anchor Society members enjoy perks such as priority boarding and disembarkation, private cocktail parties, fresh fruit, and bathrobes for the cruise.*

on board to your cabin – after going through security checks, of course.

Decor

The interior decor of all the ships is bright and contemporary, but not as neon-intensive and glitzy as Carnival's ships. There is much Scandinavian design influence, with some eclectic sculpture and artwork. The "you are here" signage and deck plans are excellent, so finding your way around should be easy. The furniture in public lounges tends to include small "tub" chairs that are often broken by large passengers unwise enough to use them.

Gratuities

Gratuities can be paid in cash or added to your onboard account daily at the suggested rate of $9 per person. Also, 15% is added to all bar, wine and spa charges. The onboard currency is the US dollar, except for ships operating out of the United Kingdom.

Cuisine/Dining

Most ships have large dining halls that are two or three decks high, giving a sense of space and grandeur. Few tables for two are available, most being for four, six, or eight persons. All dining rooms and eateries are non-smoking. The efficient dining operation emphasizes highly programmed, extremely hurried service that many find insensitive. There are no fish knives.

The cuisine in the main dining rooms is typical of mass banquet catering with stan-

ABOVE: internet access, *Brilliance of the Seas*.
LEFT: a gyroscope keeps the table steady.
RIGHT: a bar aboard *Mariner of the Seas*.

dard fare comparable to that found in American family-style restaurants ashore. The food costs per passenger are well below those for sister company Celebrity Cruises, so you should not expect the same food quality. Dinner menus typically include a Welcome-Aboard Dinner, French Dinner, Italian Dinner, International Dinner, and Captain's Gala Dinner, and all offer plenty of choice. Menu descriptions sound tempting, but the food, although well enough prepared, is unmemorable. A decent selection of light meals is provided, and there is a vegetarian menu.

While the USDA prime beef supplied is good, other meats are often disguised with gravies or heavy sauces. Most fish (except salmon) and seafood items tend to be overcooked and lack taste. Green vegetables are scarce, although salad items are plentiful. Rice is often used as a source of carbohydrates, potatoes being more expensive. Breads and pastry items are generally good, although some items, such as croissants, may not be made on board. Dessert items are standardized and lack flavor, and the cheese selection and crackers are poor. The selection of breads, rolls, and fruit could be better. Caviar – once a standard menu item – incurs a hefty extra charge.

Although prices are moderate, the wine list is not extensive, and almost all wines are very young. Only small glasses are provided. The waiters tend to be overly friendly for some tastes – particularly on the last night of the cruise, when tips are expected.

● **Casual Eateries:** All RCI ships have casual eateries called Windjammer Café for fast-food items, salads, and other casual meals. Some are of the single line type (move along with your tray), while the newest ships have more active stations and individual islands for variety and fewer lines. However, the actual quality of cooked food items is nutritionally

---

ALTERNATIVE DINING VENUES

All Freedom, Radiance and Voyager-class ships have two additional dining venues: Chops Grill Steakhouse (for veal chops and steaks; cover charge $30 per person), and Portofino (for Italian-American cuisine; cover charge $25 per person). Both serve food that is of a much higher quality than in the main dining room. Reservations are required in both venues. Dinner is usually served between 6pm and 11pm.

Vision-class ships have just one extra-charge

venue, Portofino, serving Italian-American cuisine. You should be prepared to eat a lot of food – perhaps this justifies the cover charge – from Texas-sized portions presented on large plates. Menus do not change throughout the cruise. The dress code is smart casual.

poor, as are the rather tacky salad dressings.

Breakfast buffet items are virtually the same each day, monotonous and even below the standards of diner food. The same is true of lunchtime salad items, which have little taste. The beverage stations have only the

> *During each cruise, a "Galley Buffet" allows passengers to go through a section of the galley collecting food while noting its spotless, stainless steel backdrop – cleaner than in most land-based dining facilities.*

most basic items. Hamburgers and hot dogs in self-serve buffet locations are generally left in steam tables. They are steamed rather than grilled, although you can ask for one to be grilled in front of you.

Freedom and Voyager-class ships also have Johnny Rockets diners ($3.95 extra charge, per person, whether you eat in or take out). These serve hamburgers, hot dogs and sodas, although the typical waiting time is about 30 minutes – pagers are provided, in case you want to wander off while waiting for a table.

Drinks packages are available in bars, in the form of cards or stickers. This means that you can pre-pay for a selection of standard soft drinks and alcoholic drinks. However, the rules for using the pre-paid packages are a bit cumbersome.

● **The Coffee/Tea Factor:** Regular Coffee: Weak, poor quality. Score: 1 out of 10. Espresso/Cappuccino coffees (Seattle's Best): Score: 4 out of 10 – it comes in paper cups.

For Children

Adventure Ocean is RCI's "edutainment" area. Junior passengers are divided into four age-appropriate groups: Aquanaut Center (ages 3–5); Explorer Center (6–8); Voyager Center (9–12); and Optix Teen Center (13–17). An unlimited soda and juice package for under-17s costs $4 a day. There are lots of activities for children, and a host of children's counsellors, so they will never be bored.

● **Best ships for children:** *Adventure of the Seas, Explorer of the Seas, Freedom of the Seas, Independence of the Seas, Liberty of the Seas, Mariner of the Seas, Navigator of the Seas, Voyager of the Seas.* **Ships that are acceptable, but with fewer facilities:** *Brilliance of the Seas, Enchantment of the Seas, Grandeur of the Seas, Jewel of the Seas, Legend of the Seas, Radiance of the Seas, Rhapsody of the Seas, Serenade of the Seas, Splendour of the Seas, Vision of the Seas.* **Ships with few facilities for children:** *Majesty of the Seas, Monarch of the Seas.*

Entertainment

The entertainment is upbeat (in fact, it's hard to get away from music and noise) – what you would find in a resort hotel in Las Vegas. Production shows are colorful, fast-paced, high volume razzle-dazzle spectaculars, but with

The Windjammer Café is RCI's casual eatery.

An RCI atrium creates a sense of spaciousness.

little or no storyline, poor linkage between themes and scenes, and basic choreography. The live band is augmented by prerecorded backing tracks to make it sound like a big, professional orchestra. Each ship has its resident troupe of singers and dancers.

Then there are silly audience participation (summer camp-style, but often funny) events and activities – something that RCI has always done well.

All showlounges are non-smoking venues.

Spa/Fitness Facilities

The Spa facilities in RCI ships are operated by the Steiner Leisure concession, whose offerings are similar to those already described for Celebrity Cruises and Costa Cruises.

For the more sporting, all RCI ships have a rock-climbing wall, with several separate climbing tracks. There is a 30-minute instruction period before anyone is allowed to climb, and this is done in pairs. It's free, and all safety gear is included, but you'll need to sign up. It's worth remembering that it's quieter on port days, but the hours of operation are limited – typically two hours each in the morning and afternoon.

Playing a round of golf in the golf simulator costs $25 per hour – which covers up to four persons.

STAR CRUISES

Ships

MegaStar Aries (1991); *MegaStar Taurus* (1991); *Star Pisces* (1990); *SuperStar Aquarius* (1993); *SuperStar Gemini* (1992); *SuperStar Libra* (1988); *SuperStar Virgo* (1999)

About the company

Star Cruises, the world's third largest cruise operator, was set up in 1993 as a subsidiary of the Genting Group, founded in 1965. The company operates ships dedicated to specific markets, and its brands include Star Cruises, Norwegian Cruise Line (NCL), NCL America, and Cruise Ferries.

Star Cruises is the only cruise line to have its own ship simulators – useful training tools when a captain these days may be in charge of a speeding vessel measuring more than 150,000 tons. It also owns and operates the cruise terminal at its base in Port Klang, Malaysia, and the pier facility in Langkawi.

ABOVE: karaoke session, *SuperStar Pisces*.
BELOW: a game of mahjong, *SuperStar Aquarius*.

A deck barbecue aboard *SuperStar Gemini*.

So what's it really like?

Star Cruises' ships are best suited to adult couples and singles, and families with children. They are good for those who enjoy big city life, constant activity accompanied by plenty of music, late nights, and abundant food. Star Cruises was the originator of the "Freestyle Cruising" concept, which offered more flexibility and was later adopted by NCL. A strictly casual dress code prevails aboard all the ships.

> *A popular show is "Kingdom of Kung-Fu," whose 30-strong cast highlights the power and form of the Shaolin Masters in an action-packed martial arts performance.*

Star Pisces, SuperStar Libra and *SuperStar Aquarius* are based in Hong Kong, mainly for the local gaming market, and specialize in short cruises. *SuperStar Virgo*, based in Hong Kong and Singapore, operates 2-, 3-, and 5-night cruises for the local market. *MegaStar Aries* and *MegaStar Taurus* are boutique ships

available only for charter or private parties, and are based in Singapore. All these ships have gaming casinos, including members-only private gaming rooms for serious players – a major attraction for Asian passengers.

● **Embarkation:** There are basically two distinct passenger segments – those that book "balcony-class" cabins, and those that don't. "Balcony Class" passengers and members of the Star VIP Club check-in in a separate area to "non-balcony" class passengers.

Decor

The ships have stunning Asian interior decor, with bright, fresh, happy, warm colors, and carpets with rich patterns. Many cabins have rich lacquered wood furniture and highly polished wood accents, with colorful soft furnishings as accompaniments. Some ships have original artwork costing millions.

Gratuities

Gratuities are included aboard all Star Cruises ships, and drink prices already include a service charge, so no extra tipping is expected.

Cuisine/Dining

Star Cruises provides a wide variety of food

to suit both Asian and Western tastes. However, the cuisine is still of a mainstream market standard – you'll find butter in packets. At self-serve buffets, salt and pepper are typically provided on each table, not in packets as aboard many other cruise lines. Espresso and cappuccino (Lavazza brand Italian coffee) are available fleet-wide, at extra cost. Service aboard the ships is usually by Asian staff, many from China and the Philippines.

ABOVE: Hong Kong-based *SuperStar Aquarius*.
BELOW: *SuperStar Virgo*'s executive suite.

Some ships have up to 10 restaurants and eateries; some are included in the fare, while others cost extra and serve à la carte items.

● **Room service:** Continental breakfast typically costs extra, and room service snacks are also available at extra cost throughout the day. A basket of fruit is provided to all cabins at embarkation, and is replenished daily for suite-grade accommodation.

For Children

Children are divided into three age groups, with facilities, activities and entertainment to match: for children from 6 to 9 years; for children 10–13; for teens 14–17. There's also a StarKids Club (for Singapore residents only), created for children below 12 who sail aboard *SuperStar Virgo*.

The facilities and play areas are extensive aboard *SuperStar Virgo*, and less so aboard the other ships.

The Out of Africa bar, *SuperStar Virgo*.

Entertainment

The main production shows are colorful, visual shows, particularly aboard the largest ships. Brazilian dancers, Chinese acrobats, and many top Asian entertainers are featured.

Small units provide live music for dancing or listening, but there is no real show band. Production shows are performed to pre-recorded backing tracks. Each ship has karaoke rooms for rent.

Spa/Fitness Facilities

The spas are an in-house operation, with Asian staff. Thai massage is the house specialty. Examples of prices: Thai Massage, S$60 (60 minutes); Hot Stones Massage, S$80 (75 minutes). A Singapore dollar is worth roughly 66 cents (US) or 33p (UK). ❏

WHEN ONLY THE BEST WILL DO

Of the 80-plus cruise lines operating internationally, only a handful provide, at a price, the kind of ships and service that can truly be called "luxury"

The word "luxury" has been degraded by marketing people, but comparing true luxury cruising with "premium" service is like pitting a Bentley against a Hyundai. On true luxury ships, staff will remember your name, they will escort you to and from your dining table as in a top-class restaurant, the chef may invite you to join him on visits to local food markets, there will be no jarring loudspeaker announcements, and you will be able to embark and disembark at leisure. Even the deck chairs will radiate quality.

A quiet spot is easier to find on upscale ships.

But it's not just the standard of service provided by the generous staffing – which comes, it must be said, at a premium price. There are practical benefits, too. These smaller ships can get into ports that larger ships can't. In Russia, for instance, large and mid-size ships have to dock about one hour from the center of St Petersburg, while boutique ships can dock right next to the Hermitage Museum in the heart of the city. And the personal service of luxury ships really comes into its own in mass-market destinations such as the Caribbean and Alaska, where, by contrast, the big operators organize shore excursions through the same specialist tour operators with their "one size fits all" approach.

Hapag-Lloyd Cruises' award-winning *Europa*.

More space, better service

All 16 ships that I classify as luxury *(see table on right)* have an excellent amount of open deck and lounging space, and almost all have a better ratio of crew to passengers than the large resort ships. In warm weather areas, the ships of SeaDream Yacht Cruises and Seabourn Cruise Line – all have fold-down platforms at the stern of each ship – provide jet skis, kayaks, snorkeling gear, windsurfers and the like at no extra cost, typically for one day each cruise. Hapag-Lloyd's *Europa*

ABOVE: *Seabourn Pride* takes pride in its cuisine.
RIGHT: *SeaDream* anchored off Portofino, Italy.

also has a fleet of Zodiac rigid inflatable craft for in-depth exploration and shore adventures. Tall passengers should also note that its mattresses are 7 ft (2.1 meters) long.

Fine dining

Fine dining is a highlight. Expect plenty of tables for two, a refined dining atmosphere, open or one-seating dining by candlelight, high-quality china and silverware, large wine glasses, fresh flowers, a connoisseur wine list, and competent sommeliers.

It's really about non-repetitive, highly creative menus, high-quality ingredients (fresh whenever possible), moderate portions, attractive presentation, and skilful cooking. Some luxury ships provide even more special touches. *Europa*, for example, makes its own breakfast preserves, while *Hebridean Spirit* provides its own bottled water.

Typically, lunch and dinner menus are provided in your suite/cabin in advance, and ordering off menu is often possible. Meals can be served, course by course, in your suite or cabin, either on the balcony or inside on special portable tables. It is also possible to have a special dinner set up on deck, which can be wonderful in the right location, with all the finery and individual service you would expect of private dining.

All the companies listed except for Crystal Cruises and Hapag-Lloyd Cruises provide complimentary wines with dinner; Seabourn and Silversea also include wine with lunch.

The Crystal and Regent Seven Seas ships are mid-size (600–1,600 passengers) and include entertainment in the form of production shows and cabaret acts. To a lesser extent, so do the Seabourn ships and Hapag-Lloyd's *Europa*. The other ships do not have entertainment as such.

To their discredit, *Crystal Serenity* and *Crystal Symphony* conduct art auctions, which detract from the otherwise fine ambience, although these two vessels do have good-quality bistros, which none of the other ships do.

As in five-star hotels on dry land, luxury comes with a significant price tag. You'd probably pay three to four times as much for a similar itinerary on one of these ships as you would on a large resort ship. But the experiences would have nothing in common except the ocean. ❑

WHO RUNS THE WORLD'S TOP SHIPS

These 16 ships, listed alphabetically by company, belong to seven cruise lines, and are the "cream" of the cruise industry in terms of style, staff training, cuisine, service, hospitality and finesse.

● **Crystal Cruises**
Crystal Serenity, Crystal Symphony
● **Hapag-Lloyd Cruises**
Europa (shown above)
● **Hebridean International Cruises**
Hebridean Spirit
● **Regent Seven Seas Cruises**
Seven Seas Mariner, Seven Seas Navigator, Seven Seas Voyager
● **Seabourn Cruise Line**
Seabourn Legend, Seabourn Pride, Seabourn Spirit
● **SeaDream Yacht Cruises**
SeaDream I, SeaDream II
● **Silversea Cruises**
Silver Cloud, Silver Shadow, Silver Whisper, Silver Wind

WHAT ABOUT THE SMALLER LINES?

While the major cruise lines dominate the
mass market, dozens of other companies
cater for more specialist tastes

The international cruise industry is com-
prised of around 80 companies with
ocean-going cruise ships providing vacations to more than 16 million passengers each
year. Most of the major cruise lines are owned
and operated by large corporations. Other
operators are family-owned cruise lines. Still
others are small, with just a couple of really
compact ships. Some cruise companies do not
actually own their own ships, but charter them
from ship owning and ship management companies for year-round or seasonal operation –
for example, specialized ships outfitted for Arctic and Antarctic expedition cruises only.

Barcelona, a stop on many Mediterranean tours.

WHY CALL THEM CRUISE "LINES"?

This is because a company owns a line of ships. However, the term is really a hand-me-down from when
passenger ships undertook what were called line
voyages, between Point A and Point B, in the days of
grand ocean liner travel. A good example is Cunard
Line, which operates regularly scheduled "crossings"
of the North Atlantic almost year-round.

Some cruise lines are actually tour operators
– vacation packagers, mostly in Europe, that
put together airlines, hotels, car rentals, and
cruises. Some own their own charter airlines.
Tour operators have transferred some of their
land-based tourists to the sea, aboard
ships that move the destinations for
them. These are the equivalent of the
package vacation that first became popular in Europe in the 1970s – for example, Thomson Cruises.

The listing

In the pages that follow, we provide
mini-profiles of all the cruise lines that
have small- or mid-size ships and small
fleets, or those with a small number of
large resort ships, or those that have tall
ships (with either real working sail
propulsion or computer-controlled
assistance), or those that specialize in
hardy or "soft" expedition cruises, or
those which cruise along coastal and
inland waterways. To make it easier for
you to find a particular cruise line, they
are listed in alphabetical order, and
some background information is given.

Cheetahs, the world's fastest mammals (at 70mph/112km/h), are an attraction in Kenya.

The major cruise lines

The big companies are profiled comprehensively on pages 54–103 and so are not included in this section. They are:

Carnival Cruise Lines
Celebrity Cruises
Costa Cruises
Cunard Line
Holland America Line
MSC Cruises
Norwegian Cruise Line (NCL)
P&O Cruises
Princess Cruises
Royal Caribbean Cruise Line
Star Cruises

Abercrombie & Kent (A&K)

Geoffrey Kent started A&K as a safari company in 1962 – there was no Mr Abercrombie, it just sounded good – and then specialized in upscale train journeys around the globe for small groups. The company got started in the cruise business when it went into a marketing agreement with the long-defunct Society Expeditions in 1990.

Two years later it bought the little expedition ship *Society Explorer* (formerly *Lindblad Explorer*) when Society Expeditions ceased operations. The ship, renamed *National Geographic Explorer*, now belongs to Lindblad Expeditions. Today, A&K charters various ships, such as those of Clipper Cruise Lines, for its cruise programs, taking passengers to the more remote destinations such as the Antarctic.

African Safari Club (Star Line Cruises)

Founded in 1967, African Safari Club specializes in vacations to Kenya and the Indian Ocean. The company owns and operates one ship, the 200-passenger *Royal Star*, and owns a charter airline to fly participants from the UK to Africa. The company also owns and operates safari lodges and hotels in Kenya and cruise/safari packages for passengers who want to combine different experiences in one vacation. While the standards of food and service aboard the ship are not high, the ship is a comfortable reminder of life in relax mode.

AIDA Cruises

The former East German shipping company Deutsche Seereederei (DSR) was assigned the traditional cruise ship *Arkona* as part of the east-west integration in 1985, which included a contractual agreement with the Treuhandanstalt to build a new ship. It did this in 1996

Hurtigruten's *Nordnorge* can cope with extremes during polar expeditions, yet provides luxuries such as Jacuzzis aboard.

with the newly built *Aida*, designed to appeal to young, active German-speaking families. The concept was to create a seagoing version of the popular Robinson Clubs – a sort of German Club Med concept. When *Aida* first debuted, there were almost no passengers and the company struggled.

In 1998 the company sold itself to Norwegian Cruise Line, who sold it back to its original Rostock-based owners. Now a very successful multi-ship brand belonging to the Carnival Corporation, it is well-known in German-speaking countries for its ultra-casual cruising, with two main self-serve buffet restaurants instead of the traditional sit-down-and-be-served method of cruising.

The entertainment is extremely good, and is provided in conjunction with the Schmidt Theatre in Hamburg.

American Canadian Caribbean Line

Founded in 1966 by the late Luther H. Blount, who built his ships in his own shipyard in Warren, Rhode Island, ACCL started as, and continues today, as a family-run company. Today, the company is run by his daughter, Nancy Blount.

Cruises are operated like private family outings, using two unpretentious ships that were specially constructed to operate in close-in coastal areas and inland waterways of the eastern US seaboard, with forays to the Bahamas and Caribbean during the winter.

The onboard experience is strictly no-frills cruising in very, very basic, down-to-earth surroundings that have a 1950s feel. Its early-to-bed passengers – average age 72 years – are typical of those who don't like glitz or trendy, and don't need much other than basic American food. Bring your own if you want a drink – the line supplies only tonic and soft drinks – so forget wine with dinner unless you supply your own bottle.

ACCL serves up fresh New England corn.

American Cruise Lines

ACL was originally formed in 1974, although it went bankrupt in 1989, the ships were sold off, and the company lay dormant. That is, until the original owner, Charles Robertson, a renowned yachtsman who used to race 12-meter America's Cup yachts resurrected the company in 2000, and built its own ships in its own small shipyard in Salisbury, Maryland, on the Chesapeake Bay.

ACL's four ships ply the inter-coastal waterways and rivers of the USA's east coast (between Maine and Florida), and provide an up-close, intimate

ABOVE: setting up dinner, *Azamara Journey*.
RIGHT: cruising memorably through the Corinth Canal.

experience for passengers who don't need luxury or much pampering, but do like American history and culture.

The company also formed Pearl Seas Cruises, whose two ships are being constructed in Canada.

Aurora Expeditions

This Australian company was founded in 1993 by Australian Mount Everest veteran and geologist Greg Mortimer and adventure travel specialist Margaret Werner. The company uses the chartered expedition ship *Marina Svetaeva* for its Antarctic expedition cruise programs. Other destinations include Papua New Guinea and Russia's Far East.

10 MEMORABLE CRUISING EXPERIENCES

❶ Arriving in Halong Bay, Vietnam, in the thick morning mist.
❷ Cruising through the Swedish archipelago towards Stockholm.
❸ Cruising through the Le Maire Channel in the Antarctic Peninsula.
❹ Cruising through the Norwegian fjords.
❺ Cruising through the Corinth Canal, Greece.
❻ Cruising through the Panama Canal.
❼ Cruising through the Chilean fjords.
❽ Cruising the Inside Passage, Alaska.
❾ Cruising up the River Amazon to Manaus.
❿ Arriving in Sydney in the early morning.

Azamara Cruises

Azamara Cruises is an offshoot of Celebrity Cruises, and was created in 2007. It consists of two 700-passenger ships *(for ratings, see page 237)*, taking people to smaller ports that some of the large resort ships cannot get into. The company specializes in providing high-quality dining. Its ships are in direct competition with those of Oceania Cruises.

The onboard experience is similar to that aboard the ships of parent company Celebrity Cruises, but modified to suit those who want a more personal cruise experience aboard smaller ships. The company's strengths are its food and service, and each ship has two alternative (extra-charge) restaurants, in addition to the main dining venues.

CDF Croisières de France

Founded and wholly owned by Royal Caribbean International, CDF Croisières de France was founded in 2007, with headquarters in Paris. It devotes all its resources to cruising for French-speaking passengers, with one ship, *Bleu de France* (the former *Europa*).

CIP Cruises

CIP Cruises (La Compagnie des Iles du Ponant) is a subsidiary of CMA CGM, the world's third largest container shipping com-

Crystal Serenity visits Portofino in Italy.

pany. The Company, whose head office is in Marseille, France, was created in April 1988, and presently operates three boutique-sized ships (*Le Diamant, Le Levant,* and *Le Ponant*) for the French-speaking market.

In 2004, the company acquired the Paris-based tour operator, Tapis Rouge International, which specializes in upscale travel.

Classic International Cruises

This small, family-owned company is based in Lisbon, Portugal. It buys or charters older (pre-owned) deep-draft ships that have "traditional" decor and lovingly refurbishes them. George Potamianos and his two sons run the company, which either operates the ships itself, or charters them to various cruise/tour operators. Nautical officers and most service staff are Portuguese.

Cruise West's 39-cabin *Spirit of Alaska*.

Club Med Cruises

Club Med itself became renowned for providing hassle-free vacations for the whole family. The first Club Med village was started in 1950 on the island of Mallorca, but the concept became so popular that it grew to over 100 vacation villages throughout the world.

Club Med Cruises began as an offshoot of the French all-inclusive vacation clubs, and in 1990 when it introduced its first ocean-going cruise vessel, the computer-controlled sail-cruise ship *Club Med II*. Aboard the all-inclusive ship, it's the Gentils Ordinaires, who serve as both super-cruise staff and "rah-rah" cheerleaders for the mainly French-speaking passengers. *Club Med II* has a sister ship, Wind Star Cruises' *Wind Surf*, which provides a more relaxed onboard experience.

Cruceros Australis

Cruceros Australis, based in Santiago, Chile, operates cruise ships on soft expedition cruises to the Chilean fjords, Patagonia and Tierra del Fuego. Catering increasingly to an international clientele, with Spanish as the official onboard language, cruising with this company is all about Chile and its dramatic coastline. But don't expect high standards aboard its two ships.

Cruise West

Former bush pilot Chuck West founded Cruise West in 1954. He chartered two small ships, *Glacier Queen* and *Yukon Star*, for Alaska cruises. The cruises were marketed by Alaska Cruise Line, with offices in Seattle, Washington. Their hulls – they were converted ex-Canadian Navy corvettes – were painted black, and the superstructure blue and gold.

In 1971, he sold Westours to Holland America Line. In 1973, he set up Alaska Sightseeing, dedicated to small ship travel; this became Cruise West in 1983.

The young, mostly college-age hotel service personnel are willing, but lack service finesse and knowledge about the food served.

Because, under US maritime procedures, its ships measure under 100 tons, the company is allowed to enter Alaska's Glacier Bay without having to bargain for the limited number of entry permits granted each year.

Crystal Cruises

Crystal Cruises was founded in 1988 by Nippon Yusen Kaisha (NYK), the world's largest freighter and transportation logistics companies, which currently have more than 700 ships. The American-managed company is based in Century City, Los Angeles. *Crystal Harmony*, the company's first ship, was built in Japan, and debuted in New York in May 1990 to great acclaim. Meanwhile, Crystal Cruises introduced two new ships, *Crystal Symphony* in 1995, and *Crystal Serenity* in 2000, one built in Finland, the other in France.

In 2006 *Crystal Harmony* was transferred to parent company NYK as *Asuka II* for its Asuka Cruise division, for Japanese-speaking passengers. Crystal Cruises continues to provide fine food and service aboard its ships, which operate worldwide.

Delphin Cruises

Founded by Mr Herbert Hey, and based in Offenbach, Germany, this small cruise line specializes in providing superb itineraries for its German-speaking passengers. The company owns one ship, *Delphin*, and operates another ship, *Delphin Voyager*, under a long-term charter agreement. Passengers like the friendly staff and service, as well as the destination-rich itineraries, coupled with the fact that most cruises are of 14 days or longer.

Disney Cruise Line

In 1932, a Disney cartoon, Steamboat Willy, depicted Micky Mouse at the wheel of a ship, but it took 60 years until Disney decided to get into the cruise business, as an extension of

ABOVE: the Disney brands are never far away.
BELOW: since 1998 Disney Cruise Line has had its own private island, Castaway Cay, in the Bahamas.

its resort stay business, offering a "seamless vacation package."

Its two large resort ships (*Disney Magic* and *Disney Wonder*) cater to loyal Disney followers, and everything aboard the ships is Disney – every song, every piece of artwork, every movie and production show. Its first ship debuted in 1998, the second, in 1999. The company has two more ships on order to keep Mickey's fans happy. Disney is all about families with children, and the ships cater to both. One innovation is that passengers dine in three different restaurants, in rotation. You can buy a package combining a short stay at a Disney resort and a cruise. Disney also has its own cruise terminal at Port Canaveral, and Mickey's ears can be found on the funnels of the company's ships.

easyCruise.com

Sir Stelios Haji-Iouannou, founder of many "easy" businesses including the successful airline easyJet, started easyCruise.com as an antidote to regular cruise lines. The company's two ships, *easyCruise One* and *easyCruise Life,* operate in the Mediterranean, particularly around the Greek Islands, and in the Caribbean. They provide no-frills cruises, with a two-night minimum stay.

The company's ships are second-hand, and refitted to easyCruise.com's minimalist design, although the original concept has been somewhat modified recently, and the ships now operate more in a traditional cruise manner. But, with minimal soft furnishings, it's all noise and no poise – more of a bus service, really.

Aboard Fred Olsen Cruise Lines' *Black Watch.*

Elegant Cruises & Tours

New York-based Elegant Cruises & Tours was founded in 1989 by Captain Mato Stanovich, initially to provide cruises and tours to Croatia. The company has two small vessels: *Monet,* for cruises along the Dalmatian coast in Croatia; and *Andrea,* a former Hurtigruten ship aimed at the "soft" adventure and expedition cruise market.

Fred Olsen Cruise Line

This is a Norwegian family-owned and family-run company which was founded in Hvitstein, a town on Oslofjord, Norway, in 1848 by three Olsen brothers – Andreas, Frederik Christian, and Peter. Today, the fifth generation Olsen, Fred Jr., runs the company from its headquarters in Suffolk, England. The group also has interests in the hotels, aviation, shipbuilding, ferries, and offshore industries.

The company specializes in cruises for adults who are usually retired and of senior years – typically over 65. Aboard the ships, interior design reflects traditional design features. The ships cruise year-round out of UK ports (Dover, Southampton, Liverpool, Newcastle,

easyCruise Life doubled the easyCruise fleet in 2008.

Greenock, Leith, Belfast and Dublin), with some ships operating out of Caribbean ports during the winter.

Galápagos Cruises

Metropolitan Touring, Ecuador's foremost tour and travel company, is based in Quito, Ecuador, and sells its cruises through general sales agents such as the USA's Dallas-based Adventure Associates.

Its boutique ships, *Isabela II* and *Santa Cruz*, are well-run vessels, featuring cruises in the highly protected Galápagos Islands, with all-Ecuadorean crew and food.

Hansa Touristik

Founded in the late 1990s, Hansa Touristik is based in Bremen, Germany. It charters low-budget cruise ships for cruises for a cost-conscious German-speaking clientele.

The ships have basic but comfortable facilities, with adequate and reasonable food. The service is limited by the low cruise fares, but provide good value for money.

Hapag-Lloyd Cruises

Germany's two most famous ocean liner companies from the mid-1900s, the Bremen-based

Norddeutscher Lloyd and the Hamburg-based Hamburg America Line, merged in 1970 to become Hapag-Lloyd.

Today, Hapag-Lloyd operates four ships. Two small ships are in the specialized expedition cruise market (*Bremen* and *Hanseatic*); one is in the mid-priced market (*C. Columbus*), and one ship (*Europa*) is in the luxury market. All feature destination-intensive cruises aimed at the German-speaking market, with occasional cruises for the English-speaking market.

Hebridean International Cruises

Hebridean International Cruises (formerly Hebridean Island Cruises) was set up under the Thatcher government's British Enterprise Scheme in 1989. Its headquarters is in Skipton, Yorkshire. The company operates two all-inclusive boutique ships, *Hebridean Princess* and *Hebridean Spirit*, that feature English country-house settings, and specialize in cruises for mature adults. Gratuities and all port taxes are included, as are most excursions. One ship operates cruises around the Scottish islands, while the other offers cruises in the Aegean, Mediterranean and Indian Ocean.

Hurtigruten

The company is an amalgamation of two shipping companies (OVDS and TVDS) and pro-

Hapag-Lloyd Expedition Cruises explore Antarctica.

Hurtigruten cruises from Norway include the North Cape (above), Viking carvings (right) and an Inuit village (below).

vides year-round service along the Norwegian coast, calling at 33 ports in 11 days. Hurtigruten has also recently developed expedition-style cruises, albeit aboard ships that have been converted for the purpose, rather than aboard ships built specifically for expedition cruises. So, as long as you think utilitarian and modest decor, you'll get the idea of life aboard one of the Hurtigruten ships, which are practical rather than beautiful.

Crown Princess Mette-Marit of Norway was the godmother of the company's newest ship, the *Fram*, a 318-berth expedition vessel built for cruising in Greenland.

Iberocruceros

Founded originally as one of the Iberojet (tour-operator) companies, 75% of the company is now owned by the Carnival Corporation. The company's ships feature all-inclusive cruises for the Spanish-speaking market, in direct competition to Pullmantur Cruises.

Imperial Majesty Cruise Line

The company's single ship, *Imperial Majesty*, operates two-night cruises from Florida to the Bahamas. Despite the company's claims to international gourmet dining, *Regal Empress* provides a highly programmed, but basic party getaway cruise, with friendly staff and service. The setting is that of a traditional old ship that has been well maintained, but is now approaching its sell-by date.

Indian Ocean Cruises

Indian Ocean Cruises was formed in 2006 to offer cruises to the Lakshadweep Islands, a union territory of India off the coast of Kerala in the Arabian Sea, and the Malabar Coast. The cruise company is owned by the Foresight Group, an Indian operation set up in 1984 and based in the UK.

The company's only ship, the 1965-built *Ocean Odyssey*, is an aging vessel that has been quite nicely refurbished.

Island Cruises

Island Cruises was founded as a joint venture between Royal Caribbean Cruises and the British tour operator First Choice Holidays. Its first ship started operations in 2002. In 2007, First Choice merged with travel company TUI to become TUI Travel.

The two ships presently in the fleet, *Island Escape* and *Island Star*, provide mainly British passengers with an active cruise experience in casual surroundings. Its self-serve buffet meals, enabling you to eat when you want, are the mainstay of its culinary offerings.

Kristina Cruises

This Finnish Partanan family-owned company was founded in 1985 as Rannikkolinjat to operate short cruises on Lake Saimaa. In 1987 the company purchased its first ship and started to open Baltic and Russian-owned ports on the Gulf of Finland to international cruise passengers.

Today, Kristina Cruises owns and operates two vintage-style ships, principally on cruises in the Baltic and Mediterranean, and continues to preserve nautical traditions on board.

Lindblad Expeditions

Lars-Eric Lindblad started the whole concept of expedition cruising with a single ship, *Lindblad Explorer*, in 1969, taking adventurous travellers to remote regions of the world. Today, his son, Sven-Olof Lindblad, runs the company, but with an array of small ships.

It's all about wilderness, wildlife, off-the-beaten-path adventures, and learning. Zodiac inflatable craft are used to ferry participants ashore in remote areas such as the Arctic and Antarctic sub-continents.

The onboard product features excellent lecturers, who are more academic than entertaining. In partnership with the National Geographic Society, the company operates the wholly owned *National Geographic Endeavour*, *National Geographic Explorer*, *National Geographic Islander* and *National Geographic Polaris*, together with other small ships for coastal or soft expedition-style cruising.

Louis Cruise Lines

The late Louis Loizou's vision of promoting tourism in Cyprus in 1935 is what started his quest to provide travel services to people that had not seen the beauty of their own country. Louis and Pavlos Loizou formed "Brotherhood" in 1935 to promote tourism to fellow compatriots. In 1942 Louis Loizou sold Brotherhood to his brother and, in his quest to place Cyprus on the world tourism map, founded the Louis Tourist Agency. Louis Loizou, a deeply humane man, became the undisputed father of tourism in Cyprus.

A visitor to a Cyprus eatery hopes it's not on the menu.

Initially chartering ships to take passengers to neighbouring countries, Louis Cruise Lines was formed by Louis Loizou to provide inexpensive but comfortable short cruises from Cyprus. The Louis Organization today, run by sons Costakis and Vakis Louizou, owns hotels in Cyprus, provides the duty-free shopping at Moscow's Sheremetrevo Airport, and operates resort hotels in Cyprus and Greece, buses in Cyprus and "meet and greet" services for other cruise lines and tour operators.

The fleet consists of mainly older, small- and mid-size ships under charter to other companies, such as the tour operator Thomson Cruises, or operated by its two brands, Louis Cruise Lines, and Louis Hellenic Cruises.

Mitsui OSK Passenger Line

Osaka Shosen Kaisha was founded in 1884 in Osaka, Japan. In 1964 it merged with Mitsui Steamship, to become Mitsui OSK. It is now one of the oldest and largest shipping companies in the world.

It entered cruise shipping in 1989 with *Fuji Maru*, the first cruise ship in the Japanese-speaking domestic market. The company

NCL America's *Pride of America* leaves New York.

specialized in incentive, meetings and groups at sea rather than cruising for individuals. But the company (now known as MOPAS) steadily changed to more cruises for individuals and caters to passengers seeking low-cost cruises aboard ships that are comfortable but lack the facilities of more upscale ships. The company operates two ships, *Fuji Maru* and *Nippon Maru*, both based in Japan for Japanese-speaking passengers, with *Fuju Maru* dedicated exclusively to the charter market.

Monarch Classic Cruises

The company, formerly Majestic International Cruises, was formed in 2006; it is a Greek-owned company, based in Piraeus. The company has older, more traditional ships in the mid-size category, carrying up to 800 passengers, with service by a Greek crew. Cruises aboard the company's two ships, *Blue Monarch* and *Ocean Countess*, are typically sold by numerous international tour operators.

NCL America

NCL America is a subsidiary of NCL Corporation, owners of Norwegian Cruise Line, or NCL *(profiled on pages 83–7),* but with a single ship *(Pride of America)* specifically constructed for inter-island family cruises in Hawaii, based year-round in Honolulu. The ship flies the US flag, and is crewed mainly by American officers and hotel staff.

Resort casual cruising is featured, as well as an extensive shore excursion program, with everything tailored to Hawaii.

Noble Caledonia

Based in London, Noble Caledonia owns one boutique-sized ship, *Corinthian II,* but sells cruises aboard a wide range of small and specialist expedition cruise companies, specifically for British passengers of mature years, featuring cruises with cultural interest themes.

NYK Line

Nippon Yusen Kaisha (NYK Line) is the largest shipping company in the world, and owns the well-known US-based upscale brand, Crystal Cruises. It created its own NYK Cruise division – today called Asuka Cruise – in 1989 with one Mitsubishi-built ship, *Asuka,* for Japanese-speaking passengers. In 2006, the company sold the original *Asuka* to Germany's Phoenix Reisen, and the former *Crystal Harmony* was transferred from Crystal Cruises to become *Asuka II.*

The ship, known for its excellent Japanese and western food, includes an authentic sushi bar as well as a main restaurant, and a Shiseido health spa. It operates an annual around-the-world cruise, together with an array of short cruises in the Asia-Pacific region.

Ocean Village

Ocean Village was founded in 2003 as a casual cruising division of P&O Cruises. With headquarters in Southampton, England, the company operates two ships, offering fly-cruises from Palma de Mallorca and Heraklion in the summer and Barbados in the winter.

This is really like the UK equivalent of AIDA Cruises, with large self-serve buffet-style restaurants, and one or two extra-cost dining venues under the watchful eye of celebrity chef James Martin. It's a youthful product, with more potential for growth as the demand for casual unstuffy cruises increases.

Oceania Cruises

Oceania Cruises was founded by Frank del Rio (ex-Renaissance Cruises) and Joe Watters (ex-Royal Viking Line), with substantial investment from Apollo Catering. The ships provide faux English charm in a country-club atmosphere – ideal for middle-aged and older couples looking for a relaxing week at sea. Fine dining, comfortable accommodations and warm, attentive service are its trademarks.

In 2006, Oceania Cruises was bought by Apollo Management (no relation to Apollo Catering), a private equity company that owns Regent Seven Seas Cruises, and 50% of NCL. The brand was placed under the umbrella of Apollo's brand, Prestige Cruise Holdings.

With *Insignia*, *Nautica* and *Regatta* now operating, and three new ships on order, the company is set to grow. With multiple-choice dining at no extra cost, the present 700-

Equine artwork on a balcony in Palma de Mallorca.

passenger ships suit people who prefer this size of ship to the large resort vessels.

Orion Expedition Cruises

This Australia-based expedition cruise company was created by Sarina Bratton, specifically for soft expedition-style cruises to Antarctica, Australia's Kimberley region, and Papua New Guinea and its islands. The ship, *Orion*, built in Germany, is a little gem, with hand-crafted cabinetry in every cabin.

P&O Cruises (Australia)

This Australian division of P&O Cruises was founded in 1932. Today it provides fun in the sand and sun cruises for the beer and bikini brigade and their families. With a maturing market, the company has larger, more contemporary hand-me-down ships from Carnival Corporation companies, and continues to thrive, specializing in cruises in the Pacific and to New Zealand.

Page & Moy Cruises

This Leicester-based British company does not own any ships, but charters one (*Ocean Majesty*) for its many loyal passengers who want to travel widely aboard a ship with intimate dimensions.

The Parthenon in Athens, an Oceania Cruises port of call.

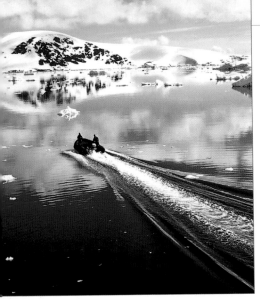
The Antarctic, a major destination for Quark Expeditions.

The company has long been booking and providing cruises for low-budget passengers of mature years, and today acts as a booking agency for cruises on many different lines.

Pearl Seas Cruises

Connecticut-based Pearl Seas Cruises is a sister company to American Cruise Lines, and was founded to build and operate two ships for the upscale coastal cruising sector, but also usable in international waters. Being SOLAS compliant *(see page 158)*, they will carry more passengers and be more luxurious than the ACL ships. Pearl Seas Cruises' first ship, *Pearl*, entered service in 2008, with the second ship to follow in 2009.

Onboard service is provided by an all-American crew, consisting of well-educated youngsters who smile a lot.

Peter Deilmann Ocean Cruises

An ex-ship navigation officer, the late Peter Deilmann saw an opportunity when he "came ashore." He started by chartering rivercruise boats for cruises along some of Europe's grand rivers and waterways.

He branched into ocean-going cruise ships in 1982, when *Berlin* was acquired. This ship was sold when the company introduced its *Deutschland*. Peter Deilmann's love of music and art translated into much personal artwork being placed aboard his ships. The legacy of this self-made man lives on in the company, based in Neustadt in Holstein, Germany, under the direction of his two daughters.

Phoenix Reisen

Based in Bonn, Germany, the company for many years operated low-budget, tour-operator-style destination-intensive cruises for its German-speaking clientele. It now has a loyal, more upscale audience and more contemporary ships. It provides extremely good itineraries for its passengers, and provides excellent value for money.

Plantours & Partner

This company provides low-budget cruises aboard its single small cruise ship, *Vistamar*, for German speakers.

Pullmantur Cruises

The company was set up as part of Pullmantur, the Spain-based holiday tour operator. Its cruising division was established in 2000 when it bought *Oceanic* from the long-defunct Florida-based operator Premier Cruise Lines. In 2006, Pullmantur Cruises was purchased by Royal Caribbean Cruises. The company serves the Spanish-speaking market, and operates all-inclusive cruises for families with children, to the Caribbean and Europe.

Quark Expeditions

The company was founded in 1991 by Lars Wikander, and silent-partner Christer Salen (formerly of Salen-Lindblad Cruises). It is based in Darien, Connecticut, and specializes in providing up-close-and-personal expedition cruises to some of the world's most remote regions and inaccessible areas.

In its formative years, Quark Expeditions chartered Russian ice-breakers to take adventurous, hardy outdoor types to the Polar regions, and has perhaps the most experience in taking participants to Antarctica. Quark Expeditions has always been committed to minimising the environmental impact of operating in ecologically sensitive areas.

In 2007, it was sold to the UK's First Choice Holidays (founded in 1973), merged with Peregrine Shipping, and then in 2007 was bought, along with First Choice, by the large German travel company TUI.

Cruising with Quark Expeditions is all about being close to nature, wilderness, wildlife, off-the-beaten-path adventures, and learning. The company still specializes in chartering nuclear- and diesel-powered Russian icebreakers, the most powerful in the world, to provide participants with a truly memorable expedition experience. This is adventure cruising for toughies.

Regent Seven Seas Cruises

Part of the Carlson group of companies, it was formerly called Radisson Seven Seas Cruises following the merger in 1995 of Radisson Diamond Cruises and Seven Seas Cruises.

Carlson Hospitality Worldwide ventured into cruising via its Radisson Hotels International division – hence, Radisson Diamond Cruises. Regent Seven Seas Cruises strives to pay close attention to detail and provide high-quality service aboard its small fleet of mid-sized cruise ships. One ship is based year-round in Tahiti, while the others operate world-wide itineraries.

In 2007 the company was purchased by US-based Apollo Management, an investment group, and, together with Oceania Cruises, was placed under the umbrella of its Prestige Cruise Holdings.

Regent Seven Seas Cruises stages large-scale shows.

Saga Cruises

Saga, based in Folkestone, England, was created by Sydney de Haan as a company offering financial services and holidays to the over-60s (reduced to the over-50s in 1995 as the company's success grew). Its popular travel flourished because it was good at providing extra personal attention and competent staff. Instead of sending passengers to ships operated by other companies, it decided to purchase its own ships and market its own product under the Saga Holidays brand.

Saga Shipping (Saga Cruises), the cruising division of Saga Holidays, was set up in 1997 when it purchased *Saga Rose* (ex-*Sagafjord*), followed not long after by *Saga Ruby* (ex-*Vistafjord*). The cruise company today is run mainly by former Cunard executives, with strong British seamanship and training aboard the company's present fleet of three ships, all of which manage to retain the feel of traditional elegant, child-free cruising.

Saga Rose and *Saga Ruby* are restricted to the over-50s.

Sea Cloud Cruises

The company was founded in 1979 by a consortium of shipowners and investors known as the Hansa Treuhand (active in commercial vessel management, engineering, and construction), and has its headquarters in Hamburg, Germany. It presently owns and operates two tall ships (sailing vessels), the legendary *Sea Cloud* and *Sea Cloud II*, and two European rivercruise boats, *River Cloud I* and *River Cloud II*. It has another tall ship, *Hussar,* on order.

The company has many corporate clients who charter the two tall ships, while a number of upscale cruise and travel companies sell cruises to individuals.

The onboard style and product delivery is quite upscale, with elegant retro decor and fine food and service.

Seabourn Cruise Line

Originally founded in 1986 as Signet Cruise Line, the company, then owned by Norwegian businessman Atle Brynestad, was forced to change its name in 1988 as a result of a lawsuit brought by a Texas company that had already registered the name *Signet Cruise Lines* (no ships were ever built). The Carnival Corporation acquired 100% of Seabourn Cruise Line in 1999.

The company aims its product at affluent, sophisticated, well travelled North Americans, with small ships providing a high level of

Seabourn Spirit cruising in Halong Bay, Vietnam.

European-style service, open-seating dining, all-inclusive drinks, great attention to detail and personal pampering.

SeaDream Yacht Cruises

Larry Pimentel and Norwegian partner Atle Brynestad jointly created the cruise line (Brynestad formerly founded Seabourn Cruise Line), purchasing the former Sea Goddess Cruises' ships and introducing them in 2001 to an audience anxious for exclusivity, personal pampering, and cuisine that is prepared à la minute.

SeaDream II is well-equipped for watersports.

The two ships have been refreshed several times, and are often chartered by companies or private individuals who appreciate the refined, elegant, but casual atmosphere on board. The 100-passenger ships operate year-round in the Caribbean and Mediterranean, and provide all-inclusive beverages and open-seating dining at all times, and a high degree of personalized service, all in a cozy, club-like atmosphere, with great attention to detail and personal idiosyncracies.

Silversea Cruises

Silversea Cruises is a mostly privately owned cruise line. It was founded in 1992 by the Lefebvre D'Ovidio family from Rome (previously co-owners of Sitmar Cruises: 90% partners being the Lefebvre D'Ovidio; 10% by V-Ships), and is based in Monaco.

Antonio Lefebvre D'Ovidio was a maritime lawyer and professor of maritime law before acquiring and operating cargo ships and ferries in the Adriatic. He took the family into partnership with Boris Vlasov's Vlasov Group (V-Ships) to co-own Sitmar Cruises until that company merged with Princess Cruises in 1988.

Silversea Cruises has generated a tremendous amount of loyalty from its frequent passengers, who view the ships as their own. All four Silversea ships feature teak verandas, and all-inclusive beverages. Open-seating dining prevails at all times, and the company is known for its partnership with the hospitality organization, Relais et Châteaux.

Star Clippers

Swedish-born yachtsman Mikhail Krafft founded Star Cruises in July 1991 with the introduction of *Star Flyer,* sister to *Star Clipper*, introduced in May the following year. The first ship should have been named *Star Clipper,* but, due to litigation with Clipper Cruise Line over the name, Krafft decided to switch names. The dispute was resolved, because Clipper Cruise Line operated motor-driven vessels, while Star Clippers' ships were true tall ships.

The company went on to build the largest tall ship presently sailing, the five-mast *Royal Clipper*. It is now building the largest-ever tall ship. Good food and service in a laid-back setting, under the romance of sail, is what Star Clippers are all about.

Swan Hellenic Cruises

Founded in 1954 By R.K. Swan, the company chartered small cruise ships for years. The company was purchased by P&O Cruises in 1982, and then it changed hands once more when the Carnival Corporation merged with P&O in April 2004.

In 2007, the Carnival Corporation disbanded Swan Hellenic, and its single ship (*Minerva II*) was transferred to the Princess Cruises fleet to become *Royal Princess*. Some months later, a semi-retired Lord Sterling purchased the brand from the Carnival Corporation and joined partners with the UK's Voyages of Discovery to be operated as a separate brand. So, the 'swanners,' as its intellectual passengers are called, now have their very own ship (*Minerva*) and product.

Champagne welcome aboard a Silversea cruise.

Antarctica is served by many specialist cruise lines.

Thomson Cruises

Thomson Cruises' first foray into cruising was in 1973 when it chartered two ships, *Calypso* and *Ithaca* (Ulysses Line). It was not a success, and the company withdrew from cruising two years later. Ulysses Line became known as Useless Line.

The company started again in 2002 after seeing rival tour operator Airtours operate ships successfully. Unlike Airtours' Sun Cruises, which no longer exists, Thomson Cruises charters its ships instead of owning them outright, preferring instead to leave ship operations, management and catering to specialist maritime companies. The company operates cruises for the whole family aboard the fleet of six ships (exception: *The Calypso*, a child-free ship). The onboard currency is the pound, and basic gratuities are included.

Transocean Tours

Founded in 1954, Transocean Tours headquarters are in Bremen, Germany. The company specializes in providing low-cost but high-value cruises aboard ships that are under long-term charter, with traditional decor and excellent itineraries. Gratuities and port charges are included.

In 2008, *Marco Polo*, a ship known for operating destination-intensive "soft-expedition" style cruises, was introduced.

Travel Dynamics International

Founded by brothers George and Vasos Papagapitos, the company specializes in providing small and boutique cruise ships to its audience of culturally minded passengers. Long a provider of vacations and cruises to university alumni, cultural associations, and museum groups, the company seeks out unusual itineraries and destinations according to a group's interest or travel theme.

Van Gogh Cruises

Created as the UK-based travel company Travelscope Cruises in the late 1990s, it operated a single ship under charter, providing extremely low-cost. The company quickly became a victim of rising fuel prices and credit crunch in 2007 and folded.

Van Gogh Cruises was quickly formed by the ship's owners, Holland-based Club Cruise, and the ship, named *Van Gogh*, now carries on cruising for its low-budget English-speaking passengers. The ship's home base is Falmouth, in the southwest of England.

Venus Cruise

Founded in 1988, the company's headquarters are in Osaka, Japan. Venus Cruise was first known as Japan Cruise Line, which is owned by four ferry companies: Shin Nipponkai Ferry, Kyowa Shoji, Hankyu Ferry, and Kanko Kisen. As Japan Cruise Line, the company at first operated company and incentive charter cruises before branching out into cruises for individuals.

The company presently has one ship, *Pacific Venus*, and caters exclusively to Japanese-speaking passengers, operating an annual around-the-world cruise as well as shorter Asia-Pacific cruises.

Vision Cruises

Spain-based Vision Cruises was founded in the late 1980s to provide low-cost, all-inclusive tour operator-style cruises for Spanish-speaking families with children. It doesn't own any ships, but charters them from other owners such as Classic International Cruises and Club Cruise.

The company charters small ships and provides popular destination cruises in a casual setting, with food and service that is adequate, but nothing more.

Voyages of Discovery

UK-based Roger Allard and Dudley Smith jointly founded the company to offer low-cost cruises aboard comfortable, roomy mid-sized ships, to UK-based passengers, but with good food and service. The company's *Discovery* is one of the former "Love Boats" of US television fame. The company went public in 2006 and, with the help of Lord Sterling of Plaistow, purchased Swan Hellenic Cruises. It now operates both brands from its headquarters in the south of England.

Windstar Cruises

Founded by New York-based Karl Andren in 1984 as Windstar Sail Cruises, the company's concept was to build high-class sail-cruise ships with computer-controlled sails, and outfit them in a contemporary decor designed by

Wind Surf carries 347 passengers and 163 crew.

Marc Held. The first ship, *Wind Star*, debuted in 1986 to much acclaim, and was followed by *Wind Spirit* (1988) and *Wind Surf* (1990).

Windstar Cruises was sold to Holland America Line in 1988. The company, with headquarters in Seattle, USA, was sold again in 2007 to the Ambassadors Cruise Group, wholly owned by Ambassadors International.

The onboard style is casual and totally unregimented, but smart, with service by Indonesian and Filipino crew. The ships carry watersports equipment, accessed from a retractable stern platform.

Zegrahm Expeditions

This small expeditions cruise company was founded in 1990 to take inquisitive travelers to remote or unusual destinations, including the Arctic and Antarctica. Although it doesn't own any ships, it charters high-quality specialized vessels, and it also sells cruises operated by other expedition companies. Two- or three-week expedition cruises are headed by experienced leaders and expert naturalists. ❑

Voyages of Discovery's destinations include Rio de Janeiro.

THE BEST SHORE EXCURSIONS

Guided tours in ports of call cost extra, but
they are often the best way to get a nutshell
view of a destination and make the most
efficient use of your limited time ashore

Shore excursions used to be limited to city tours and venues that offered folkloric dances by local troupes. Today's excursions are almost limitless, and include flightseeing, floatplane rides, cross-country four-wheel drive trips, mountain biking, ziplining, dog sledding and overland safaris. It's possible to spend far more on shore excursions than the price of the cruise.

Most excursions are escorted by ship's staff, who will usually carry first-aid kits. If you explore independently and need medical help, you could risk missing the ship when it sails. Unless the destination is a familiar one, first-timer cruisegoers are probably safer booking

THRILLING SHORE EXCURSIONS

● **St. Petersburg, Russia:** Take a Russian MIG jet flight over Moscow – great for that flying fast feeling.
● **Monte Carlo, Monaco:** Driving an exhilarating Formula One racing car.
● **Abu Dhabi, United Arab Emirates:** Four-wheel dune bashing in the Liwa Oasis among the world's tallest sand dunes.
● **Seward, Alaska:** Taking part in an Iditarod Trail Sled Dog Race Tour, held in March.

excursions organized by the ship because they will have been vetted by the cruise line. Also, if you have a problem during a tour, the cruise line should be able to sort it out on the spot.

If you do go it alone, always take the ship's port agent and telephone numbers with you, in case of emergencies (they are normally printed in the Daily Program). Allow plenty of time to get back to your ship before sailing time – the ship won't wait. Make sure your travel insurance covers you fully.

How tiring are excursions?

Most tours will involve some degree of walking, and some require extensive walking. Most cruise lines grade their excursions with visual symbols to indicate the degree of fitness required.

Are there private excursions?

Yes, aboard some of the more upscale ships such as those of Hebridean International Cruises, Hapag-Lloyd Cruises, Regent Seven Seas Cruises, SeaDream

Waterfront and Table Mountain, Cape Town, South Africa.

ABOVE: the Acropolis in Greece.
RIGHT: the Petronas Twin Towers in Kuala Lumpur, Malaysia.

Yacht Cruises, Seabourn Cruise Line and Silversea Cruises, you can have shore excursions tailored to your specific needs. But even large resort ship lines like Norwegian Cruise Line (NCL) can book something special under its Freestyle Private Touring program.

What if my first choice is sold out?

Some excursions do sell out, owing to limited space or transport, but there are sometimes last-minute cancellations. Check with the shore excursion manager on board.

What should I take with me?

Only what's necessary; leave any valuables aboard ship, together with any money and credit cards you do not plan to use. Groups of people are often targets for pickpockets in popular sightseeing destinations. Also, beware of excursion guides who give you a colored disk to wear for "identification" – they may be marking you as a "rich" tourist for local shopkeepers. It's always prudent to wear comfortable rubber-soled shoes, particularly in older ports when there may be cobblestones or other uneven surfaces.

How can I make a booking?

Aboard some ships, where shore excursions can be booked before the sailing date via the internet, they can sell out fast. So book early.

Payment aboard ship is normally made via a ship's central billing system. Most ships do not accept personal checks.

If you need to cancel a shore excursion, you usually need to do so at least 24 hours before its advertised departure time. Otherwise, refunds are at the discretion of the cruise line. In many cases, you will be able to sell your ticket to another passenger. Tickets do not normally have names or cabin numbers on them, except those that involve flights or overland arrangements. Check with the shore excursion manager to make sure it's okay to resell.

How can I know which are good?

If it's your first cruise, try to attend the shore excursion briefing. Read the excursion literature and circle tours that appeal. Then go to the shore excursion office and ask any other questions you may have before you book. A few helpful tips:

● Shore excursions are put together for general interest. If you want to see something that is not described in the excursion literature, do not take it. Go on your own or with friends.

● Brochure descriptions of shore excursions, often written by personnel who haven't visited the ports of call, can be imprecise. All cruise lines should adopt the following definitions in their descriptive literature and for their lectures and presentations: The term "visit" should mean actually entering the place or building concerned. The term "see" should mean viewing from the outside – as from a bus, for example.

● City excursions are basically superficial. To get to know a city intimately, go alone or with a small group. Go by taxi or bus, or walk directly to the places that are of most interest.

● If you do not want to miss the major sightseeing attractions in each port, organized shore excursions provide a good solution. They also provide an ideal opportunity to get to know fellow passengers with similar interests.

● In the Caribbean, many sightseeing tours cover the same ground, regardless of the cruise line you sail with. Choose one and then do something different in the next port. The same is true of the history and archaeology excursions in the Greek Isles.

What if I lose my ticket?

Report lost or misplaced tickets to the shore excursion manager. Aboard most ships, excursion tickets, once sold, become the sole responsibility of the purchaser, and the cruise line is not generally able to issue replacements.

The shore excursion office

This is located centrally, often close to the main-lobby reception desk. Here you'll find details of excursions and descriptive literature about ports of call, with information on the history, language, population, main attractions, shopping areas, sports facilities, and transportation. For more specific information, see the shore excursion manager or visit the ship's library.

Going ashore independently

If you hire a taxi for sightseeing, negotiate the price in advance, and don't pay until you get back to the ship or to your final destination. If you are with friends, hiring a taxi for a full- or half-day sightseeing trip can often work out far cheaper than renting a car – and it's probably safer. Try to find a driver who speaks your language.

Exploring independently is ideal in the major cruise ports of Alaska, the Bahamas, Bermuda, the Caribbean, the Mexican Riviera, the Canary Islands, the Mediterranean, Aegean ports, and the South Pacific's islands.

If you don't speak the local language, carry some identification (but not your

The Bibi-ka-Maqbara tomb, Aurangabad, near Mumbai, India.

ABOVE: the dynamic port of Hong Kong, where you can buy souvenir terracotta warriors from Xian (**RIGHT**).

passport), the name of your ship and the area in which it is docked. If the ship is anchored and you take a launch tender ashore, take note of exactly where the landing place is by observing nearby landmarks, and write down the location. This will be invaluable if you get lost and need to take a taxi back to the launch.

Some small ships provide an identification tag or boarding pass at the reception desk or gangway, to be handed in each time you return to the ship. Remember that ships have schedules – and sometimes tides – to meet, and they won't wait for individuals who return late.

If you are in a launch port in a tropical area and the weather changes for the worse, the ship's captain could well make a decision to depart early to avoid being hemmed in by an approaching storm; it has happened, especially in the Caribbean. If it does, locate the ship's agent in the port – he's likely to be carrying a walkie-talkie – who will try to get you back.

Planning on going to a quiet, secluded beach to swim? First check with the cruise director or shore excursion manager, as certain beaches may be considered off-limits because of a dangerous undertow, drug pushers, or persistent hawkers. And don't even think of going diving alone – even if you know the area well. Always go diving with at least one companion (the "buddy" system). ❏

10 GREAT OVERLAND EXCURSIONS

❶ Buenos Aires, Argentina
Tour to the splendors of Iguazu Falls (2–3 days)

❷ London, England
The royal Scotsman luxury train tour to the Scottish Highlands (4–5 days)

❸ Mombasa, Kenya
Safari in the shadow of Kilimajaro, including the Amboseli National Park and the wonders of the Masai Mara (4–5 days)

❹ Mumbai (Bombay), India
Glory of the Mughals Tour to the Taj Mahal in Agra (3–4 days)

❺ Santiago or Valparaiso, Chile
Tour to the Incas' mountain city of Machu Picchu in the Andes Mountains (3–4 days) including the Hiram Bingham luxury train

❻ Shanghai, China
Fly tour to Beijing, and to see Xian to see the famous terracotta warriors (2–5 days)

❼ Singapore
Tour to Phnom Penh and Angkor Wat in Cambodia (4–5 days)

❽ Sydney, Australia
Outback Discovery Tour, including Alice Springs (4–5 days)

❾ Tokyo, Japan
Bullet train (shinkansen) to Kyoto to visit the ancient temples (2–3 days)

❿ Venice, Italy
Overland to Milan, Lake Como and delightful lakeside towns like Bellagio (3–4 days)

100 POPULAR SHORE EXCURSIONS AROUND THE WORLD

THE CARIBBEAN

Antigua
❶ Tour to Shirley Heights and Nelson's Dockyard
Aruba, Netherlands Antilles
❷ Full-day Jeep eco-adventure trip
Barbados
Party cruise aboard the *Jolly Roger* pirate boat
Grand Cayman
❸ Go snorkeling with the sting rays at Sting Ray City
Grenada
❹ Eco-hiking tour to the Seven Sisters waterfall
Hamilton, Bermuda
❺ Guided Walking Tour of the former capital, St. George's
Jamaica
❻ Excursion to Dunn's River Falls and Prospect Plantation (Ocho Rios)
❼ Horseback riding on the beach (Montego Bay, Ocho Rios)
❽ Zip-line forest canopy tour
Nassau, Bahamas
❾ Go swimming with the dolphins
San Juan, Puerto Rico
❿ El Yunque Rain Forest Tour & Hike
St Lucia
⓫ Jungle Eco-Tour by Jeep
St. Maarten, Netherlands Antilles
⓬ Join the America's Cup Regatta Adventure tour and compete in an actual yacht race
St. Thomas, US Virgin Islands
⓭ The Coral World Underwater Aquarium and Island Drive Tour
⓮ The "Screemin' Eagle" Jet Boat thrill ride
Tortola, British Virgin Islands
⓯ Hiking tour to the peak of Sage Mountain (National Park)
Virgin Gorda, British Virgin Islands
⓰ Excursion to "The Baths" in Virgin Gorda

MEXICO / CENTRAL AMERICA

MEXICO AND CENTRAL AMERICA
Acapulco, Mexico
⓱ Excursion to see the famous rock divers
⓲ Tour to the Silver City of Taxco
Belize, Central America
⓳ Horseback riding and more in the jungles of Belize

Dunn's River Falls in Jamaica.

Cabo San Lucas, Mexico
⓴ Personal dolphin encounter (for children) at the Cabo Dolphin Center
Cozumel, Mexico
㉑ Tour to 12th-century Mayan ruins of Tulum and Xel-Ha national park

EUROPE AND THE BALTIC

Amsterdam, Holland
㉒ Go to the Anne Frank Museum
Athens (Piraeus, the port for Athens), Greece
㉓ Tour to the Acropolis and museums of ancient Athens
Barcelona, Spain
㉔ City tour to see Gaudi's architecture, the Sagrada Familia cathedral, and the Ramblas
Casablanca, Morocco
㉕ Casablanca, including the Hassan II Grand Mosque, and Rabat
Catania/Messina, Sicily
㉖ Visit to Mt. Etna and Taormina
㉗ Sicilian Cooking Class tour
Copenhagen, Denmark
㉘ Guided walking tour of the famed Tivoli Gardens
Dublin, Ireland
㉙ Visit the original Guinness brewery

Dubrovnik, Croatia
㉚ Guided walking tour of the old walled city
Edinburgh, Scotland
㉛ Visit Edinburgh Castle and the city
㉜ The Whisky Distillery Tour
Flam/Gudvangen
㉝ Take the mountain railway excursion from Flam to Gudvangen
Helsinki, Finland
㉞ Art, city highlights and Sibelius concert tour
Istanbul, Turkey
㉟ Tour to Topkapi Palace and the Grand Bazaar
Kusadasi
㊱ Tour to historic Ephesus, and the house of the Virgin Mary
La Coruna, Spain
㊲ Tour to Santiago de Compostela, home to the mystery of St. James
Lisbon, Portugal
㊳ Tour to the Alfama (old) quarter of Lisbon and the Maritime Museum
Livorno, Italy
㊴ Full-day tour to Florence and the Leaning Tower of Pisa
London, England
㊵ River cruise along the banks of the historic River Thames for a different view of London
㊶ London by Night, including a West End musical or play
Madeira, Portugal
㊷ The toboggan ride excursion
Monte Carlo, Monaco
㊸ Tour to the Royal Palace and Grand Casino (jacket and tie required)
Naples, Italy
㊹ Tour to the Isle of Capri by boat to visit the famous Blue Grotto caves
Nice, France
㊺ Tour to Ez and the Corniche
Oslo, Norway
㊻ Tour to the Viking Museum and the warship Wasa
Palma de Mallorca
㊼ Tour to former Carthusian monastery of Valldemosa (Frederick Chopin and George Sand lived here in 1838)
Rhodes, Greece
㊽ Follow in the footsteps of St. Paul
Rome (Civitavecchia, the port for Rome), Italy
㊾ Guided "Roman Holiday" walking tour, including the Colosseum

Visit to the Vatican, including the Sistine Chapel

Santorini, Greece
Donkey ride tour up the hillside

Sorrento, Italy
Visit to the ruins of Pompeii and the Amalfi Coast

St. Petersburg, Russia
Guided walking tour through the Hermitage Museum
Excursion to St. Catherine's Summer Palace
Night tour to a ballet or classical music performance at the Mariinsky Theater

Stockholm, Sweden
Tour to the Nobel Prize Museum

Venice, Italy
Romantic gondola ride excursion
Guided walking tour to the Guggenheim Museum

Warnemunde, Germany
Excursion to Berlin

ICELAND

Reykyavik, Iceland
Tour to the warm geothermal waters of the Blue Lagoon

INDIAN OCEAN AND THE MIDDLE EAST

Aqaba, Jordan
Tour to the "Rose Red City" of Petra

Dubai, UAE
4 x 4 Dune Drive Safari Tour

Male, Seychelles
Flightseeing of the atolls and inlets

Mumbai, India
Mumbai City Sights
Buddhist Trail tour to the Kanheri Caves

Alexandria or Port Said, Egypt
Tour to the amazing temple of Karnak in Luxor

Sharm el Sheik, Egypt
Go diving and snorkeling

Tripoli, Libya
Tour to historic Leptis Magna and Tripoli's Medina

THE UNITED STATES

Hilo, Hawaii
Kilauea Volcano tour in Volcanoes National Park

Juneau, Alaska
Flightseeing trip to Mendenhall Glacier, and Alaska salmon bake

Ketchikan, Alaska
Misty Fjords flightseeing trip

Key West, Florida
The Conch Train Tour in Ernest Hemingway's favorite city

Los Angeles, California
Tour past the Hollywood homes of top movie stars

New York City
Take a Circle Line boat cruise around Manhattan

Skagway, Alaska
The historic White Pass & Yukon Route Railway train tour

Sitka, Alaska
Sea Otter and Wildlife Quest

AUSTRALIA, NEW ZEALAND AND THE SOUTH PACIFIC

Auckland, New Zealand
Tour to one of West Auckland's wineries and micro-breweries

Hamilton Island, Australia
Cruise/tour to Great Barrier Reef

Melbourne, Australia
Guided walking and tram tour, including the Gold Treasury
Shark diving in the aquarium tour on the banks of the Yarra River

Sydney, Australia
Full-day catamaran tour taking in

Floatplane rides are popular in Alaska.

the Blue Mountains and Featherdale Wildlife Park

SOUTHEAST ASIA

Bali, Indonesia
Balinese music and dance show

Bangkok (Laem Chabang, the port for Bangkok), Thailand
Tour to the Royal Palace and the sacred halls of Wat Phra Kaew

Ha Long Bay, Vietnam
Junk tour through the misty waters and limestone monuments

Ho Chi Minh City, Vietnam
Tour to the (Vietnam) War Museum

Hong Kong, China
The Harbour Bay cruise tour

Kuala Lumpur, Malaysia
Visit the Petronas Twin Tower building and night market

Osaka, Japan
Tour to Kyoto, the former capital city of Japan and the historic monuments of the ancient city, now a Unesco World Heritage site

Singapore
The Night Safari Tour

Yokohama, Japan
Tour to the famous Ginza shopping area in Tokyo
Kabuki Theater Performance tour

SOUTH AMERICA

Rio de Janeiro, Brazil
Tour to Sugar Loaf Mountain
Corcovado Tour & Christ the Redeemer Monument

Buenos Aires, Argentina
Steak and Tango night tour

Ushuaia, Argentina
Ride world's southernmost train

Puerto Madryn, Chile
The Penguin Safari tour (encounter 250,000 penguins, and the landscape of Patagonia)

SOUTH AFRICA

Cape Town, South Africa
Cape Town/Table Top Mountain
Vintage car tour to Mount Nelson Hotel for afternoon tea

Mombasa, Kenya
Tour to Tsavo National Park (Kenya's oldest game preserve)

Walvis Bay, Namibia
Moon landscape and Welwitschia Plains Tour

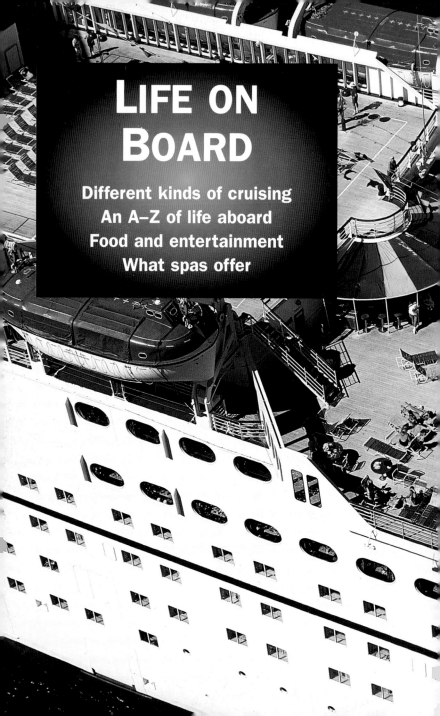

LIFE ON BOARD

Different kinds of cruising
An A–Z of life aboard
Food and entertainment
What spas offer

CRUISES FOR FAMILIES

Many cruise lines, recognizing the needs of parents, have added a whole variety of children's programs to their daily activities

There are few better vacations for families than a ship cruise, especially during school breaks. Active parents can have the best of all worlds: family togetherness, social contact, and privacy. Cruise ships provide a safe, crime-free, encapsulated environment, and give junior passengers a lot of freedom without parents having to be concerned about where their children are at all times. Because the days aboard are long, youngsters will be able to spend time with their parents or grandparents, as well as with their peers. They can also meet senior officers and learn about the navigation, radar, and communications equipment. They will be exposed to different environments, and experience many types of food. They will discover different cultures during shore excursions.

Although children may not like organized school-like clubs, they will probably make new friends quickly in the surroundings of a cruise ship. Whether you share a cabin with them or book an adjoining cabin, there will be plenty to keep them occupied.

Some cruise lines have token family programs, with limited activities and only a couple of general staff allocated to look after children, even though their brochures might claim otherwise. Other lines dedicate teams of counselors who run special programs off-limits to adults. They also have provide practical facilities such as high chairs in the dining room, cots, and real playrooms.

Small children who are not toilet-trained will not generally be allowed in the swimming pool, and it may be difficult to bathe small children in cabins with no bathtub but only a shower enclosure with a fixed-head shower.

Children's entertainment

Most entertainment for children is designed to run simultaneously with adult programs; few ships have dedicated children's entertainers. For those cruising with very young children, baby-sitting services may be available. For example, *QM2* has children's nurses and even fully qualified English

Holland America Line runs cookery classes for children.

ABOVE: having a ball during a Princess cruise.
RIGHT: the waterpark aboard *Freedom of the Seas*.

nannies. *Aurora*, *Oceana* and *Oriana* have a "night nursery" for two- to five-year-olds.

Some ships have children's pools and play areas, as well as junior discos, video rooms, and teen "chill-out" centers. Not to be outdone by Disney, Carnival Cruise Lines has "Fun Ship Freddy," a lifesized mascot with a head shaped like the company's distinctive funnels.

In some ships, stewards, stewardesses, and other staff may be available as private baby-sitters for an hourly charge; otherwise, group babysitting may be offered. Make arrangements at the reception desk. Aboard some ships, evening baby-sitting services may not start until late – check details before booking.

Cruise lines serious about children typically divide them into distinct age groups: Toddlers (ages 2–4); Juniors (ages 5–7); Intermediate

Children under two travel free on most cruise lines and airlines. If they're older, however, you have to pay.

(ages 8–10); Tweens (ages 11–13); and Teens (ages 14–17). It often seems to be children under 12 who get the most from a cruise.

Safety tips

Because young children love to climb, they should never be left alone on a balcony. On the open decks, ships have railings – either horizontal bars through which a children can't get their heads, or they are covered in glass or plexiglass under a thick wooden top rail.

Although children find their way around easily, walk with them between your cabin and an activity so that you both know the way. Discuss safety issues with them, and warn them not to walk into "Crew Only" areas at any time. For identification, most cruise lines provide children with colored wristbands, which must be worn at all times.

The right food

Selected baby foods, along with cribs and high chairs, are stocked by ships that cater to children, but ask your travel agent to check first. If you need a special brand of baby food, or a high chair in the restaurant, a crib, baby bathtub, baby stroller (few ships have them to rent), or monitoring service, let your travel agent know well in advance, and obtain confirmation in writing that the facilities will be available. Given enough notice, most cruise lines will try to obtain what is needed.

Parents using organic baby foods, such as those obtained from health food stores, should be aware that cruise lines buy their supplies from major general food suppliers and not the smaller specialized food houses.

Activities for children

Although many ships have full programs for children during days at sea, these may be limited when the ship is in port. Ships expect you to take your children with you on organized

excursions, which sometimes have lower prices for children. If the ship has a playroom, find out if it is open and supervised on all days of the cruise.

When going ashore, remember that if you want to take your children swimming or to the beach, it is wise to telephone ahead to a local hotel with a beach or pool. Many hotels will be happy to show off their property to you, hoping to gain your future business.

Some cruise ships in the Caribbean have the use of a "private" island for a day, including waterpark areas for kids and adults. A lifeguard will be on duty, and there will be water sports and snorkeling equipment you can rent. But remember that the beaches on some "private" islands are fine for 200 passengers, but with 2,000 they quickly become crowded, forcing you to stand in line for beach barbecues and toilet facilities.

Although the sun and warm sea might attract juniors to the Caribbean, children aged seven and over will find a Baltic, Black Sea, or Mediterranean cruise a delight. They will have a fine introduction to history, languages, and different cultures.

Activities for teens

Many large resort ships have dedicated "no adults allowed" zones. Teen-only activities include deck parties, pool parties, games, karaoke, discos, dances, computer gaming consoles and talent shows. Some Royal Caribbean International ships provide musical instruments for jam sessions. Sports include rock-climbing and basketball. There's usually almost unlimited food, too, although some of it may not be very nutritious.

Disney goes cruising

In 1998, Disney Cruise Line entered the family cruise market with a splash. The giant entertainment and theme park company

---

Goofy entertainment aboard Disney's ships.

ABOVE: kiss and tell during a shore excursion.
RIGHT: large resort ships have teens-only activities.

introduced the first of two large resort ships to cater to families with children, with cruises of 3, 4 and 7 days. *Disney Magic* and *Disney Wonder* cater to 1,750 adults and up to 1,000 children (sometimes more), and have ambitious entertainment programs.

Disney has its own passenger terminal –

designed after the original Art Deco-inspired 1930s Ocean Terminal in Southampton, England – and facilities at Port Canaveral, Florida, as well as a fleet of motorcoaches. One ship also sails in the Mediterranean in summer, from Barcelona. Disney has two more ships on order, for delivery in 2010 and 2011.

THE SHIPS THAT CATER BEST FOR CHILDREN

These cruise lines and ships have been selected for the quality of their children's programs and care:

Aida Cruises: *AIDAcara, AIDAaura, AIDAbella, AIDAvita, AIDAdiva*

Carnival Cruise Lines: *Carnival Conquest, Carnival Destiny, Carnival Freedom, Carnival Glory, Carnival Legend, Carnival Liberty, Carnival Pride, Carnival Spirit, Carnival Splendor, Carnival Triumph, Carnival Valor, Carnival Victory, Carnival Ecstasy, Carnival Elation, Carnival Fantasy, Carnival Fascination, Carnival Imagination, Carnival Inspiration, Carnival Paradise, Carnival Sensation*

Celebrity Cruises: *Celebrity Century, Celebrity Constellation, Celebrity Eclipse, Celebrity Galaxy, Celebrity*

Carnival has strong children's programs.

Infinity, Celebrity Mercury, Celebrity Millennium, Celebrity Solstice, Celebrity Summit

Cunard Line: *Queen Mary 2, Queen Victoria*

Disney Cruise Line: *Disney Magic, Disney Wonder*

Norwegian Cruise Line: *Norwegian Dawn, Norwegian Gem, Norwegian Jade, Norwegian Jewel, Norwegian Pearl, Norwegian Spirit, Norwegian Star, Norwegian Sun*

P&O Cruises: *Aurora, Oceana, Oriana, Ventura*

Princess Cruises: *Crown Princess, Diamond Princess, Emerald Princess, Golden Princess, Grand Princess, Ruby Princess, Sapphire Princess, Star Princess*

Royal Caribbean International: *Adventure of the Seas, Explorer of the Seas, Freedom of the Seas, Independence of the Seas, Liberty of the Seas, Mariner of the Seas, Navigator of the Seas, Voyager of the Seas*

Star Cruises: *Star Pisces, SuperStar Aquarius, SuperStar Libra, SuperStar Virgo*

Thomson Cruises: *Thomson Celebration, Thomson Destiny, Thomson Spirit*

Children's rates

Most cruise lines offer special rates for children sharing their parents' cabin. The cost is often lower than third and fourth person share rates. To get the best rates, it's wise to book early. If you don't anticipate spending much time in your cabin, consider a cheaper interior (no-view) cabin.

Although many adult cruise rates include

> *If you're planning an active vacation which won't involve spending much time in your cabin, consider booking a cheaper interior cabin without a view.*

airfare, most children's rates don't. Also, although some lines say children sail "free," they must pay port taxes as well as airfare. The cruise line will get the airfare at the best rate, so there is no need to shop around. If you have very young children and can get to your ship without having to fly, you'll save yourself the hassles of struggling though airports.

Single parents

Only a few cruise lines have introduced their versions of the "Single Parent Plan." This offers an economical way for single parents to take their children on a cruise, with parent and child sharing a two-berth cabin, or parent and children sharing a three-berth cabin.

Single parents will pay about one-third the normal single-person rate for their children.

Family reunions

A cruise can provide the ideal place for a family get-together, with or without children. Let your travel agent make the arrangements and ask for a group discount there are more than 15 of you.

Take care to choose a cruise line with a suitable ambience. Book 12 months in advance if possible so that you can arrange cabins close to each other. If the ship operates two dinner seatings, you may also wish to arrange for everyone to be at the same one.

Birthday specials

If anyone in the group has a birthday or anniversary, tell your travel agent to arrange a special cake – most cruise lines don't charge extra for this. Special private parties can also be arranged, at a price. If the group isn't too large, you may be able to request to dine at the captain's table. Shore excursions, too, can be booked in advance for a group.

Finally, get everything in writing, particularly cabin assignments and locations. ❏

Scuba diving off St. Maarten during an RCI cruise.

CRUISES FOR SOLO PASSENGERS

**Cruise prices are geared towards couples.
Yet more than one in four cruise passengers
travels alone or as a single parent**

Many solo passengers are prejudiced against cruising because most lines charge them a single occupancy supplement. The reason is that the most precious commodity aboard any ship is space. Since a solo-occupancy cabin is often as large as a double and is just as expensive to build, cruise lines feel the premium price is justified, What's more, because solo-occupancy cabins are at a premium, they are unlikely to be discounted.

Single supplements

If you are not sharing a cabin, you'll be asked to pay either a flat rate or a single "supplement" if you occupy a double cabin. Some lines charge a fixed amount – $250, for instance – as a supplement, no matter what the cabin category, ship, itinerary, or length of cruise. Such rates vary between lines, and sometimes between a line's ships. Because there are so few single-occupancy cabins, it's best to book as far ahead as you can.

Lines that charge low single supplements include Crystal Cruises, Peter Deilmann Ocean Cruises, and Voyages of Discovery. Only a few of the smaller cruise lines, such as Saga Cruises and Voyages of Discovery, have no additional supplements for singles.

Guaranteed singles rates

Some lines offer singles a set price for a double cabin but reserve the right to choose the cabin. So you could end up with a rotten cabin in a poor location or a wonderful stateroom that happened to be unallocated.

Guaranteed share programs

These allow you to pay what it would cost each half of a couple for a double-occupancy cabin, but the cruise line will find another passenger of the same sex (and preferences such as smoking or non-smoking) to share it with you. If the line does not find a cabin-mate, the single passenger may get the cabin

Pampering a sunbather aboard *Celebrity Millennium*.

Cruising for single women

A cruise ship is at least as safe for single women as any major vacation destination, but that doesn't mean it is entirely hassle-free.

It's easy to strike up conversations with other passengers, and cruising is not a "meat market" that keeps you under constant observation. The easiest way to meet other singles, however, is to participate in scheduled activities. Single black women may find there is often a dearth of single black men for dancing or socializing with.

Beware of embarking on an easy affair with a ship's officer or crew member. They meet new people on every cruise and could consequently transmit sexual diseases.

Gentlemen cruise hosts

The female-to-male passenger ratio is typically high, especially among older people, so some cruise lines provide male social hosts. They may host a table in the dining room, appear as dance partners at cocktail parties and dance classes, join bridge games, and accompany women on shore excursions.

These men, usually over 55 and retired, are outgoing, mingle easily, and are well groomed. First introduced aboard Cunard Line's *QE2* in the mid-1970s, gentlemen hosts are now employed by a number of cruise line, including Crystal Cruises, Cunard Line, Holland America Line, Regent Seven Seas Cruises, and Silversea Cruises.

If you think you'd like such a job, do remember that you'll have to dance for several hours most nights, and be proficient in just about every kind of dance. ❏

to himself or herself at no extra charge. Some cruise lines do not advertise a guaranteed-share program in their brochures but will often try to accommodate such bookings, particularly when demand for space is light.

Solo dining

A common complaint concerns dining arrangements. Before you take your cruise, make sure that you request a table assignment based on your personal preferences; table sizes are typically for 2, 4, 6, or 8 people. Do you want to sit with other singles? Or do you like to sit with couples? Or perhaps

> *Jack Lemmon and Walter Matthau played gentlemen dance hosts intent on defrauding rich widows aboard a Caribbean cruise ship in the 1997 movie Out to Sea.*

with a mixture of both? Or with passengers who may not speak your language?

When you are on board, make sure that you are comfortable with the dining arrangements, particularly in ships with fixed table assignments, or ask the maître d' to move you to a different table. Aboard ships with open seating or with several different dining venues, you can choose which venue you want to eat in, and when; Norwegian Cruise Line (NCL) is an excellent example of this arrangement, with its Freestyle Dining.

A leisurely breakfast in the luxury of a stateroom.

CRUISES FOR ROMANTICS

No need to worry about getting to the church on time – you can be married at sea, or get engaged, or have a second honeymoon

Two famous TV shows, *The Love Boat* (US) and *Traumschiff* (Germany), boosted the concept of cruising as a romantic vacation, though the plots didn't always match reality. The real captain of one ship, when asked the difference between his job and that of the captain of *The Love Boat*, remarked: "On TV they can do a retake if things aren't right the first time around, whereas I have to get it right the first time."

Getting engaged aboard ship

Princess Cruises has a special "Engagement Under the Stars" package that allows you to propose to your loved one in a personal video that is then screened just before an evening movie at a large outdoor screen aboard some of the company's ships. Current cost: $695.

Getting married at sea

Instead of the hassle of arranging flights, hotels, transportation and packages, you can

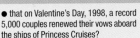

DID YOU KNOW...

● that on Valentine's Day, 1998, a record 5,000 couples renewed their vows aboard the ships of Princess Cruises?

● that Princess Cruises even has a "Department of Romance" dedicated to creating eventful romantic packages, settings and celebrations?

let a specialist wedding planner do it all for you. As in all those old romantic black-and-white movies, a ship's captain can indeed marry you when at sea if properly certified – unless the ship's country of registry prohibits or does not recognize such marriages.

You first need to inquire in your country of domicile whether such a marriage is legal, and ascertain what paperwork and blood tests are required. The onus is on you to prove the validity of such a marriage. The captain could be held legally responsible if he married a couple not entitled to be wed.

10 ROMANTIC PORTS OF CALL

Fowey (Cornwall, UK)
Hvar (Croatia)
Hydra, Greece
La Rochelle, France
Nice (France),
Portofino, Italy
St George's (Bermuda)
St Jean de Luc, France
Venice, Italy
Villefranche (France)

It's relatively easy to get married aboard almost any cruise ship when it is alongside in port. Carnival Cruise Lines, Holland America Line, and Princess Cruises, among others, offer special wedding packages. These include the services of a minister to marry you, wedding cake, champagne, bridal bouquet and matching boutonnière for the bridal party, a band to perform at the ceremony, and an album of wedding photos. Note that US citizens and "green card" residents may need to pay sales tax on wedding packages.

Several cruise lines can arrange a marriage ceremony on a Caribbean beach – a dream for

The ocean air can be remarkably invigorating.

many. For example, Princess Cruises offers weddings on a beach in St. Thomas (prices range from $525 to $1,175 per package). Or how about a romantic wedding Disney-style on its private island, Castaway Cay?

Azamara Cruises, Celebrity Cruises and Princess Cruises offer weddings aboard many of their ships – your travel agent should check with a cruise line's wedding coordinator. The ceremonies can be performed by the captain, who is certified as a notary, when the ships' registry – Bermuda or Malta, for example – recognizes such unions.

Expect to pay about $2,500, plus about $500 for licensing fees. Harborside or shore-side packages vary according to the port. A wedding coordinator at the line handles all the details, enabling you to be married aboard ship and honeymoon aboard, too.

Even if you don't get married aboard ship, you could have your wedding reception aboard one. Many cruise lines offer good facilities and provide complete services to help you plan your reception. Contact the Director of Hotel Services at the cruise line of your choice. The cruise line should go out of its way to help, especially if you follow the reception with a honeymoon cruise – and a

cruise, of course, also makes a fine, no-worry honeymoon *(see below)*.

UK-based passengers should know that P&O Cruises hosts a series of cruises called the "Red-Letter Anniversary Collection" for those celebrating 10, 15, 20, 25, 30, 35, 40, 45, 50, 55, or 60 years of marriage; the cruise comes with a complimentary gift, such as a brass carriage clock, leather photograph album, or free car parking at Southampton.

Renewal of vows

Many cruise lines now perform "renewal of vows" ceremonies. A cruise is a wonderful setting for reaffirming to one's partner the strength of commitment. A handful of ships have a small chapel where this ceremony can take place; otherwise it can be anywhere aboard ship – a most romantic time is at sunrise or sunset on the open deck. The renewal of vows ceremony is conducted by the ship's captain, using a non-denominational text.

Carnival takes the romance of cruising to heart.

Although some companies, such as Carnival Cruise Lines, Celebrity Cruises, Holland America Line, P&O Cruises and Princess Cruises, have complete packages for purchase, which include music, champagne, hors d'oeuvres, certificate, corsages for the women, and so on, most other companies do not charge – yet.

Cruising for honeymooners

Cruising is the new hot honeymoon. The advantages are appealing: you pack and unpack only once; it is a hassle-free and crime-free environment; and you get special attention, if you want it. It is also easy to budget in advance, as one price often includes airfare, cruise, food, entertainment, several destinations, shore excursions, and pre- and post-cruise hotel stays.

Once you are married, some cruise lines make a point of offering discounts to entice you to book a future cruise to celebrate an anniversary. Just think: no cooking meals, everything will be done for you.

Although no ship as yet provides bridal suites (hint, hint), many ships have suites with king- or queen-sized beds. Some also provide tables for two in the dining room should you wish to dine together without having to make friends with others.

Some cruise ships feature Sunday departures, so couples can plan a Saturday wedding and reception before traveling to their ship. Pre- and post-cruise hotel accommodation can also be arranged.

Most large resort ships accommodate honeymoon couples well. However, if you want to plan a more private, intimate honeymoon without the crowds, it would be a good idea to try one of the smaller, yacht-like cruise vessels such as those of Seabourn Cruise Line, Regent Seven Seas Cruises, Silversea Cruises, or Windstar Cruises.

And what could be more romantic for honeymooners than to stroll, all by themselves, on deck to the forward part of the ship, near the ship's bridge. This is the quietest (except perhaps for some wind noise) and most dimly lit part of the ship – ideal for stargazing and romancing.

Togetherness in a hot tub, on deck at dusk, and on a private balcony.

Package deals

Cruise lines offer a variety of honeymoon packages, just as hotels and resorts on land do. Although not all cruise lines provide all services, a typical selection might include:

- ❤ Private captain's cocktail party for honeymooners.
- ❤ Tables for two in the dining room.
- ❤ Set of crystal champagne or wine glasses.
- ❤ Honeymoon photograph with the captain, and photo album.
- ❤ Champagne and caviar for breakfast.
- ❤ Complimentary champagne (imported or domestic) or wine.
- ❤ Honeymoon cruise certificate.
- ❤ Flowers in your suite or cabin.
- ❤ Complimentary cake.
- ❤ Special T-shirts.

An essential checklist

Finally, take a copy of your marriage license or certificate, for immigration (or marriage) purposes, as your passports will not yet have been amended.

Also, remember to allow extra in your budget for things like drinks, shipboard gratuities, shore excursions, and spending money while ashore.

If your romance includes the desire to share a large bed with your loved one, check with your travel agent and cruise line to make sure

the cabin you have booked has such a bed. Better still, book a suite if you can afford to. But it's important to check and double-check to avoid disappointment.

If you need to take your wedding gown aboard for a planned wedding somewhere along the way – in Hawaii or Bermuda, for example – there is usually space to hang it in the dressing room next to the stage in the main showlounge, especially aboard the large resort ships. ❏

20 STUNNING HARBORS

Cape Town, S. Africa
Funchal, Madeira
Gibraltar
Hamburg, Germany
Hamilton, Bermuda
Hobart, Tasmania
Honolulu, Hawaii
Hong Kong, China
Monte Carlo, Monaco
Naples, Italy
New York, USA
Oslo, Norway
Rio de Janeiro, Brazil
St Petersburg, Russia
Singapore
Shanghai, China
Stockholm, Sweden
Sydney, Australia
Venice, Italy
Valletta, Malta

CRUISES FOR GAYS AND LESBIANS

Some cruise lines are known to be more gay-friendly than others, and some agencies charter entire ships for gays and lesbians only

S everal US companies specialize in ship charters or large group bookings for gay and lesbian passengers. These include the California-based Atlantis (tel: 310-859 8800; www.atlantis events.com), San Francisco's lesbian specialist Olivia (www. olivia.com) or New York's Pied Piper Travel (tel: 212-239 2412; http://home.att. net/~gaygroupcruises).

One drawback of gay charters is that they're as much as 20% more expensive than the equivalent general cruise. Another is that they have been greeted with hostility by church groups on some Caribbean islands such as Grand Cayman, Jamaica and Bermuda. One Atlantis cruise was even denied the right to dock. But their great advantage is that they provide an accepting environment and gay-geared entertainment, with some big-name comedians and singers.

Another approach is to join a gay affinity group on a regular cruise at normal prices; these groups may be offered amenities such as private dining rooms and separate shore excursions.

Many gays, of course, have no wish to travel exclusively with other gays but may worry that, on a mainstream cruise, they might be seated for dinner with unsympathetic companions. They would prefer to sit where they want, when they want, and such open seating is offered by Norwegian Cruise Line and Princess Cruises, and by more upscale lines such as Crystal, Silversea and Seabourn. Open seating is not offered by Carnival, Celebrity or Royal Caribbean International.

That doesn't mean that any of the major

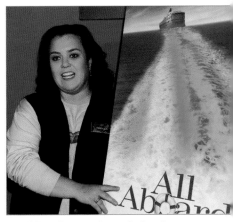

Rosie O'Donnell promotes her gay family cruise.

cruise companies are not gay-friendly – many hold regular "Friends of Dorothy" gatherings, sometimes scheduled and sometimes on request – though it would be prudent to realize that Disney Cruise Line, for example, will not offer the ideal entertainment and ambience. Among the smaller companies, Windstar's sail-powered cruise yachts have a reputation for being gay-friendly.

Gay familes are catered for by R Family Vacations (tel: 866-732 6822; www.rfamily-vacations.com), although it's not essential to bring children. Events may include seminars on adoption and discussion groups for teenagers in gay families. One of the company's founders was the former TV talk show host Rosie O'Donnell, herself a lesbian mother. ❏

CRUISES TO SUIT SPECIAL NEEDS

Cruising for the physically challenged offers one of the most hassle-free vacations possible, with a wide choice of ships and itineraries, a clean environment, and almost all of the details taken care of before you go

Cruise ships have become much more accessible for people with most types of disabilities. Many new ships also have text telephones, listening device kits for the hearing-impaired (including show lounges and theaters aboard some ships). Special dietary needs can often be accommodated, and many cabins have refrigerators (useful for those with diabetes who need to keep supplies of insulin cool). Special cruises cater for dialysis patients and for those who need oxygen regularly.

If you use a wheelchair, take it with you, as ships carry only a limited number for emergency hospital use only. An alternative is to rent an electric wheelchair, which can be delivered to the ship on your sailing date.

The disadvantages

It is as well to begin with the disadvantages of a cruise for the physically challenged:
● Unless cabins and bathrooms are specifically designed, problem areas include the entrance, furniture configuration, closet hanging rails, beds, grab bars, height of toiletries cabinet, and wheel-in shower stall.
● Elevators: the width of the door is important; in older ships, controls often cannot be reached from a wheelchair.
● Few ships have access-help lifts installed at swimming pools (exception: P&O Cruises) or angled steps with handrail, or thalassotherapy pools or shore tenders (exception: Holland America Line).

During an inspection, the author or one of his inspectors wheels around each ship to check wheelchair accessibility. The chart on pages 236–51 includes their ratings for more than 350 cruise ships.

● It can be hard to access some areas such as self-serve buffets.
● Some insurance companies may prohibit smaller ships from accepting passengers with severe disabilities.
● Only five cruise ships have direct access ramps to lifeboats: *Amadea, Asuka II, Crystal Serenity, Crystal Symphony* and *Europa*.

12 tips to avoid pitfalls

❶ Start by planning an itinerary and date, and find a travel agent who knows your needs. But follow up on all aspects of the booking yourself to avoid slip-ups; many cruise lines have a department or person to handle requests from disabled passengers.
❷ Choose a cruise line that permits you to select a specific cabin, rather than one that merely allows you to select a price category. If the ship does not have any specially equipped cabins, book the best outside cabin in your price range, or choose another ship.
❸ Check whether your wheelchair will fit through your cabin's bathroom door, or into the shower area whether there is a "lip" at the door. Don't accept "I think so" as an answer. Get specific measurements.
❹ Choose a cabin close to an elevator. Not all elevators go to all decks, so check the deck

Elevators such as *Oosterdam*'s make life easier.

plan carefully. Smaller and older vessels may not even have elevators, making access to even the dining room difficult.
❺ Avoid, at all costs, a cabin down a little alleyway shared by several other cabins, even if the price is attractive. It's hard to access a

---

WHY DOORS CAN PRESENT A PROBLEM FOR WHEELCHAIR USERS

The design of ships has traditionally worked against the mobility-limited. To keep water out or to prevent water escaping from a flooded area, raised edges ("lips") – unfriendly to wheel-chairs – are often placed in doorways and across exit pathways. Also, cabin doorways, at a standard 24 inches (60cm) wide, are often not wide enough for wheelchairs – about 30 inches (76 cm) is needed.

Bathroom doors, whether they open outward or inward, hinder maneuverability, for the same reason. An electrically operated sliding door would be better.

Bathrooms in many older ships are small and full of plumbing fixtures, often at odd angles, awkward when moving about in a wheelchair.

The author tests accessibility.

Those aboard new ships are more accessible, but the plumbing may be located beneath the complete pre-fabricated module, making the floor higher than that in the cabin, which means a ramp is needed.

Some cruise lines will, if given

advance notice, remove a bathroom door and hang a fabric curtain in its place. Many lines will provide ramps for the bathroom doorway if needed.

Access to outside decks is usu-ally provided through doors that must be opened manually rather than via electric-eye doors that open and close automatically.

It's not cheap to provide facilities for wheelchair-bound passengers. Trained crew members are needed to assist them, which translates to two crew members per eight-hour shift. Thus, six crew members would be required according to the latest safety and evacuation regulations solely to provide support for one wheelchair-bound passenger – a big drain on labor resources.

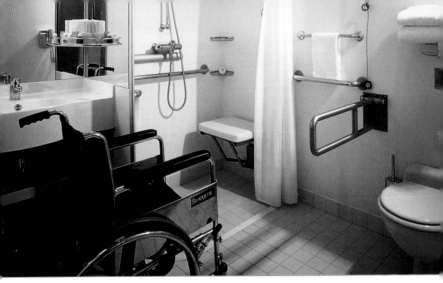

Modern ships' bathrooms are fairly accessible.

cabin in a wheelchair from such an alleyway.

6 Cabins located amidships are less affected by vessel motion, so choose something in the middle of the ship if you are concerned about possible rough seas. The larger – and therefore more expensive – the cabin, the more room you will have to maneuver in. And a tub provides more space than a shower.

7 Hanging rails in the closets on most ships are positioned too high for someone in a wheelchair to reach – even the latest ships seem to repeat this basic error. Many cruise ships, however, have cabins specially fitted out to suit the mobility-limited. They are typically fitted with roll-in closets and have a pull-down facility to bring your clothes down to any height you want.

8 Meals in some ships may be served in your

cabin, on special request – an advantage should you wish to avoid dressing for every meal. But few ships have enough space in the cabin for dining tables. If you opt for a dining room with two fixed-time seatings for meals, choose the second – it's more leisurely. Alert the restaurant manager in advance that you would like a table that leaves plenty of room for your wheelchair.

9 Hand-carry medical records. Once on board, notify the reception desk that help may be needed in an emergency.

10 Make sure that the contract specifically states that if, for any reason, the cabin is not available, that you will get a full refund and transportation back home as well as a refund on any hotel bills incurred.

11 Advise the cruise line of the need for proper transfer facilities such as buses or vans with wheelchair ramps or hydraulic lifts.

12 If you live near the port of embarkation, arrange to visit the ship to check its suitability (most cruise lines will be accommodating).

Ship-to-shore launches

Cruise lines should – but don't always – provide an anchor emblem in brochures for those ports of call where a ship will be at anchor instead of alongside. If the ship is at anchor, the crew will lower you and your wheelchair into a waiting tender and then, after a short boat-ride, lift you out again onto a rigged gangway or integral platform. If the sea is

---

HOW TO COPE WITH EMBARKATION

The boarding process can pose problems. If you embark at ground level, the gangway may be level or inclined. It will depend on the embarkation deck of the ship and/or the tide in the port.

Alternatively, you may be required to embark from an upper level of a terminal, in which case the gangway could well be of the floating loading-bridge type, like those used at major airports. Some have flat floors; others may have raised lips at regular intervals. The lips can be awkward to negotiate in a wheelchair, especially if the gangway is made steeper by a rising tide.

calm, this maneuver proceeds uneventfully; if the sea is choppy, it could vary from exciting to somewhat harrowing.

This type of embarkation is rare except in a busy port with several ships sailing the same day. Holland America Line is one of the few companies to make shore tenders accessible to the disabled, with a special boarding ramp and scissor lift so that wheelchair passengers can see out of the shore tender's windows.

Help for the hearing impaired

Difficulties for such passengers include hearing announcements on the public address system; using the telephone; and poor acoustics in key areas such as boarding shore tenders.

Take a spare hearing aid battery. More new ships have cabins specially fitted with colored signs to help those who are hearing impaired. Crystal Cruises' *Crystal Serenity* and *Crystal Symphony*, and Celebrity Cruises' *Celebrity Century*, *Celebrity Galaxy*, and *Celebrity Mercury* have movie

theaters fitted with special headsets for those with hearing difficulties.

Finally, when going ashore, particularly on organized excursions, be aware that most destinations, particularly in Europe and Southeast Asia, are simply not equipped to handle people with hearing impairment.

The latest improvements

Things are getting better. For example, the large resort ships *Norwegian Gem*, *Norwegian Jewel* and *Norwegian Pearl* provide:
● 11 wheelchair-accessible public toilets throughout each ship (including the spa).
● 27 wheelchair-accessible cabins, including suites. All have collapsible shower stools mounted on shower walls; all bathroom toilets have collapsible arm guards and lower washbasin. Other cabin equipment includes a vibrating alarm clock, door beacon (light flashes when someone knock on the door), television with closed caption decoders, and a flashing light as fire alarm.
● Hearing-impaired kits on request.
● Dedicated wheelchair positions in the showlounge (including induction systems).
● Electrical hoist to access pool and hot tubs.
● All elevators and cabins have Braille text. ❏

AN A–Z OF PRACTICAL TIPS

How do I get laundry done? Are baby-sitters available? Who should I tip? What television stations can you receive at sea? Can I access the internet? This alphabetical survey of facilities available aboard has the answers

Air-conditioning

Cabin temperature can be regulated by an individually controlled thermostat, so you can adjust it to suit yourself. Public room temperatures are controlled automatically. Air temperatures are often kept cooler than you may be used to. Note that in some ships, the air-conditioning cannot be turned off.

Art auctions

Beware of these. Aboard most large resort ships, intrusive art auctions form part of the "entertainment" program, with flyers, brochures, and forceful announcements that almost demand that you attend. They may be fun participation events – though the "free champagne" given to entice you is mostly sparkling wine and *not* champagne – but don't expect to purchase an heirloom, as most of the art pieces (lithographs and seriographs) are rubbish. It's funny how so many identical pieces can be found aboard so many ships.

Note that art "appraisal prices" are done in-house by the art provider, a company that *pays* a cruise line to be onboard. Watch out for the words: "retail replacement value". Also, listen for phrases such as "signed in the stone" – it means that the artists did not sign the work – or "pochoire" (a stencil print less valuable than an original etching or lithograph). If you do buy something, do so because it will look good hanging on your wall, not as an investment. But read the fine print, and buy only with caution.

Baby-sitting

In some ships, stewards, stewardesses, and other staff may be available as babysitters for an hourly fee. Make arrangements at the reception desk. Aboard some ships, evening baby-sitting services may not start until late; check times and availability before you book a cruise.

Beauty salon/Barber shop

Make appointments as soon after boarding as possible, particularly on short cruises. Appointment times fill

Childcare facilities aboard Disney Cruise Line.

Low stakes on the high seas aboard a Seabourn ship.

up rapidly, especially before social events such as a captain's cocktail party. Charges are comparable to those ashore. Typical services: haircut for men and women, styling, permanent waving, coloring, manicure, pedicure, leg waxing. *See Shipboard Spas page 170–7.*

Cashless cruising

It is now the norm to cruise cash-free, and to settle your account with one payment (by cash or credit card) before disembarking on the last day. An imprint of your credit card is taken at embarkation or when you register online, permitting you to sign for everything. Before the end of the cruise, a detailed statement is delivered to your cabin. Some cruise lines, irritatingly, may discontinue their "cashless" system for the last day of the cruise. Some may add a "currency conversion service charge" to your credit card account if it is not in the currency of the cruise line.

Ships visiting a "private island" on a Bahamas/Caribbean itinerary will probably ask you to pay cash for beverages, water sports and scuba diving gear, and other items that you purchase ashore.

Casino gaming

Many cruise ships have casinos, where the range of table games includes blackjack or 21, Caribbean stud poker, roulette, craps, and baccarat. Under-18s are not allowed in casinos, and photography is usually banned inside them. Customs regulations mean that casinos generally don't open when the ship is in port.

Gaming casino operations aboard cruise ships are unregulated. However, some companies, such as Celebrity Cruises and Royal Caribbean International, abide by Nevada Gaming Control Board regulations. Most table games have a $5 minimum and $200 maximum – but, for serious players, Carnival Cruise Lines' casinos have blackjack tables with a $25 minimum and $500 maximum.

Some cruise lines have "private gaming club" memberships, with regular newsletters, rebates and special offers (example: Star Cruises). Slot machines can also in evidence and, as on shore, make more than half a casino's profits.

Note that, for American citizens and resident aliens in the US, slot machine winnings may be subject to WG-2 tax withholding.

> Most cruise lines give free lessons in how to play the various table games. And shipboard casinos have no entrance charge.

Comment cards

On the last day of the cruise you will be asked to fill out a company "comment card." Some lines offer "incentives" such as a bottle of champagne. Be truthful, as the form serves as a means of communication between you and the cruise line. Pressure from staff to write "excellent" for everything is rampant aboard cruise ships. But if there have been problems, say so, or things are less likely to improve.

Daily program

This contains a useful list of the day's activities, entertainment, and social events. It is normally delivered to your cabin the evening before the day that it covers.

Departure Tax

If you are disembarking in a foreign port and flying home, there could be a departure tax to pay, in local currency, at the airport.

Disembarkation

This can be the most trying part of any cruise. The cruise director will already have given an informal talk on customs, immigration, and disembarkation procedures. The night before the ship reaches its destination, you will be given a customs form to fill out. Include any duty-free items, whether purchased aboard or ashore. Save the receipts in case a customs officer asks for them.

The night before arrival, place your main baggage outside your cabin on retiring, or before 2am. It will be collected and off-loaded on arrival. Leave out fragile items, liquor, and the clothes you intend to wear for disembarkation and onward travel – it is amazing just how many people pack absolutely everything. Anything left in your cabin will be considered hand luggage to be hand-carried off when you leave.

On disembarkation day, breakfast will probably be early. It might be better to miss breakfast and sleep later, providing announcements on the ship's public address system do not wake you (it may be possible to turn off such announcements). Even worse than early breakfast is the fact that aboard many ships you will be commanded – requested, if you are lucky – to leave your cabin early, only to wait in crowded public rooms, sometimes for hours. To add insult to injury, your cabin steward – after he has received his tip, of course – will knock on the door to take the sheets off the bed so the cabin can be made up for the incoming passengers. This will not

Disembarking can sometimes be a dreary business.

ABOVE: the internet café aboard RCI's *Navigator of the Seas*.
RIGHT: the shopping promenade aboard *Freedom of the Seas*.

happen aboard the smaller "upscale" ships.

Some companies now offer a slightly more relaxed system that allows you to stay in your cabin as long as they wish, or until your tag color is called, instead of waiting in public areas, where it's difficult to avoid the mass of wheeled luggage waiting to trip you up.

Before leaving the ship, remember to claim any items you have placed in your in-cabin personal safe. Passengers cannot go ashore until all baggage has been offloaded, and customs and/or immigration inspections or pre-inspections have been carried out. In most ports, this takes two to three hours after arrival. It is wise to leave at least three hours from the time of arrival to catch a connecting flight or other transportation. Once off the ship, you identify your baggage on the pier before going through customs inspection. Porters may be there to assist you.

Duty-free liquor purchases

If you buy a box of "duty-free" liquor in the Caribbean, it will be taken from you at the gangway as you reboard and given back to you the day before you disembark. Also, be aware that if you fly home from a US airport after your cruise, you are not permitted to take any liquid items larger than 100ml in your hand luggage. Unless you place the liquor in your checked baggage, there's no point purchasing it – it will be confiscated.

Engine room

For insurance and security reasons, visits to the engine room are seldom allowed. In some ships, a technical information leaflet may be available. Aboard others, a Behind the Scenes video may be shown on cabin TV system.

Gift shops

The gift shop/boutique/drugstore offers souvenirs, gifts, toiletries, logo and duty-free items, as well as a basic stock of essential items. Opening hours are posted at the store and in the Daily Program.

Internet access and email

Most large resort ships have internet access, for a fee. This can be slow, due to uplink/downlink to satellites, and the fact that ships often move out of the satellite's "footprint." Charges are typically 50–75 cents per minute, although bulk packages of 30, 60, or 100 minutes may be available. If you can wait, an internet café ashore will be faster and cheaper.

Almost all large resort ships have wi-fi for your computer or cell phone. You can send and receive emails – but at a price, because all internet connection is via satellite.

Launch (shore tender) services

Enclosed or open motor launches ("tenders") are used when your cruise ship is unable to berth at a port or island. In such cases, a regular launch service is operated between ship and shore for the duration of the port call.

When stepping on or off a tender, extend "forearm to forearm" to the person who is assisting you. Do not grip their hands because this has the unintentional effect of immobilizing the helper.

Laundry and dry cleaning

Most ships offer a full laundry and pressing service. Some ships may also offer dry cleaning facilities. A detailed list of services, and prices, can be found in your cabin. Your steward will collect and deliver your clothes.

Some ships have self-service launderettes, equipped with washers, dryers, and ironing facilities. There may be a charge for washing powder and for use of the machines.

Library

Most cruise ships have a library offering a good selection of books, reference material, and periodicals. A small, refundable deposit may be required when you borrow a book.

A quiet moment in *Sun Princess*'s library.

Aboard small luxury ships, the library is open 24 hours a day, and no deposit is required. Aboard the large resort ships, the library may be open only a couple of hours a day.

Aurora, *Oriana*, *QM2* and *Queen Victoria* are examples of ships with full-time, qualified librarians sourced by the specialist company Ocean Books. Aboard most other ships a member of the cruise staff or entertainment staff – with little knowledge of books or authors – staffs the library. The library may also have board games such as Scrabble, backgammon and chess.

Lido

This is a deck devoted to swimming pools, hot tubs, showers, and recreation. Aboard most cruise ships, it has a self-serve buffet.

Lost property

Contact the reception desk immediately if you lose or find something on the ship. Notices

The Skylight chapel aboard *Mariner of the Seas*.

regarding lost and found property may be posted on the bulletin boards.

Mail

You can buy stamps and mail letters aboard most ships, at the reception desk. Some ships use the postal privileges and stamps of their flag of registration, while others buy local stamps at ports of call. Mail is usually taken ashore by the ship's port agent just before the ship sails. You will receive a list of port agents and mailing addresses with your tickets and documents, so you can advise friends and family how they can send mail to you.

News and sports bulletins

The world's news and sports results are reported in the ship's newspaper or placed on a bulletin board near the reception desk or in the library. For sports results not listed, inquire at the reception desk.

Photographs

Professional photographers take digital pictures of passengers during embarkation and throughout the cruise. They cover all the main events and social functions, such as the captain's cocktail party. The pictures can be viewed without any obligation to purchase, but the prices may surprise. The cost is likely to exceed $10 for a postcard-sized photograph, and a 10 x 8-inch embarkation photo aboard *Queen Mary 2* will set you back a whopping $27.50.

Postcards and writing paper

These are available from the writing room, library, or purser's office/reception desk. Some ships charge for them.

Reception desk

This is also known as the Purser's Office, guest relations, or information desk. Centrally located, it is the nerve center of the ship for general passenger information and problems. Opening hours – in some ships, 24 hours a day – are posted outside the office and given in the Daily Program.

Religious services

Interdenominational services are conducted on board, usually by the captain or staff captain. A few older ships and Costa Cruises' ships have a small private chapel. Denominational services may be taken by clergy traveling as passengers.

Room service

Beverages and snacks are available at most times. Liquor is normally limited to the opening hours of the ship's bars. Some ships may charge for room service.

Sailing time

In each port of call, sailing and all-aboard times are posted at the gangway. The all-aboard time is usually half an hour before sailing. If you miss the ship, it's entirely your responsibility to get to the next port of call to re-join the vessel.

Shipboard etiquette

Cruise lines want you to have a good vacation, but there are some rules to be observed.
● In public rooms, smoking and nonsmoking sections are available. In the dining room, cigar and pipe smoking are banned.
● If you take a video camera with you, be aware that international copyright laws will prohibit you from recording any of the professional entertainment shows.

A nursery pool is designed to keep kids cool.

● It is all right to be casual when on vacation, but not to enter a ship's dining room in just a bathing suit. Nor are bare feet permitted here.
● If you are uncomfortable eating with the typical 10-piece dining room cutlery setting, some cruise lines have introduced etiquette classes to help you.

Shopping

Many cruise lines operating in Alaska, the Bahamas, the Caribbean, and the Mexican Riviera engage an outside company that provides the services of a "shopping lecturer." This person promotes "selected" shops, goods, and services heavily, fully authorized by the cruise line (which receives a commission). This relieves the cruise director of responsibility, together with any questions concerning his involvement, credibility, and financial remuneration. Shopping maps, with "selected" stores highlighted, are placed in your cabin, and sometimes include a guarantee of satisfaction valid for 30 days.

When shopping time is included in shore excursions, be wary of stores recommended by tour guides – they are likely to be receiving commissions from the merchants. Shop around before you buy. Good shopping hints and recommendations are often given in the port lecture at the start of your cruise. When buying local handicrafts, make sure they have indeed been made locally. Be wary of "bargain-priced" name brands, as they may be counterfeit. For watches, check the guarantee.

The ship's shops are also duty-free and, for the most part, competitive in price. The shops on board are closed while in port, however, due to international customs regulations. Worthwhile discounts are often offered on the last day of the cruise.

Swimming pools

Most ships have outdoor or indoor swimming pools, or both. They may be closed in port owing to local health regulations or cleaning requirements. Diving is not allowed – pools are shallow.

Parents should note that most pools are unsupervised. Some ships use excessive chlorine or bleaching agent; these could cause bathing suit colors to run.

Telephone calls

Most ships have a direct-dial satellite telephone system, so you can call from your cabin to anywhere in the world. All ships have an internationally recognized call sign, a combination of letters and digits.

Satellite calls can also be made when the ship is in port. Satellite telephone calls cost between US$5 and $15 a minute, depending on the type of equipment the ship carries, and are charged to your onboard account.

To reach any ship dial the International Direct Dial (IDD) code for the country you are calling from, followed by the ship's telephone number.

Anyone without a direct-dial telephone should call the High Seas Operator (in the

Shopping in Mexico during an RCI cruise.

Waters sports off Holland America's Half Moon Cay.

United States, dial 1-800-SEA-CALL). The operator will need the name of the ship, together with the ocean code (Atlantic East is 871; Pacific is 872; Indian Ocean is 873; Atlantic West/ Caribbean/US is 874).

Television

Programming is obtained from a mixture of satellite feeds and onboard videos. Some ships lock on to live international news programs such as CNN or BBC World, or to text-only news services. Satellite TV reception can be poor because ships constantly move out of the narrow beam transmitted from the satellite.

Tipping

Gratuities, at about $10 per person, per day, are added automatically to onboard accounts by almost all the major cruise lines. Gratuities are included in the cruise fare aboard a small number of ships, principally those in the luxury end of the market, where no extra tipping is permitted – at least in theory.

In some ships, subtle suggestions are made regarding tips; in others, cruise directors get carried away and dictate rules. Although some cruise brochures state "tipping is not required," it will be expected by the staff.

Here are the accepted industry guidelines: dining room waiter, $3–$4 per person per day; busboy (assistant waiter), $1.50–$2 per day; cabin steward or stewardess, $3–$3.50 per person per day; Butler: $5–$6 per person per day. Tips are normally given on the last evening of a cruise of up to 14 days' duration. For longer cruises, you would hand over half of the tip halfway through and the rest on

your last evening. Aboard many ships, a gratuity of 10 or 15 percent is automatically added to your bar check, whether you get good service or not, and to spa treatments.

Valuables

Most ships have a small personal safe in each cabin, but items of special value should be kept in a safety deposit box in the purser's office. This is accessible during the cruise.

Water sports

Some small ships have a water sports platform that is lowered from the ship's stern or side. These ships carry windsurfers, waterski boats, jet skis, water skis, and scuba and snorkel equipment, usually at no extra charge. Some may have an enclosed swimming "cage" if local fish are unwelcoming.

Such facilities look good in brochures, but ships are often reluctant to use them. This is because many itineraries have too few useful anchor ports. Also, the sea must be in an almost flat calm condition – seldom the case. Insurance regulations can be restrictive too.

Wine and liquor

The cost of drinks on board is generally lower than on land, since ships have access to duty-free liquor. Drinks may be ordered in the dining room, at any of the ship's bars, or from room service. Dining rooms have extensive and reasonably priced wine lists.

Some ships sell duty-free wine and liquor to drink in your cabin. You can not normally bring these into the dining room or public rooms, nor any duty-free wine or liquor bought in port. These rules protect bar sales, a substantial source of onboard revenue. ❑

My 50 Pet Peeves

It's not all bliss aboard some cruise ships. Douglas Ward pinpoints the things that irritate him most

❶ Shore-side porters who take your bags when you get off the bus, or out of your car, then stand there until you tip them before they move your bags or drop them. The worst ports for this are Fort Lauderdale and Miami.

❷ Lining up for ages to collect passports.

❸ "Family" cabins with four berths, but one bathroom and only two toiletry storage cabinets.

A Renoir aboard *Norwegian Dawn* lifts the spirits, but some ships relentlessly promote art auctions.

❹ Art auctions, carpet auctions, and the obnoxious sales persons who conduct them.

❺ Fine paintings and sculptures displayed, but with the cruise line not caring or knowing enough about them to place the name of the artist and the year of creation alongside.

❻ Tacky trinket tables set up as tourist traps outside the onboard shops.

❼ Tiny tub chairs suitable only for tiny people.

❽ Sugar and sugar substitutes in packets.

❾ Sugar packet containers filled with enough sugar for 100 people.

❿ Foil-wrapped butter that always ends up all over your fingers.

⓫ Foil-wrapped jam and marmalade – the kind you get in an American diner.

⓬ Paper, plastic, or polystyrene plastic cups for drinks of any kind.

⓭ Paper napkins for meals or informal buffets; they should be linen or cotton.

⓮ Plastic plates, often too small, for buffets.

⓯ Buffets where only cold plates are available, even for hot food items.

⓰ Repetitious breakfast and luncheon buffets and uncreative displays.

⓱ Baked Alaska parades in the dining room.

⓲ Mini-bar/refrigerators that do not provide limes and lemons for drink mixes.

⓳ The appalling number of merchandising flyers that come under the cabin door.

⓴ User-unfriendly automated telephone answering systems that provide number options to connect you to various services – you start to wonder whether the answering service is located in a call center in India.

㉑ Fluorescent lighting in the bathroom.

㉒ Bathroom mirrors that steam up.

㉓ Aboard large resort ships, getting Cabin Services, or the "Guest Relations Desk," or anyone to answer the telephone can be an exercise in frustration and patience.

㉔ The use of mobile phones in public rooms.

㉕ Constant, irritating, and repetitive announcements for bingo, horse racing, art auctions, and the latest gizmos for sale in the shops.

㉖ "Elevator music" that is played continuously in passageways and on open decks. Even worse: rock and rap music.

㉗ Any announcement that is repeated. Any announcement that is repeated.

㉘ In-cabin announcements at any time, except for emergencies; they are unnecessary for programmed events and shore excursions.

㉙ Flowers in one's cabin which are not watered or refreshed by the stewardess.

㉚ Pool towels provided in passenger cabins. This is user-unfriendly for anyone on the lowest accommodation decks, who are expected to carry them up to exterior decks, and down again, when they may be wet and heavy.

The shows are spectacular – but can be too loud.

31 Bathrobes provided but never changed during the cruise.

32 Toilet tissue paper that is too thin (2-ply) so you need twice as much.

33 Facial tissues (often made of cellulose) that make you feel you need reconstructive surgery after you use them.

34 Mechanically challenging bath plugs.

35 Toilet paper folded to a point, then sealed with a gummed label.

36 Lavatory seats with unnecessary "sanitized" seals across them.

37 Soap bars that are not large enough to wash the hands of a leprechaun.

38 Non-lathering shampoos.

39 All-in-one shampoo/conditioner/bodywash/detergent/pesticide.

40 Skimpy towels.

Baked Alaska often entails a pointless parade.

41 Garnishes, when "parsley with everything" seems to be the unbending rule for entrées.

42 Shopping lecturers and shopping videos.

43 Cabin stewards and stewardesses who insist on placing small folded pieces of paper in cabin door frames to indicate when their passengers have left their cabins.

44 Audiovisual technicians who think that the volume level of the show should equal that for a major rock concert.

45 Private island days, when the tender ride to get to the island seems to be longer than the flight to get to the ship.

46 Ships that ask you to settle your shipboard account before the morning of disembarkation.

47 If you want to reduce, or otherwise change, the "automatic gratuities" charged to your cabin aboard the large resort ships, you may have to provide the reason, in writing, to present to the reception desk.

48 Aboard most ships, 15% is automatically added to wine bills. Thus, a wine waiter makes much more money on a more expensive bottle of wine, whether he knows anything about that wine (or how to decant and serve it) or not. Insist on adding your own gratuity, and politely refuse to be told how much you have to tip.

49 Cruise brochures that use models, and provide the anticipation of an onboard product that a ship cannot deliver, thus disappointing passengers.

50 Brochures that promise a "small ship feel, big ship choice" when the ship caters to more than 2,000 people – and often more than 3,000. ❑

ARE CRUISE SHIPS SAFE?

Ships and icebergs don't mix well, of course.
But how likely is an accident at sea? What if
there's a fire? Is lifeboat training provided?
How good are are medical facilities aboard?

You can't always stop passengers having too much to drink and falling over balconies. But, as far as maritime accidents are concerned, cruising can claim the travel industry's best safety record, with fewer than 20 passenger fatalities during the past 20 years. Eleven of those happened when the *Royal Pacific* sank off Malaysia in 1992 after colliding with a Taiwanese trawler.

International regulations require all crew to undergo basic safety training *before* they are allowed to work aboard any cruise ship. On-the-job training is no longer enough. And safety regulations are getting more stringent all the time, governed by an international convention called SOLAS (Safety of Life at Sea).

Safety measures

All cruise ships built since July 1, 1986, must have either totally enclosed or partially

enclosed lifeboats with diesel engines that will operate even if the lifeboat is inverted.

Since October 1997, cruise ships have had:
● All stairways fully enclosed in self-contained fire zones.
● Smoke detectors and smoke alarms fitted in all passenger cabins and all public spaces.
● Low-level lighting showing routes of

> All cruise ships must meet standards set by the International Maritime Organization (IMO) and the International Convention for Safety of Life at Sea (SOLAS).

escape (such as in corridors and stairways).
● All fire doors throughout the ship controllable from the ship's navigation bridge.
● All fire doors that are held open by hinges capable of release from a remote location.
● Emergency alarms audible in all cabins.

Since July 2002, ocean-going cruise ships on international voyages have been required to carry voyage data recorders (VDRs), similar to black boxes carries by aircraft.

In October 2010, SOLAS regulations will prohibit the use of combustible materials in cruise ship construction. This means that as many as 60 pre-1974 vessels will either have to be withdrawn or be expensively upgraded.

Crew members attend frequent emergency drills, the lifeboat equipment is regularly tested, and the fire-detecting devices, and alarm and fire-fighting systems are checked.

Today's crews have had thorough safety training.

It doesn't help to have seen *Titanic*.

Any passenger spotting fire or smoke is encouraged to use the nearest fire alarm box, alert a member of staff, or contact the bridge.

Lifeboat drill

Few recent incidents have required the evacuation of passengers, although two cruise ships were lost following collisions (*Jupiter* in 1988, and *Royal Pacific* in 1992), one after striking an iceberg near Antarctica (*Explorer* in 2007) and one after foundering on a reef off the Greek island of Santorini (*Sea Diamond* in 2007).

A passenger lifeboat drill, announced publicly by the captain, must be held within 24 hours of leaving the embarkation port. Attendance is compulsory. Make sure you know your boat station or assembly point and how to get to it in the event of an emergency. If other passengers are lighthearted about the drill, don't be distracted. Note your exit and escape pathways and learn how to put on your lifejacket correctly. The drill takes no more than 15 minutes and is a good investment in playing safe – the *Royal Pacific* took less than 20 minutes to sink after its collision.

Medical services

Except for ships registered in the UK or Norway, there are no mandatory international maritime requirements for cruise lines to carry a licensed physician or to have hospital facilities aboard. However, in general, all ships carrying over 50 passengers do have medical facilities and at least one doctor.

The standard of medical practice and of the doctors themselves may vary from line to line.

Most shipboard doctors are generalists; there are no cardiologists or neurosurgeons. Doctors are typically employed as outside contractors and will charge for use of their services, including seasickness shots.

Regrettably, many cruise lines make medical services a low priority. Most shipboard physicians are not certified in trauma treatment or medical evacuation procedures, for example. However, some medical organizations, such as the American College of Emergency Physicians, have a special division for cruise medicine. Most ships catering to North American passengers carry doctors licensed in the United States, Canada, or Britain, but doctors aboard many other ships come from a variety of countries and disciplines.

Cunard Line's *QM2*, with 4,344 passengers and crew, has a fully equipped hospital with one surgeon, one doctor, a staff of six nurses, and two medical orderlies; contrast this with *Carnival Sensation*, which carries up to 3,514 passengers and crew, with just one doctor and two nurses.

Any ship operating long-distance cruises,

WHEN SOMEONE DIES AT SEA

Typically, this happens more on long cruises, where passengers are generally older. Bodies are put in a special refrigeration unit for removal at the port of disembarkation, or the body can be flown home from a wayward port of call – complicated, owing to the paperwork, and very expensive. Bodies cannot be buried at sea these days. But some people have the deceased cremated at home, return to their favorite cruise ship, and have the ashes scattered into the ocean.

Dialysis facilities are available aboard a few ships.

with several days at sea should have better medical facilities than one engaged in a standard 7-day Caribbean cruise, with a port of call almost every day.

Ideally, a ship's medical staff should be certified in advanced cardiac life support. The equipment should include an examination room, isolation ward/bed, X-ray machine (to verify fractures), cardiac monitor (EKG) and defibrillator, oxygen-saturation monitor, external pacemaker, oxygen, suction and ventilators, hematology analyzer, culture incubator, and a mobile trolley intensive care unit.

Wear sensible shoes with rubber soles (not crepe) when walking on deck or going to pool and lido areas. A ship does move, so leave the high heels at home.

Any existing health problems requiring treatment on board must be reported when you book. Aboard some ships, you may be charged for filling a prescription as well as for the cost of prescribed drugs. There may also be a charge if, as a result of being unwell, you have to cancel a shore excursion and need a doctor's letter to prove that you are ill.

Shipboard injury

Slipping, tripping, and falling are the major sources of shipboard injury. There are things you can do to minimize the chance of injury.
● Aboard many pre-1980 ships, raised thresholds separate a cabin's bathroom from its sleeping area. Don't hang anything from the fire sprinkler heads on the cabin ceilings.
● On older ships, it is wise to note how the door lock works. Some require a key on the inside in order to unlock the door. Leave the key in the lock, so that in the event of a real emergency, you don't have to hunt for the key.
● Aboard older ships, take care not to trip over raised thresholds in doorways leading to the open deck.
● Walk with caution when the outer decks are wet after being washed, or if they are wet after rain. This applies especially to solid steel decks – falling onto them is really painful.
● Do not throw a lighted cigarette or cigar butt, or knock out your pipe, over the ship's side. They can easily be sucked into an opening in the ship's side or onto an aft open deck area, and cause a fire.

Legal action: If you do suffer from injury aboard ship, feel it is the cruise line's fault, and want to take legal action against the company, you should be aware of the following, which applies to American passengers:

In the United States, Appendix 46, Section 183(b) of the US Civil Code requires that "the injured passenger notify the cruise line in writing within six months from the date of the injury to file a claim and suit must be filed within one year from the date of injury." So, if you file a claim after the one-year period, the cruise line will probably seek a summary judgment for dismissal.

First, however, read your ticket. The passenger ticket is a legal contract between passenger and cruise line. It will invariably state that you must file suit in the state (or country) designated in the ticket. Thus, if a resident of California buys a cruise, and the cruise line is based in Florida, then the lawsuit must be filed in Florida. If you reside in the US and you purchase a cruise in the Mediterranean and the ship's registry is Italy, then you would have to file suit in Italy. This is known as the Forum Clause.

Surviving a shipboard fire

Shipboard fires can generate an incredible amount of heat, smoke, and often panic. In the unlikely event that you are in one, try to remain calm and think logically and clearly.

When you board the ship and get to your cabin, check the way to the nearest emergency exits fore and aft. Count the number of cabin doorways and other distinguishing features to the exits in case you have to escape without the benefit of lighting, or in case the passageway is filled with smoke. All ships use "low location" lighting systems.

Firefighters are required to hold regular training sessions.

Exit signs are normally located just above your head – this is virtually useless, as smoke and flames rise. Note the nearest fire alarm location and know how to use it in case of dense smoke. In future, it is likely that direc-tional sound evacuation beacons will be mandated; these will direct passengers to exits, escape-ways and other safe areas and may be better than the present inadequate visual aids.

If you are in your cabin and there is fire in the passageway outside, put on your lifejacket. If the cabin's door handle is hot, soak a towel in water and use it to turn the handle. If a fire is raging in the passageway, cover yourself in wet towels and go through the flames.

Check the passageway. If there are no flames, or if everything looks clear, walk to the nearest emergency exit or stairway. If there is smoke in the passageway, crawl to the nearest exit. If the exit is blocked, go to an alternate one. It may take considerable effort to open a heavy fire door to the exit. Don't use the elevators: they may stop at a deck that's on fire, or they may stop working.

If there's a fire in your cabin or on the balcony, report it immediately by telephone. Then get out of your cabin, close the door behind you, sound the alarm, and alert your neighbors. ❑

IS SECURITY GOOD ENOUGH?

Cruise lines are subject to stringent international safety and security standards. Passengers and crew can embark or disembark only by passing through a security checkpoint. Cruise ships maintain zero tolerance for onboard crime or offences against the person. Trained security professionals are employed aboard all cruise ships. In the case of the USA, where more than 60 percent of cruise passengers reside, you will be far more secure aboard a cruise ship than almost anywhere on land.

It is recommended that you keep your cabin locked at all times when you are not there. All new ships have encoded plastic key cards that operate a lock electronically; older ships have metal keys. Cruise lines do not accept responsibility for any money or valuables left in cabins and suggest that you store them in a safety deposit box at the purser's office, or, if one is provided, in your in-cabin personal safe.

You will be issued a personal boarding pass when you embark. This typically includes your photo, lifeboat station, restaurant seating, and other pertinent information, and serves as identification to be shown at the gangway each time you board. You may also be asked for a government-issued photo ID, such as a passport.

WHAT'S THE FOOD LIKE?

There's a lot of it, and you could eat round-
the-clock aboard many ships. But the quality
doesn't always match the quantity

Rubberized duck, rock-hard lobster, brittle pizza, elasticized croissants, grenade-quality fruit, coffee that tastes like army surplus paint... you can find all this and more in the cruise industry's global cafeteria. On the other hand, you can enjoy the finest caviar and vintage champagne. The message to remember is this: generally speaking, as in most restaurants on land, you get what you pay for.

High-quality food ingredients cost money, so it's pointless expecting low-cost cruises to offer anything other than low-cost food. It's not that the cruise lines don't try. They know that you will spend more time eating on board

Extra-cost restaurants try to match fine dining ashore.

than doing anything else, so their intention is to cater as well as they can to your palate while keeping the cruise price competitive. They even boast about their food, but the reality is that meals aboard most ships are not gourmet affairs. How could they be when a kitchen has to turn out hundreds of meals at the same time? Most of the cuisine compares favorably with "banquet" food in a family restaurant – in other words, often tasteless. What you will find, therefore, is a good selection of palatable, pleasing, and complete meals served in comfortable surroundings. Maybe you will even dine by candlelight, which at least creates some atmosphere.

Fresh versus frozen

Aboard low-priced cruises, you will typically be served portion-controlled frozen food that has been reheated. Fresh fish and the best cuts of meats cost the cruise lines more, and that cost is reflected in the cruise price. Aboard some ships, the "fresh" fish – often described as "Catch of the Day" (but *which* day?) – has clearly had no contact with the sea for quite some time.

Sushi bars are the latest fad but, in 90% of cases, fish used in sushi (with rice) is cooked, and raw (sashimi-style, without rice) fish is not available, as storage and preparation facilities are inadequate. The only ships with authentic sushi bars and authentic sushi/sashimi are *Asuka II*, *Crystal Serenity*, *MSC Musica* and *MSC Poesia*.

ABOVE: pizzas, popular on resort ships.
RIGHT: *Hanseatic*'s buffet in the Arctic.
BELOW: authentic sushi is hard to find.

Note also that many items of "fresh" fruit may have been treated with 1-MCP (methylcyclopropene) to make them last longer – apples, for example, may be up to a year old.

A typical day

From morning till night (and beyond), food is offered to the point of overkill, even aboard the most modest cruise ship. Aboard the large resort ships, pizzas, hamburgers, hot dogs,

> Alcohol usually costs extra. Expect to pay around $5.50 for a palatable glass of wine, or between $20 and $30 for a bottle.

ice-cream and frozen yoghurt are almost always available. And if you're still hungry, there's 24-hour room service. Some ships also have extra-charge cafés and patisseries.

If you prefer to eat at set times rather than graze, these are the options:

● **6am:** hot coffee and tea on deck for early risers (or late-to-bed types).
● **Full breakfast:** typically with as many as 60 different items, in the main dining room. For a more casual meal, you can serve yourself buffet-style at an indoor/outdoor deck café, although the choice may be more restricted.

● **Lunchtime:** with service in the dining room, buffet-style at a casual café, or at a separate grill for hot dogs and hamburgers, and a pizzeria, where you can watch the cooking.
● **4pm:** Afternoon tea, in the British tradition, complete with finger sandwiches and cakes. This may be served in a main lounge to the accompaniment of live music (it may even be a "tea-dance") or recorded classical music.
● **Dinner:** the main event of the evening, and apart from the casualness of the first and last nights, it is generally formal in style.
● **Light Bites:** sometimes served in public rooms late at night. These have mostly replaced the traditional midnight buffet.
● **Gala Midnight Buffet:** It's almost extinct, but if there is one, it is usually held on the penultimate evening of a cruise when the chefs pull out all the stops. It features a grand, colorful spread, with much intricate decoration that can take up to 48 hours to prepare.

The dining room

Many lines contract the running and staffing of dining rooms to a specialist maritime catering organization. Ships that cruise far from their home country find that professional catering companies do a good job. However, ships that control their own catering staff and food often try very hard for good quality.

Seating arrangements

On ships with open seating, you can sit at any available table, with whomever you wish, at any time within dining room opening hours – just like going out to a restaurant ashore.

On ships without open seating, unless you are with your own family or group of friends, you will be seated next to strangers. Tables for two are a rarity; most tables seat four, six, or eight. It is a good idea to ask in advance to be seated at a larger table, because if you are a couple seated at a table for four and you don't get along with your table partners, there is no one else to talk to. And remember, if the ship is full, it may be difficult to change tables once the cruise has started.

Depending on the size of the ship, it may have one, two or four seatings:

● **Single Seating:** you can choose when you wish to eat (within dining room hours) but have the same table assigned for the cruise.

● **Two Seatings:** you are assigned (or choose) one of two seatings, early or late. Typical meal times for two-seating ships are: Breakfast: 6.30am–8.30am; Lunch: 12 noon–1.30pm; Dinner: 6.30pm–8.30pm.

Some ships operate two seatings for all meals and some just for dinner. Dinner hours may vary when the ship is in port to allow for the timing of shore excursions. Ships that operate in Europe and the Mediterranean or in South America may have later meal times.

● **Four Seatings:** Only Carnival Cruise Lines operates four seatings – with dinner, for example, at 5.30pm, 6.45pm, 7.30pm or 8.45pm (except *Carnival Legend, Carnival Miracle, Carnival Pride* and *Carnival Spirit*, each with two seatings). You choose a time, and cannot change it later.

Alternative Dining

"Alternative" restaurants are trendy, particularly aboard the large resort ships, and are ideal for escaping from huge, noisy dining halls and singing, table-dancing waiters. These are typically smaller, à la carte venues where you must make a reservation, and pay an extra charge of between $6 and $30 a person. In return, you get better food, wines, service and ambiance.

The costs can soon add up, just as when you dine out ashore. As an example, take David's Supper Club aboard *Carnival Pride*. The food is very good, and the ambiance is refined. But a couple having two glasses of decent wine each can, with the cover charge, easily end up paying $100 for dinner.

Asian stir-fry aboard *Crystal Symphony*.

ABOVE: David's Supper Club, *Carnival Pride*.
RIGHT: *Noordam*'s vibrant dining room.

Special needs

Cruise lines tend to cater to general tastes. If you are allergic to any kind of ingredients (such as nuts or shellfish), do let the cruise line know in writing well ahead of time and, once on board, check with the restaurant manager.

Vegetarians should make sure that soups are not made with a chicken stock, as many so-called "vegetarian" soups are.

Menus are typically displayed outside the dining room each day so that you can preview each meal. Menus are delivered to suites.

Plate service vs. silver service

PLATE SERVICE: When the food is presented as a complete dish, it is as the chef wants it to look. In most cruise ships, "plate service" is

CELEBRITY CHEFS

Several cruise lines have signed up well-known chefs to devise menus for their alternative dining venues. Celebrity Cruises, for example, worked with three-star Michelin chef Michel Roux from 1989 until 2007. The partnership was successful because Roux insisted that the cruise line purchase high-quality ingredients and make everything from scratch, avoiding pre-made sauces, soup mixes and the like.

Other celebrated chefs have included Georges Blanc (Carnival Cruise Lines), Nobu Matsuhisa (Crystal Cruises), Todd English (Cunard Line), Gary Rhodes and Marco Pierre White (P&O Cruises), and Charlie Palmer (Seabourn Cruise Line).

now the norm. It works well and means that most people seated at a table will be served at the same time and can eat together, rather than let their food become cold.

SILVER SERVICE: When the component parts are brought to the table separately, so that the diner, not the chef, can choose what goes on the plate and in what proportion. Silver service is best when there is plenty of time, and is rare aboard today's ships. What some cruise lines class as silver service is actually silver service of vegetables only, with the main item, be it fish, fowl, or meat, already on the plate.

Self-serve buffets

Most ships have self-serve buffets for breakfast and luncheon (some also for dinner), one of the effects of discounted fares and dumbing down – and fewer staff are needed. Strangely, passengers don't seem to mind lining up for self-service food (reminiscent of school lunches and army canteens). But while buffets look fine when they are fresh, they don't after a few minutes of passengers helping themselves. And, one soon learns, otherwise sweet little old ladies can become ruthlessly competitive at opening time.

Passengers should not have to play guessing games when it comes to food, but many cruise lines forget to put labels on food items; this slows down any buffet line. Labels on salad dressings, sauces, and cheeses would be particularly useful.

What's not good is that if you ask anyone behind the self-serve buffet counters what kind of apples are in the fruit bowl they haven't a clue, "red" or "green" being the

WHAT YOU'RE MOST LIKELY TO FIND ON A TYPICAL MENU

HEALTHY CHOICE MENU
This menu reflects today's awareness of lighter, more balanced diets. Princess Cruises, for example, offers dishes that are low in cholesterol, fat, and sodium but high in flavor.
USA: Fresh Fruit Cup California Style
China: Won Ton and Vegetable Soup
New Zealand: John Dory Fillet Maori Style
Austria: Kranz Cake, Warm Vanilla Custard Sauce

VEGETARIAN MENU
USA: Fresh Fruit Cup California Style
Greece: Greek Salad, Mediterranean Dressing
Italy: Risotto with Asparagus
France: Puff Pastry Vegetable Roll with Tomato Sauce
Switzerland: Vacherin Suisse
Assorted International Cheese and Crackers

ALWAYS AVAILABLE
Classic Caesar Salad
Broiled North Sea Silver Salmon Fillet
Grilled Skinless Chicken Breast
Grilled Black Angus Sirloin Steak
Baked Potato and French Fries can be requested in addition to the daily vegetable selection.

APPETIZERS
Italy: Cocktail di Granseola Costa Esmeralda
Crabmeat Served in Half Cantaloupe Melon with Aurora Sauce
France: Smoked Breast of Strasbourg Duckling

England: Cured York Rolls on a Bed of Fresh Baby Leaves
USA: Fresh Fruit Cup California Style

SOUPS
China: Won Ton and Vegetable Soup
Scotland: Mutton and Barley Soup
Polynesia: Chilled Tropical Fresh Fruit Cream Soup

SALAD
Greece: Greek Salad, Mediterranean Dressing
Italy: Risotto con Pollo e Asparagi (*combination of Italian Carnaroli rice with green asparagus tips and strips of chicken finished with freshly grated Parmesan cheese and herbs*)

ENTRÉES
New Zealand: John Dory Fillet, Maori Style
Norway: Rainbow Trout Seven Sisters Fjord Fashion
Poached and Served with a Delicate Dill Sauce. Potatoes au Gratin
Holland: Glazed Milk-Fed Veal Leg Ancienne
Sliced and Served with a Mushroom Morel Cream Sauce, Hollandaise Potatoes
Australia: Oven-baked Spring Leg of Lamb Aussie-style
Coated with Mustard and Aromatic Herbs flavored with mint
USA: Surf and Turf (*Filet Mignon and Jumbo Shrimp from the grill with browned red new potatoes and bâtonnet vegetables*)

10 RECOMMENDED ALTERNATIVE RESTAURANTS

L'Enoteca *MSC Orchestra*
Le Champagne *Silver Shadow*
Le Cordon Bleu *Seven Seas Voyager*
Nobu's Sushi Bar *Crystal Serenity (pictured below)*
Olympic Restaurant *Celebrity Millennium*
Oriental Restaurant *Europa*
Palo's *Disney Wonder*
Queens Grill *Queen Victoria*
Teppanyaki Grill *Norwegian Pearl*
Umihiko *Asuka II*

ABOVE: cooking with brio in *Celebrity Millennium*'s top-rated – and extra-cost – Olympic Restaurant.

usual answer (red apples, for example, could be Braeburn, Egremont Russet, Gala, Pink Lady, Starking Delicious, or Worcester Pearmain). Staff should know – but seldom do – the most basic details about food on display.

Healthy eating

It's easy to gain weight when cruising – but not inevitable. First, weight-conscious passengers should exercise self-restraint, particularly at self-service buffets. Second, most ships have "heart-healthy" or "lean and light" options on the menu, or "spa" menus, with calorie-filled sauces replaced by spa cuisine. Third, there are plenty of opportunities for exercise, either in the spa or gym, on the jogging track often found above the main swimming pool deck, or by signing up for active shore excursions involving biking, hiking or river-rafting.

If you are vegetarian, vegan, macrobiotic, counting calories, want a salt-free, sugar-restricted, low-fat, low-cholesterol, or any other diet, advise your travel agent when you book, and get the cruise line to confirm that the ship can meet your needs. Cruise ship food tends to be liberally sprinkled with salt, and vegetables are often cooked with sauces containing dairy products, salt, and sugar.

Most cruise ships don't cope well with those on vegan or macrobiotic diets who regularly need fresh-squeezed juices; most large resort ships use commercial canned or bottled juices containing preservatives and can't provide really fresh juices in their bars.

Smoking/Nonsmoking

Most ships now have totally nonsmoking dining rooms, while some still provide smoking (cigarettes only, not cigars or pipes) and non-smoking sections. Those wishing to sit in a no-smoking area should tell the restaurant manager when reserving a table.

At open seating breakfasts and luncheons in the dining room or at a casual self-serve buffet venue, smokers and nonsmokers may be seated close together. ❏

Carnival Line tempts cruisegoers with calories.

ARE THE SHOWS WORTH SEEING?

After food, the most subjective part of any mainstream cruise is the entertainment. It has to be diversified and innovative but never controversial – which can mean bland

Many passengers, despite having paid so little for their cruise, expect to see top-notch entertainment, provided by big names. There are many reasons why this is not realistic. International star acts are accompanied by an entourage of managers, musicians, even hairdressers. One-night shows are not logistically or economically possible on a a cruise ship, as they are on land. It's tough to play to an audience of mixed nationalities – and languages. And not every entertainer likes the idea of living so closely with their audiences for several days, or even weeks. So,

when some upscale cruises do attract big names, they tend to be yesteryear's big names. However, cruise ships are the new location for vaudeville acts, where a guaranteed audience is a bonus for many former club-date acts and would-be future stars.

A certain sameness

A cruise line with several ships will normally employ an entertainment director and several assistants, and most cruise lines use agencies that specialize in entertainment for cruise ships. As a result, regular passengers will notice that they seem to see the same acts time after time on various ships. Also, aboard today's large resort ships the target is a family audience, so the fare must appeal to a broad age range.

Mistakes do happen. It is no use, for example, booking a juggler who needs a floor-to-ceiling height of 12 feet but finds that the ship has a show lounge with a height of just 7 feet (although I did overhear one cruise director ask if the act "couldn't he juggle sideways"); or an acrobatic knife-throwing act (in a moving ship?); or a concert pianist when the ship only has an upright honky-tonk piano; or a singer who sings only in English when the passengers are German-speaking.

The toughest audience is one of mixed nationalities, each of whom will expect entertainers to cater exclusively to their particular linguistic group. The "luxury" cruise lines – typically those

Hitting the high notes on the high seas.

NCL brought modern circus acts onto cruise ships.

operating small ships – offer more classical music, even some light opera, more guest lecturers and top authors than the seven-day package cruises heading for the sun.

Part of the entertainment experience aboard large resort ships is the glamorous "produc-

> Some cruise ships have coarse shows that are not becoming to either dancer or passenger – topless shows can be found aboard Star Cruises' ships, for example.

tion show," the kind of show you would expect to see in any Las Vegas show palace, with male and female lead singers and Marilyn Monroe look-alike dancers, a production manager, lavish backdrops, extravagant sets, grand lighting, special effects, and stunning custom-designed costumes. Unfortunately, most cruise line executives, who know little about entertainment, still regard plumes and huge feather boas paraded by showgirls who step, but don't dance, as being the last word.

Book back-to-back seven-day cruises – on alternating eastern and western Caribbean itineraries, for example – and you will probably find the same two or three production shows and the same acts on the second week of your cruise. The way to avoid seeing everything twice is to pace yourself. Go to some shows during the first week and save the rest for the second week.

Other entertainment
Most cruise ships organize acts that, while perhaps not nationally recognized "names," can provide two or three different shows during a 7-day cruise. These will be singers, illusionists, puppeteers, hypnotists, and even circus acts, with wide age-range appeal.

There are comedians and comedy duos who perform "clean" material and who may find employment year-round on the "cruise ship circuit." These popular comics enjoy good accommodation, are stars while on board, and often go from ship to ship on a standard rotation every few days. There are also raunchy, late-night "adults only" comedy acts aboard some ships with younger, "hip" audiences, but few have enough material for several shows. The larger a ship, the broader the entertainment program is likely to be. ❑

THE COST OF STAGING A SHOW

In today's high-tech world, staging a lavish 50-minute production show can easily cost between $500,000 and $1 million, plus performers' pay, costume cleaning and repair, royalties, and so on. To justify that cost, shows have to stay aboard a ship for 18 to 24 months.

Some smaller operators have targeted entertainment as an area for cost-cutting, so you could find yourself entertained by cheaper singers (who sound cheaper) and bands that can't read musical arrangements.

SPAS FLEX THEIR MUSCLES

The "feelgood factor" is alive and well aboard the latest cruise ships, which offer a growing array of body-pampering treatments and exercise classes. Your wallet will lose weight even if you don't

Land-based health spas have long provided a range of body treatments and services for those who wanted to hide away at a rural health farm. With an increasing emphasis on the body beautiful and the importance of well-being has come a whole new range of shipboard spas to rival those on land, particularly when it comes to body-pampering treatments. Today's cruise ships have elaborate spas where, for an extra fee, whole days of almost continuous treatments are on offer. Once the domain of women, spas now cater almost as much to men.

A visit to the ship's spa will help you to relax, remove stress, and feel soothed and pampered. Many people not used to spas may find some of the terminology daunting: aromatherapy, hydrotherapy, ionithermie, rasul, thalassotherapy. It's a good idea to visit the spa on embarkation day, when staff can show you round and answer your questions.

Facilities

Large resort ships will have a large gymnasium with ocean views, saunas, steam rooms, rasul chamber, several body treatment rooms, thalassotherapy pool, relaxation area, changing/locker rooms, and a beauty salon. Some ships even have acupuncture treatment clinics, and some have a built-in juice bar.

Thermal suites

These are private areas that provide a combination of various warm scented rain showers,

Spas offer strenuous exercise and serious pampering.

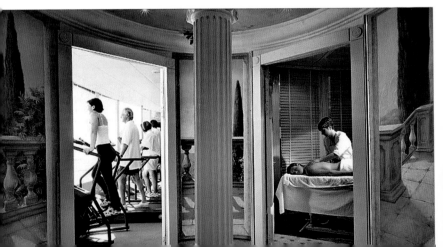

saunas, steam rooms, thalassotherapy (saltwater) pools and relaxation zones offer the promise of ultimate relaxation.

While most ships do not charge for use of the sauna or steam room, some make a per-day charge (examples: *MSC Musica* $30; *Norwegian Gem* $20; *Queen Mary 2*, $25).

Spa suites

Some ships have "spa suites," which include spa access and even a treatment or two (whereas regular cabin occupants pay extra to use the sauna/steam room/relaxation rooms), and special spa amenities (examples: *Costa Concordia, Costa Serena, Europa*), and even a special spa-food-menu-only restaurant (examples: *Celebrity Solstice, Costa Concordia, Costa Serena*).

Spa design

The latest sea-going spas have Asian-themed decor as an aid to relaxation, with warm woods and gently flowing water to provide a natural aesthetic environment aimed to caress and soothe, with therapy staff dressed in Balinese attire. But interior designers often forget to include dimmers and mood lighting, particularly in reception areas, where lighting is often too bright.

Spa facilities aboard the 2,800-passenger *SuperStar Virgo*.

Pampering treatments

Stress reducing and relaxation treatments are featured, combined with the use of seawater, which contains minerals, micronutrients, and vitamins. Massages might include Swedish remedial massage, shiatsu, and aromatherapy oils. You can even get a massage on your private balcony aboard some ships.

Having body-pampering treatments aboard a cruise ship can be wonderful, as the ship can provide a serene environment in itself; so, when enhanced by something like a massage or facial, the benefits can be more therapeutic. Ship interior designers do, however, need to pay more attention to soundproofing so that facilities can be used at all hours. Lighting dimmers are also essential – it's surprising how often this simple, but essential, item is overlooked. Examples of poor soundproofing include the treatment rooms aboard *Golden Princess, Grand Princess*, where they are located directly underneath a sports court. So, before you actually book your relaxing massage, find out if the treatment rooms are quiet enough.

Unfortunately, treatments are typically available only until about 8pm, whereas some passengers would welcome being able to have a massage late at night before retiring to bed. The problem is that most shipboard spas are run by concessions, with well-being treated as a daytime-only event. Also, be aware that

10 GREAT SHIPBOARD SPAS

AIDAdiva
Asuka II
Celebrity Solstice
Crystal Serenity
Emerald Princess
Europa
MSC Fantasia
Ocean Village Two
Queen Mary 2
Silver Shadow

Keeping fit during a Carnival cruise.

the latest "con" in the revenue game is to charge more for treatments on days at sea, and a lower fee on port days. Check the daily program for "port day specials" and packages that make prices more palatable.

Some of the smaller, more upscale ships now offer "Spa Days" with a whole day of body-pampering treatments ("wellness packages"). Expect to pay up to $500 a day, in addition to the cost of your cruise.

> Elixirs of youth, lotions and potions, creams and scrubs – all are sold by therapists, typically at the end of your treatment, for you to use when you get home. But be warned, these are expensive items.

Fitness centers

A typical large resort ship spa will include a gymnasium, probably with ocean-view windows. Virtual-reality exercise machines and weapons of mass reduction are found in the techno-gyms aboard most large resort ships, with state-of-the-art equipment muscle-pumping and body-strengthening equipment, universal stations, treadmills, bicycles, rowing machines, and free weights.

Most fitness centers are open only until early evening (one exception: NCL ships, whose gymnasiums are open 24 hours a day).

If you've forgotten your workout clothes, you can probably purchase new items on board.

Typical exercise classes

These include aerobics (for beginners, intermediate, and advanced), high intensity/low impact aerobics, step aerobics, interval training, stretch and relax, super body sculpting, fab abdominals, sit and be fit, and walk-a-mile.

Group exercycling, kick-boxing, pilates and yoga classes, body composition analysis, and sessions with a personal trainer, cost extra.

Massage

Having a massage aboard ship is a treat that more people are discovering. Today, many ships have suites and cabins with a "private" balcony, although you'll need a balcony with plenty of space in order to set up a proper portable massage table and allow the masseur room to walk around it and work from all sides. It can be a real stress-busting experience, but if it's not right it can prove frustrating, and expensive.

Make appointments for a massage as soon after embarkation as possible; some cruise lines let you book on-line ahead of the cruise so you can get the time slot you want – useful aboard the really large ships, where treatment slots can be hard to get. Large resort ships have more staff and offer more flexibile appointment times, although cruises tend to be shorter than those aboard smaller, more upscale ships. The cost averages about $2 a minute. In some ships, massage may be available in your cabin, or on your private balcony if it is large enough to accommodate a portable massage table.

A whole range of treatments and styles has evolved from the standard Swedish Remedial Massage. The most popular are:

● **Swedish Massage:** There are two main effects of massage: a reflex effect and a mechanical effect. There are four basic movements in this general massage: effleurage (the stroking movements that benefit the circulation of lymphatic fluids and drainage), petrissage (the picking, kneading, rolling and wringing movements), friction (the application of circular pressure) and tapotement (percussive tapping, flicking and hacking movements that stimulate circulation).

● **Well-being Massage:** This is really another term for general Swedish Massage but with more emphasis on effleurage movements, the use of complementary, warmed aromatic oils and four-hand massage (two therapists working rhythmically in unison).

● **Shiatsu Massage:** This literally means "finger pressure" and in Japan for thousands of years has been applied to the pressure points of the body as a preventative measure. It typically promotes a peaceful awareness of both body and mind, and is administered in a calm, relaxed environment, without oil.

● **Hot Stones Massage:** The therapist places 24 to 36 smooth basalt volcanic stones of varying sizes in a special oven. These are then applied to various key energy points of the body, using the stones to gently massage spe-

Hot stones massage aboard *Celebrity Infinity*.

cific areas and muscles. The heated volcanic stones are then left in place while the therapist works on other parts of the body. The heat from the stones helps the body to achieve a sense of deep relaxation.

● **Ayurvedic Head Massage:** Using a selection of warmed herbal oils, the therapist will apply the oil to the scalp, neck and shoulders to stimulate circulation and nourish the hair; you'll need to wash your hair afterwards, as it will be extremely oily. Shirodhara is the form of Ayurvedic medicine that involves gently pouring warm oil (made from tulsi, or holy basil) over the forehead, including the "third eye". Ayurveda is a compound word meaning life and knowledge.

● **Underwater Massage:** You soak in a large tub of warm water, possibly with rose petals floating around you, while the therapist massages joints and muscles.

● **Sports Massage:** Typically provided by a male therapist, sports massage is a deep-tissue massage that unlocks the kinks and knots.

● **Lomi-Lomi Massage:** This is a more rhythmic massage inspired by Hawaiian healing traditions that restore the free flow of "mana" or life force; it is typically given using warm aromatherapy oils, and may be a two-hand or four-hand massage.

● **Lymphatic Massage:** This massage is designed to improve circulation by releasing body toxins and nodes that build up in key lymphatic points. This massage is usually recommended for those who have poor circulation or suffer from exhaustion.

● **Thai Massage:** Uses pressure points and stretching techniques to relax muscles, improve circulation, and reduce stress.

● **Chinese Tuina:** This is a therapeutic massage based on a diagnostic evaluation, manipulation of the joints and muscle fibers, and identification and prevention of wrong body postures, habits and degenerative conditions.

> *When you charge treatments to your onboard account, remember that gratuities are often added automatically, so the real cost is 10–15% higher than you expect.*

● **Couples Massage:** Sometimes known as a "duet massage," this is typically a 90-minute session for a couple that includes a hands-on lesson from a massage specialist on the art of massaging each other.

● **Ultimate Massage:** Two therapists provide a synchronized full body massage, using Swedish massage movements to provide the ultimate in stress-busting relief. But it can be less than wonderful if the two therapists are even slightly out of sync.

Couples massage is also known as "duet massage."

OTHER TREATMENTS

While massage is the most popular shipboard spa treatment, some ships offer a whole range of body-pampering treatments, such as facials, manicures, pedicures, teeth whitening – even acupuncture. Most treatments are based on holistic Asian therapies. Some examples: Bali or Java, Indonesia (ural and pijat massage; mandi lulur, a scrub made from herbs essential oils and rice to soften the skin; Balinese boreh (a warm herb, rice, spice, galangal water and oil body wrap for detoxification); China (acupuncture); Japan (shiatsu massage; enzyme baths made from warmed finely shaved cedar chips, rice bran and vegetable enzymes to improve the metabolic system); Malaysia (Malay massage, which focuses on the body's 600,666 nerves); Philippines (Hilot massage, using virgin coconut oil and banana leaves); Thailand (Thai massage, or nuad boran).

Typically, the spa will provide items such as towels, robes and slippers, but it's best to store valuables safely in your cabin.

Don't worry about having to get naked; you'll typically change into a robe and slippers in the men's or women's changing rooms. You then go to the treatment room, and the

therapist will leave while you disrobe and lie down, placing a towel over your body, ready for massage. Some spas offer disposable panties for body treatments such as a Body Salt Glow or Seaweed Wrap. They may be optional, and sometimes the spa will insist that you wear them.

Spa staff aboard a Royal Caribbean International ship.

Acupuncture

The World Health Organization (WHO) recognizes acupuncture and its 5,000-year-old history. It can be used to prevent and remedy many maladies. Moxibustion is the treatment which involves hair-thin needles and heat transfer based on a special plant, the Artemisa Capillaris, placed into one of the more than 1,100 acupuncture points located along the meridians of the body.

Body scrub

The aim of this treatment is to cleanse and soften the skin, and to draw out impurities from within, using aromatic oils, creams, lotions, and perhaps sea salt, together with exfoliation (removal of dead skin cells) using skin brushing techniques.

Body wrap

Often called a body mask, this treatment typically includes the use of algae and seaweeds applied to the whole body. The body is then covered in aluminium foil and blankets. There are many variations on this theme, using mud from the Dead Sea or Mediterranean Sea, or sea salt and ginger, or cooling cucumber and aloe, or other combinations of herbs and oils that leave you with a warm glow. The aim of this treatment is to detoxify, firm and tone the skin, and reduce cellulite.

Dry flotation

This hydrobath gives you the sensation of floating without getting wet; you lie on a plush warm blanket between your body and the water. A therapist gently massages your head and neck while you relax.

Facials

Aromatherapy facial: This treatment typically uses aromatic oils such as lavender, sandalwood and geranium, plus a rejuvenating

Inspiring statuary in a Celebrity Cruises AquaSpa.

THE 10 RULES OF SPA ETIQUETTE

❶ It is important to wear proper attire (including shoes) in the gym.

❷ Wipe the equipment off with a clean towel (or sanitized cloth) after you have used it.

❸ Limit your time on the equipment or in the hot tub to a maximum of 30 minutes when others are waiting.

❹ Most ships allow jogging on a designated deck or area at selected times which will be posted. Adhere to the times posted because cabins are usually located directly below the designated deck and you may disturb fellow passengers who are sleeping.

❺ If there's a mixed sauna, men should not shave in it – it's unclean, and uncool.

❻ Arrive at least 10 minutes before your appointment.

❼ Take a shower or wash off all suntan lotions or oils.

❽ It's better not to talk during a massage – simply close your eyes, relax and enjoy.

❾ Shipboard spas are no-smoking zones – so no quick drag in the sauna.

❿ You can cancel an appointment up to 24 hours before your treatment time without charge. If you cancel within the 24 hours before your appointment time, you will be charged for the treatment you booked.

mask and accompanying creams and essences to "lift" the skin and facial muscles.

Rejuvenation facial: This classic French facial, which aims to reduce lines and wrinkles, uses the latest skin care products that may include essential plant and vitamin-rich oils.

Oscar's beauty salon aboard *SuperStar Virgo*.

Best foot forward in a Carnival Cruise Lines salon.

Rasul chamber

This is a steam chamber, also known as Hammam, that is typically fully tiled, featuring a domed roof and Moorish decor. When you enter, you paste yourself or your partner – it's a much better experience with a partner – with three types of mud, and sit down while gentle steam surrounds you.

The various types of mud become heated and then you're in a mud bath, after which you rub yourself, and each other, with large crystals of rock salt. Then shower, sit, and relax, all in the privacy of the chamber. Your skin will visibly glow afterwards.

Reflexology

The body's energy meridians exist as reflex points on the soles of the feet. The therapist

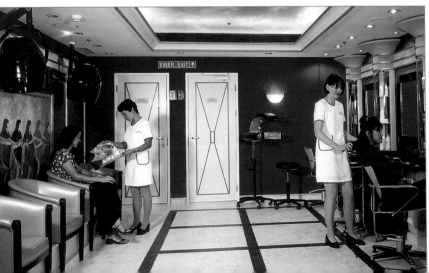

uses thumb pressure to stimulate these points to improve circulation and restore energy flow throughout the body.

Thalassotherapy

The use of seawater to promote well-being and healing dates back to ancient Greece. Today, shipboard spas have whole bath rituals involving water and flower petals, herbs or mineral salts.

Sample prices

Prices of body-pampering treatments have escalated recently, and are now equal to USA land-based spa prices. Expect to pay up to:
$190 for 75-minute Seaweed Wrap
$175 for 75-minute Hot Stones Massage
$110 for 50-minute Well-Being Massage
$110 for 50-minute Reflexology Session

Spa staff

Aboard most ships, the spa and fitness areas are operated by a specialist concession, although each cruise line may have a separate name for the spa, such as AquaSpa (Celebrity Cruises), The Greenhouse Spa (Holland America Line), Lotus Spas (Princess Cruises), etc.

Steiner Leisure *(see box below)* is by far the largest concession. Others include Blue Ocean, Canyon Ranch At Sea, Espace Elegance, Futuresse, Harding Brothers, and Mandara Spa (owned by Steiner).

Spa cuisine

Originally designed as low-fat, low-calorie (almost tasteless) meals for weight loss using grains, greens, and sprouts, spa cuisine now includes whole grains, seasonal fruits and vegetables, and lean proteins – ingredients that are low in saturated fats and cholesterol, low-fat dairy products, and reduced salt. To eat healthier meals, choose steamed or grilled items rather than baked or fried items.

Sports facilities

Sports facilities might include basketball and paddle tennis (a sort of downsized tennis court), and electronic golf simulators. Aboard some of the boutique/small "luxury" ships, kayaking, water-skiing, jet skiing, wake boarding are all included in the cruise fare. In reality, however, the watersports equipment is typically only used on one or two days, or part-days, during a 7-day cruise. ❏

Boxing clever aboard *Freedom of the Seas*.

SPECIALIST CRUISING

Expedition and nature cruises
Freighter travel
River cruises
North Atlantic Crossings

EXPEDITIONS AND NATURE CRUISES

There are still some less explored areas to be visited by the more adventurous, who want to visit them before they are spoiled

Passengers joining expeditions tend to be more self-reliant and more interested in doing or learning than in being entertained. They become "participants" and take an active role in almost every aspect of the voyage, which is destination-, exploration- and nature-intensive.

Naturalists, historians, and lecturers (rather than entertainers) are aboard each ship to provide background information and observations about wildlife. Each participant receives a personal logbook, illustrated and written by the wildlife artists and writers who accompany each cruise – a fine souvenir.

A venerable turtle on the Galápagos Islands.

You can walk on pack ice in the islands and land masses in the Arctic Ocean and Arctic Circle, explore a huge penguin rookery on an island in the Antarctic Peninsula, the Falkland Islands or South Georgia, or search for "lost" peoples in Melanesia. Or you can cruise close to the source of the Amazon, gaze at species of flora and fauna in the Galápagos Islands (Darwin's laboratory), or watch a genuine dragon on the island of Komodo – from a comfortable distance, of course.

Briefings and lectures bring cultural and intellectual elements to expedition cruise vessels. There is no formal entertainment as such; passengers enjoy this type of cruise more for the camaraderie and learning experience, and being close to nature. The ships are designed and equipped to sail in ice-laden waters, yet they have a shallow enough draft to glide over coral reefs.

Travel in comfort

Despite being rugged, expedition cruise vessels can provide comfortable and even elegant surroundings for up to 200 passengers, and offer first-class food and service. Without traditional cruise ports at which to stop, a ship must be self-sufficient, be capable of long-range cruising, and be totally environmentally friendly.

Lars-Eric Lindblad pioneered expedition cruising in the late 1960s. A Swedish American, he turned travel into adventure by going to parts of the

A group from *Hanseatic* explores the Amazon.

world tourists had not visited. After chartering several vessels for voyages to Antarctica, he organized the design and construction of a small ship capable of going almost anywhere in comfort and safety. In 1969, *Lindblad Explorer* was launched; it soon earned an enviable reputation in adventure travel. Others followed.

To put together cruise expeditions, companies turn to knowledgeable sources and advisors. Scientific institutions are consulted; experienced world explorers and naturalists provide up-to-date reports on wildlife sightings, migrations, and other natural phenomena. Although some days are scheduled for relaxation, participants are kept physically and mentally active. Thus it is unwise to consider such an adventure cruise if you are not completely ambulatory.

Adventure cruise companies provide expedition parkas and waterproof boots, but you will need to take waterproof trousers for Antarctica and the Arctic.

Antarctica

This is the ultimate place to chill-out. It was first sighted only in 1820 by the American sealer Nathaniel Palmer, British naval officer Edward Bransfield, and Russian captain Fabian Bellingshausen.

For most, it is just a wind-swept frozen wasteland – it has been calculated that the ice mass contains almost 90 percent of the world's snow and ice, while its land mass is twice the size of Australia. For others, it represents the last pristine place on earth, empty of people, commerce, and pollution, yet offering awesome icescape scenery and a truly wonderful abundance of marine and bird life. There are no germs and not a single tree.

As many as 35,000 people a year visit the continent – the only smoke-free continent on earth – yet the first human to come here did so within a generation of man landing on the moon. There is not a single permanent inhabitant of the continent, whose ice is as much as 2 miles (3km) thick. Its total land mass equals more than all the rivers and lakes on earth and exceeds that of China and India com-

bined. Icebergs can easily be the size of Belgium. The continent has a raw beauty and an ever-changing landscape.

This region is, perhaps, the closest thing on earth to another planet, and it has an incredibly fragile ecosystem that needs international protection. It contains two-thirds of all the fresh water on Earth (covered by ice, in September there are 8.5 million square miles of sea ice, but only 1.2 million in March). Antarctica lies in the southern ocean, whose global reach is a crucial link in the chain that is the Earth's heat engine; the southern Ocean absorbs heat from the atmosphere, which in turn can cause sea levels to rise through thermal expansion and ocean currents.

Helicopters are used during Celebrity's polar expeditions.

Although visited by "soft" expedition cruise ships and even "normal"-sized cruise ships with ice-hardened hulls, the more remote "far side" – the Oates and Scott Coasts, McMurdo Sound, and the famous

THE LEADING EXPEDITION CRUISE VESSELS: HOW THEY RATE

Research Vessels/ True Expedition Vessels	Rating (Facilities max: 100)	Company/Operator (1)	Built	Pass. Cabins	Max No. Passen- gers	Tonnage	Registry	Length (m)
Akademik Ioffe	48	Quark Expeditions	1988	55	110	6,460	Russia	117.10
Akademik Sergey Vavilov	50	Quark Expeditions	1988	40	110	6,231	Russia	117.80
Akademik Sholaskiy	44	Quark Expeditions	1982	22	44	2,140	Russia	71.56
Aleksey Maryshev	46	Oceanwide Expeditions	1990	22	44	2,000	Russia	70.00
Antarctic Dream	41	Antarctic Shipping	1959	39	78		Chile	83.00
Grigoriy Mikheev	46	Oceanwide Expeditions	1990	22	44	2,000	Russia	70.00
Kapitan Dranitsyn	50	Poseidon Arctic Voyages	1980	53	113	10,471	Russia	131.00
Kapitan Khlebnikov	51	Quark Expeditions	1981	54	114	12,288	Russia	132.49
Marina Svetaeva	45	Aurora Expeditions	1989	45	100		Russia	90.00
Polar Pioneer	47	Aurora Expeditions	1985	26	54	2,140	Russia	71.60
Professor Molchanov	44	Oceanwide Expeditions	1983	29	52	1,753	Russia	71.60
Professor Multanovskiy	44	Quark Expeditions	1983	29	49	1,753	Russia	71.60
Ocean Nova	48	Quark Expeditions/Albatros	1992	45	96	1,753	Greenland	73.00
Spirit of Enderby	44	Heritage Expeditions	1984	22	48	6,231	Russia	72.00
Yamal (2)	76	Quark Expeditions	1992	50	100	23,445	Russia	150.00
Other Expedition Cruise Ships								
Andrea	41	Various Tour Operators	1960	57	112	2,568	Norway	87.40
Bremen	76	Hapag-Lloyd Cruises	1990	82	184	6,752	Bahamas	111.51
Clipper Adventurer	56	Quark Expeditions	1976	61	122	5,750	Bahamas	100.01
Hanseatic	84	Hapag-Lloyd Cruises	1993	92	194	8,378	Bahamas	122.80
Lyubov Orlova	63	Quark Expeditions	1976	61	129	4,251	Malta	100.02
Marco Polo	55	Orient Lines	1965	425	915	22,080	Bahamas	176.28
Minerva	66	Swan Hellenic Cruises/ Voyages of Discovery	1996	178	474	12,500	Bahamas	133.00
National Geographic Endeavour	51	Lindblad Expeditions	1966	62	110	3,132	Bahamas	89.20
National Geographic Explorer	45	Lindblad Expeditions	1982	81	148	6,200	Bahamas	108.60
Orion	82	Orion Expedition Cruises	2003	53	139	4,050	Bahamas	102.70
Polar Star	56	Karlsen Shipping/ Polar Star Expeditions	1969	45	105	4,998	Barbados	86.50

NOTES: (1) = most expedition ships are sold by multiple expedition companies, or under full charter to one operator
(2) = nuclear powered

Ross Ice Shelf – can be visited only by genuine icebreakers such as the 114-passenger *Kapitan Khlebnikov*, the first vessel to circumnavigate Antarctica with passengers, as the katabatic winds can easily reach more than 100 mph (160 km/h).

Only 100 passengers per ship are allowed ashore at any given time, so if you choose to sail aboard one of the larger ships that claim to include Antarctica on their itineraries, it will probably be to view it – but only from the ship.

> *Do take plenty of sunscreen, as Antarctica has no pollution and it is easy to get sunburned when the weather is good.*

For real expedition cruising, choose a ship that includes a flotilla of Zodiac rubber inflatable landing craft, proper boot washing stations, and expedition equipment. Cruise ships that carry more than 500 passengers should not be allowed to sail in Antarctic waters, as the chances of rescue in the event of pack ice crushing a normal cruise ship hull, are virtually nil. So avoid the large resort ships in this region – they don't carry Zodiacs, cannot dock anywhere, and you will be disappointed.

There are no docks in Antarctica – venturing "ashore" is done by Zodiacs, which is an integral part of the experience.

Be aware that you can get stuck even aboard these specialized expedition ships, as did *Nordkapp*, which ran aground near Deception Island in 2007, and *Clipper Adventurer* in February 2000, in an ice field – it had to be rescued by an Argentine Navy icebreaker. And, in November 2007, Canadian company GAP Expeditions' *Explorer* hit

A family stroll for king penguins in Antarctica.

an iceberg in Bransfield Strait off King George Island and sank; all 91 passengers, nine expedition staff and 54 crew members were rescued thanks to the coordination efforts of the British Coast Guard and the Hurtigruten cruise ship *Nordnorge*.

Tip: Passengers would be advised to wear an identification bracelet or belt at all times while on an Antarctic expedition cruise.

Wildlife you may see or come into contact with include orcas, dolphins, the six species

Hanseatic in Le Maire Channel, Antarctic Peninsula.

Zodiac craft enable visitors to view wildlife up close.

of Antarctic seals, penguins, birds, and various species of lichen and flora, depending on the area visited.

Note to photographers: take plastic bags to cover your camera, so that condensation forms inside the bag and not on your camera when changing from the cold of the outside Antarctic air to the warmth of your expedition cruise vessel. Make sure you know how to operate your camera with gloves on – frostbite is a real danger.

The best expedition ships for conditions in the Arctic are the nuclear-powered Russian icebreakers such as Yamal, one of five "Arktika" class vessels.

The Arctic

Want some Northern Exposure? Try the Arctic. The Arctic is an ocean surrounded by continents, whereas Antarctica is an ice-covered continent surrounded by ocean. The Arctic Circle is located at 66 degrees, 33 minutes, and 3 seconds north, although this really designates where 24-hour days and nights begin.

The Arctic is best defined as that region north of which no trees grow, and where water is the primary feature of the landscape. It is technically a desert (receiving less than 10 inches of rainfall a year) but actually teems with wildlife, including polar bears, walruses, seals, and Arctic birds.

It has short, cool summers; long, cold winters; and frequent high winds. Canada's Northwest Territories, which cover 1.3 million square miles, is part of the Arctic region, as are some of Russia's northernmost islands such as Franz Josef Land.

Greenland

The world's largest island, the inappropriately named Greenland, in the Arctic Circle, is 82 percent covered with ice – actually compressed snow – up to 11,000 feet thick (3,350 meters). Its rocks are among the world's oldest (the 3.8 billion-year-old Isukasia formations), and its ecosystem is one of the newest.

The glacier at Jacobshavn, also known as Ilulissat, is the world's fastest moving and cre-

---

HOW TO PROTECT SENSITIVE ENVIRONMENTS

In the future, only ships capable of meeting new "zero discharge" standards, such as those introduced in the Arctic by the Canadian Coast Guard will be allowed to proceed through environmentally sensitive areas. Expedition cruise companies are very concerned about the environment, and they spend much time and money in educating their crews and passengers about safe environmental procedures.

The "Antarctic Traveler's Code" (whose rules are enforced by all expedition cruise companies) is based on the Antarctic Conservation Act of 1978, designed to protect the region's ecosystem, flora, and fauna.

Polar bears are threatened by global warming.

Recommendation XVIII-1, adopted at the Antarctic Treaty Meeting in Kyoto in 1994, makes it unlawful, unless authorized by permit, to take native animals or birds, to collect any special native plant or introduce species, to enter certain special areas (SPAs), or to discharge or dispose of any pollutants. To "take" means to remove, harass, molest, harm, pursue, hunt, shoot, kill, trap, capture, restrain, or tag any native mammal or bird, or to attempt to do so. Violators face civil penalties, including a fine of up to $10,000 and one-year imprisonment for each violation. The Act is found in the library of each adventure/expedition ship that visits the continent.

Will large resort ships ever cruise in Antarctica? I hope not. Ships are limited to a maximum of 400 passengers, so the likelihood of a mega-ship zooming in on the penguins with 2,000-plus passengers is unlikely. Nor would it be possible to rescue so many passengers and crew in the event of an emergency.

ates a new iceberg every five minutes. Greenland, which was granted home rule by Denmark in 1978, makes its living from fishing. It is said to have more dogs than people – its population is 68,400 – and dogs are an important means of transport.

The Galápagos Islands

The Galápagos Islands, 600 miles (960km) off the coast of Ecuador in the Pacific Ocean, are a microcosm of our planet. More than 100 islands, mineral-rich outcroppings and lava outcroppings make up the Galápagos, which are fed by the nutrient-rich Cromwell and Humboldt currents. The fertile waters can be cold, even on the equator.

Photographer at work during an Antarctica visit.

The Ecuadorians jealously guard their islands and prohibit the movement of almost all non-Ecuadorian-registered cruise vessels within its boundaries. The best way to follow in the footsteps of Charles Darwin, who visited the islands in 1835 aboard the *Beagle*, is to fly to Quito and cruise aboard an Ecuadorian-registered vessel.

The government of Ecuador set aside most of the islands as a wildlife sanctuary in 1934, while uninhabited areas were declared national parks in 1959. The national park includes approximately 97 per cent of the islands' landmass, together with 20,000 sq miles (50,000 sq km) of ocean. The Charles Darwin Research Station was established in 1964, and the government created the Galápagos Marine Resources Reserve in 1986.

Note that the Galápagos National Park tax is about $100 per person. Smoking is prohibited on the islands, and no more than 50,000 visitors a year are admitted. ❑

An iguana basks in the sun in the Galápagos.

COASTAL CRUISES

Being all at sea doesn't appeal? You can stay close to dry land by journeying round the coasts of Australia, Europe, and North and South America

AUSTRALIA

The marine wonderland of the Great Barrier Reef, a World Heritage site off the northeast coast of Australia, is the earth's largest living coral reef – it actually consists of more than 2,800 individual coral reefs. It is visited by around 70 local Australian boutique ship operators, who mostly offer 1- to 4-night cruises to the reefs and Whitsunday Islands. The area is excellent for scuba diving and snorkelers. June

ABOVE: Geiranger Fjord in Norway.
BELOW: an exotic inhabitant of the Great Barrier Reef.

through September is humpback whale-watching season; the Reef shelters the young whales while the adults nurture them in the shallow waters. Note that the Australian government levies an environmental charge of A\$5 on everyone over four years of age visiting the Great Barrier Reef and its environs.

NORWAY

There is year-round coastal cruising along the shores of Norway to the Land of the Midnight Sun aboard the ships of the Hurtigruten Group, formerly known as Norwegian Coastal Voyages. The fleet consists of small, comfortable, working express coastal packet steamers and contemporary cruise vessels that deliver mail, small packaged goods, and foodstuffs, and take passengers, to the communities spread on the shoreline.

Invariably dubbed "the world's most beautiful voyage." this is a 1,250-mile (2,000-km) journey from Bergen in Norway to Kirkenes, close to the Russian border (half of which is north of the Arctic Circle) and takes 12 days. The service started in 1893, and the name

Hurtigruten – meaning "fast route," – reflects the fact that this coastal express was once the most reliable communication link between southern Norway and its remote north. Today the company carries more than 300,000 passengers a year. It's a good way to meet Norwegians, who treat the service like a bus.

You can join it at any of the 34 ports of call and stay as long as you wish because the vessels, being working ships, sail every day of the year. At the height of summer, north of the Arctic Circle, there are 24 hours of daylight, and between November and February the northern lights create spectacular arcs across the sky. Some specialist voyages are aimed at birdwatchers and others include onboard concerts and lectures celebrating the work of Norwegian composer Edvard Grieg.

The ships can accommodate between 144 and 674 passengers. The newest ships in the fleet have an elevator that can accommodate a wheelchair passenger, but otherwise, they are fairly plain and basic, practical vessels, with food that is more bistro than restaurant. Note that alcohol prices are extremely high, as they are throughout Norway, and that the currency is the Norwegian krone.

Archipelago hopping can be done along Sweden's eastern coast, too, by sailing in the daytime and staying overnight in one of the many small hotels. One vessel sails from Norrtalje, north of Stockholm, to Oskarshamn,

Lofoten Island in northern Norway.

near the Baltic island of Öland, right through the spectacular Swedish archipelago. You can also cruise from the Finnish city of Lappeenranta to the Estonian city of Viborg without a visa, thanks to perestroika. Point-to-point coastal transportation between neighboring countries, major cities, and commercial centers is big business in Northern Europe.

The Hurtigruten Group also operates utilitarian ships for expedition-style cruising in the Arctic, Antarctic, and Greenland.

SCOTLAND

The fishing town of Oban, two hours west of Glasgow by road, perhaps seems an unlikely point to start a cruise, but it is the base for one of the world's finest cruise experiences. *Hebridean Princess* is a little gem, with Laura Ashley-style interiors – elegant enough to have been chartered by Queen Elizabeth II for a family-only celebration of her 80th birthday in 2006. The food is great, including Scottish beef, local seafood and seasonal vegetables, and there's fine personal service.

This ship, owned by Hebridean International Cruises, carries up to 49 passengers around some of Scotland's most magnificent coastline and islands. Take lots of warm clothing, however (layers are best), as the weather can be flexible and often unkind.

As an alternative, there's *Lord of the Glens*, operated by Magna Carta Steamship Company and accommodating 54 passengers. It's another treat for small ship lovers, cruising in style through Scotland's lakes and canals.

HURTIGRUTEN SHIPS			
Ship	**Tonnage**	**Built**	**Berths**
Finnmarken	15,000	2002	638
Fram	12,700	2007	328
Kong Harald	11,200	1993	490
Lofoten	2,621	1964	147
Lyngen	16,053	2003	652
Nordkapp	11,386	1996	464
Nordlys	11,200	1994	482
Nordnorge	11,386	1997	455
Nordstjernen *	2,621	1956	114
Polar Star *	4,998	1969	100
Polarlys	12,000	1996	479
Richard With	11,205	1993	483
Trollfjord	15,000	2002	648
Vesteralen	6,261	1983	316

* for expedition voyages only

SMALL COASTAL CRUISE VESSELS (more than 10 cabins)

Ship	Cruise Line	Cabins	Region	Built
American Eagle	American Cruise Lines	27	USA Coastal Cruises	2000
American Glory	American Cruise Lines	27	USA Coastal Cruises	2002
American Spirit	American Cruise Lines	50	USA Coastal Cruises	2005
American Star	American Cruise Lines	52	USA Coastal Cruises	2007
Andrea	Elegant Cruises & Tours	56	Antarctica/Patagonia	1960
Aranui 3 (coastal freighter)	Campagnie Polynesienne de Transport Maritime	63	Tahiti/Marquesas	2003
Callisto	Travel Dynamics International	17	Greek Isles	1963
Celebrity Xpedition	Celebrity Cruises	47	Galápagos Islands	2001
CoCo Explorer	CoCo Explorer Cruises	56	Philippines	1967
Contessa	Majestic America Line	25	Alaska	1986
Coral Princess	Coral Princess Cruises	27	Australia (Great Barrier Reef)	1988
Corinthian	Ecoventura/Galápagos Network	45	Galápagos Islands	1967
Discovery	EPanama Marine Adventures	12	Panama	2004
Disko II	Arctic Umiaq Line	26	Greenland	1992
Emeraude	Emeraude Classic Cruises	38	Halong Bay (Vietnam)	2003
Evolution	various	17	Galápagos Islands	2004
Fantasea Ammari	Fantasea Adventure Cruising	32	Whitsunday Islands	2007
Galápagos Legend	GlobalQuest	57	Galápagos Islands	1963
Grande Caribe	American Canadian Caribbean Line	48	USA Coastal Cruises	1997
Grande Mariner	American Canadian Caribbean Line	50	USA Coastal Cruises	1999
Halcyon	various operators	24	Greek Islands, Mediterranean	1990
Haumana	Bora Bora Cruises	19	Tahiti and Islands	1997
Independence	American Cruise Lines	52	USA Coastal Cruises	2009
Isabela II	Metropolitan Touring	21	Galápagos Islands	1989
La Pinta	South American Experience	24	Galápagos Islands	2008
Lord of the Glens	Magna Carta Cruises	27	Scotland	1985
Lycianda	Blue Lagoon Cruises	21	Yasawa Islands (Fiji)	1984
Marco Polo	CroisiEurope	100	European Coast	2006
Mare Australis	Cruceros Australis	63	Patagonia	2002
Megastar Aries	Star Cruises	33	Southeast Asia	2000
Megastar Taurus	Star Cruises	33	Southeast Asia	2000
Monet	Elegant Cruises & Tours	30	Croatian Coast	1970
Mystique Princess	Blue Lagoon Cruises	36	Yasawa Islands (Fiji)	1996
Nanuya Princess	Blue Lagoon Cruises	25	Yasawa Islands (Fiji)	1987
National Geographic Islander	Lindblad Expeditions	24	Galápagos Islands	1995
Oceanic Discoverer	Coral Princess Cruises	38	Australia (Great Barrier Reef)	2005
Pacific Aurora	British Columbia Discovery Voyages	34	British Columbia (Canada)	1962
Pacific Explorer	Cruise West	50	Central America	1970
Pearl	Pearl Seas Cruises	108	USA Coastal Cruises	2008
Pegasus	Classical Cruises	23	Greek Islands, Mediterranean	1992
Reef Escape	Captain Cook Cruises	60	Australia	1987
Safari Explorer	American Safari Cruises	18	Alaska/Mexico Coast	1998
Safari Quest	American Safari Cruises	11	Alaska/Mexico Coast	1992
Santa Cruz	Metropolitan Touring	43	Galápagos Islands	1979
Sea Bird	Lindblad Expeditions	35	Alaska, Baja	1981
Sea Lion	Lindblad Expeditions	35	Alaska, Baja	1982
Sea Voyager	Lindblad Expeditions	33	Central America	1982
Shearwater	various operators	40	Worldwide	1962
Skorpios III	GlobalQuest	50	Chilean Fjords	1988
Spirit of '98	Cruise West	48	Alaska	1984
Spirit of Alaska	Cruise West	39	Alaska	1980
Spirit of Columbia	Cruise West	39	Alaska	1979
Spirit of Discovery	Cruise West	25	Alaska	1982
Spirit of Endeavor	Cruise West	51	Alaska	1983
Spirit of Nantucket	Cruise West	51	Alaska	1984
Spirit of Oceanus	Cruise West	50	Alaska/South Pacific	1991
Spirit of Yorktown	Cruise West	69	Alaska	1988
Tia Moana	Bora Bora Cruises	37	Tahitian Islands	2003
Tu Moana	Bora Bora Cruises	37	Tahitian Islands	2003
Tropic Sun	Aquanaut Cruise Lines	24	Galápagos Islands	1967
True North	North Star Cruises	18	Australia (west coast)	2005

Cruising the inland waterways near Lake Erie.

NORTH AMERICA

Coastal cruise ships flying the American flag offer a complete change of style from the large resort cruise ships. They are American-owned and American-crewed, and informality is the order of the day. Because of their US registry, they can start from and return to a US port without being required by the Passenger Vessel Services Act to call at a foreign port along the way – which a foreign-flagged cruise ship must do.

Accommodating up to 150 passengers, the ships are more like private family affairs, and are rarely out of sight of land. These cruises are low-key, low pace, and not for active, adventurous types. Their operators seek out lesser-known areas, offering in-depth visits to destinations inaccessible to larger ships, both along the eastern and western seaboards of the USA, including Alaska.

Most passengers are over 60, and many over 70. They may prefer not to fly, and wherever possible drive or take a train to join their ship. During the summer, you might see a couple of children on board, but in general small kids are not allowed. There are no facilities for them, and no staff to look after them.

Destinations: Eastern US and Canadian seaboard cruises include the St. Lawrence River, Atlantic Coastal Waterways, New England (good for fall cruises), Cape Cod and the Islands (and Cape Cod Canal), the Great Lakes (and Welland Canal), the Colonial Deep South, and Florida waterways.

Western seaboard cruises cover Alaska, the Pacific Northwest, California Wine Country, and Baja California/Sea of Cortés. Cruises focus on historically-relevant destinations,

Getting close to the whales in Magdalena Bay, Baja California.

WHO RUNS COASTAL CRUISES IN NORTH AMERICA?

There are five cruise companies: American Canadian Caribbean Line, American Cruise Lines, American Safari Cruises, Cruise West, and Lindblad Expeditions.

What differentiates them? American Cruise Lines and American Safari Cruises provide better food and service than the others. American Cruise Lines' ships have larger cabins, and more public rooms. Drinks are included aboard the ships of American Cruise Lines only. American Canadian Caribbean Line and American Cruise Lines operate on the USA's east coast; American Safari Cruises and Lindblad Expeditions operate on the USA's west coast and Alaska.

Pearl Seas Cruises, a new company under the same ownership as American Cruise Lines, introduced two ships, the first in 2008, the second in 2009. Considerably larger than those of the other lines, they accommodate 210 passengers, have an all-American registry and crew, are certified for oceangoing voyages, have more lounges and facilities and much larger cabins, and aspire to the standards set by international boutique ships. Itineraries include cruises around Newfoundland, the Caribbean and Central America.

nature and wildlife spotting, and coastal viewing. On some cruises, these boutique ships can dock adjacent to a town, allowing easy access on foot.

The ships: These "D-class" vessels are less than 2,500 tons, and are subject neither to bureaucratic regulations nor to union rules. They are restricted to cruising no more than 20 miles (32 km) offshore, at a comfortable 12 knots (13.8mph). Public room facilities are limited. Because the vessels are American-registered, there is no casino. They really are ultra-casual, no-frills ships with the most basic of facilities, no swimming pools, little artwork, and no glitz in interior decor. They usually have three or four decks and, except for the ships of American Cruise Lines, no elevator. Stairs can be steep and are not recommended for people with walking difficulties. Because of this, some ships have an electric chair-lift on indoor or outdoor stairways.

Cabins: Accommodation is in outside-view cabins, some of which open directly onto a walking deck – inconvenient when it rains. Each has a picture window and small bathroom. They are small and basic, with very limited closet space – perhaps just a curtain across a space with a hanging rod for clothes. Many do not have a television or telephone. There's no room service, and you may have to turn your own bed down. Cabins are closer to the engines and generators than aboard the large resort ships, so generator humming noises can be disturbing at night. The quietest cabins are at the ship's bows – although there could be noise if the ship is equipped with a bow thruster – and most cruising is done in the early morning so that passengers can sleep better at night.

Tall passengers should note that the overall length of beds rarely exceeds 6 ft (1.82 meters). While soap is provided, it's best to bring your own shampoo, conditioner, and other personal toiletries. American Canadian Caribbean Line's ships do not have cabin keys, and most passengers don't feel they need to lock their doors at night anyway.

Although some of the older ships are really basic, the latest ones, particularly those of American Cruise Lines, are very comfortable. Because they are not classified for open-water cruising, though, they don't have to conform to the same rigorous shipbuilding standards that larger ocean-going cruise ships do. You may find, for example, that hot and cold water lines run close

Mexican fiesta during a Sea of Cortes trip by Cruise West.

Chicago is a stop on Great Lakes itineraries.

to each other in your bathroom, thus delivering neither really hot nor really cold water. Sound insulation could be almost non-existent.

Activities: The principal evening event is dinner in the dining room, which accommodates all passengers at once. This can be a family-style affair, with passengers at long tables, and the food passed around.

The cuisine is decidedly American, with fresh local specialties featured. However, menus aboard the ships of American Canadian Caribbean Cruise Line and Cruise West are very limited, while those aboard the ships of American Cruise Lines offer slightly more variety, including seasonal items. You'll probably be asked in the morning to choose which of two main courses you would like for dinner.

Evening entertainment consists mainly of after-dinner conversation. Most vessels are in port during the time, so you can easily go ashore for the local nightlife, although most passengers simply go to bed early.

If you have taken a cruise aboard one of the large resort ships, you'll know that standing in long lines waiting to get back on board and go through the security check can be a painful experience – in every port. However, passengers aboard the small coastal ships sometimes aren't asked to show their ID cards when rejoining a ship, because gangway staff recognize them. Another advantage is that you won't get seasick because these ships sail mostly in sheltered waters and inshore bays, inlets and rivers.

The cost: This kind of cruising is expensive, with an average daily rate of around $400–$800 a person. Suggested gratuities are high – typically about $125 per person, per 7-day cruise – but they are at least shared by all the personnel on board. ❑

Stanley Park's totems are a major Vancouver attraction.

SAILING SHIPS

Want to be free as the wind? Think about cruising under sail, with towering masts, the creak of taut ropes and gleaming white sails to power you along

There is simply nothing that beats the thrill of being aboard a multi-mast tall ship, sailing under thousands of square feet of canvas through waters that mariners have sailed for centuries. This is cruising in the traditional manner, aboard authentic sailing ships, contemporary copies of clipper ships, or aboard high-tech cruise-sail ships.

There are no rigid schedules, and life aboard equates to an unstructured lifestyle, apart from meal times. Weather conditions may often dictate whether a scheduled port visit will be made or not, but passengers sailing on these vessels are usually unconcerned. They would rather savor the thrill of being one with nature, albeit in a comfortable, civilized setting, and without having to do the work themselves. The more luxurious sailing ships are the closest most people will get to owning their own mega-yacht.

Real tall ships

While we have all been dreaming of adventure, a pocketful of designers and yachtsmen committed pen to paper, hand in pocket and rigging to mast, and came up with a potpourri of stunning vessels to delight the eye and refresh the spirit. Examples are *Royal Clipper, Sea Cloud, Sea Cloud II, Star Clipper,* and *Star Flyer.*

Of these, *Sea Cloud,* built in 1931 and restored in 1979, is the most romantic sailing ship afloat. It operates under charter for much of the year, and sails in both the Caribbean and the Mediterranean. A kind of stately home afloat, *Sea Cloud* remains one of the finest and most exhilarating travel experiences in the world.

The activities are few, and so relaxation is the key, in a stylish but unpretentious setting. The food and service are good, as is the interaction between the 69 passengers and 60 crew, many of whom have worked aboard the ship for many years. One bonus is the fact that the doctor on board is available at no charge for medical emergencies or seasickness medication.

Although passengers may be able participate occasionally in the furling and unfurling of the sails, they are not permitted to climb the

Sailing ships can be exhausting.

Star Clippers' superb *Royal Clipper* under full sail.

rigging, as may be possible aboard some of the other, more modern tall ships.

Contemporary sail-cruise ships

To combine sailing with push-button automation, try *Club Med 2* (Club Mediterranée) or *Wind Surf* (Windstar Cruises) – with five tall aluminum masts, they are the world's largest sail-cruise ships – and *Wind Spirit* and *Wind Star* (Windstar Cruises), with four masts. Not a hand touches the sails; they are computer-controlled from the navigation bridge.

A drawback for some people is that there's little sense of sailing in these oceangoing robots because the computer controls keep the ship on a steady, even keel. Also, some people find it hard to get used to the whine of the vessels' generators, which run the lighting and air-conditioning systems 24 hours a day.

From a yachtsman's viewpoint, the sail-to-power ratio is poor. That's why these cruise ships with sails have engine power to get them into and out of port. The Star Clipper ships, by contrast, do it by sail alone, except when there is no wind, which doesn't happen often.

On some itineraries, when there is little wind, you could well be under motor power for most of the cruise, with only a few hours spent under sail. The three Windstar Cruises vessels and one Club Med ship are typically under sail for about 40 percent of the time.

The Windstar ships carry mainly North American passengers, whereas the Club Med vessel caters primarily to French-speaking passengers.

Another slightly smaller but chic vessel is *Le Ponant*. This three-mast ship caters to just 64 French-speaking passengers in elegant, yet casual, high-tech surroundings, developing the original Windstar concept to an advanced state of contemporary technology.   ❑

A tall ship docked in Stockholm, Sweden.

FREIGHTER TRAVEL

These slow voyages appeal to independent types, retirees, relocating executives, those with far-flung family connections, graduates returning home from an overseas college, or professors on sabbatical

More than 3,000 passengers travel by freighter each year, and the number is growing as passengers become further disenchanted with the large resort ships that dominate the cruise industry. Traveling by freighter is also the ultimate way to travel for those seeking a totally unstructured voyage without entertainment or other diversions.

There are about 250 cargo ships (freighters and container vessels) offering berths, with German operators accounting for more than half of them. True freighters – the general breakbulk carrier ships and feeder container vessels – carry up to 12 passengers; the only exception is the Royal Mail Ship *RMS St. Helena*, which carries up to 128 passengers, animals such as goats and sheep, and goods from the UK to the island of Ascension. While *RMS St. Helena* carries a doctor, freighters do not, and remember that they are working vessels, not cruise ships.

Freighter schedules change constantly, depending on the whim of the owner and the cargo to be carried, whereas container ships travel on regular schedules. For the sake of simplicity, they are all termed freighters. But freighters have changed dramatically as cost management and efficiency have become vital. Container ships are operated as passenger liners used to be: running line voyages on set schedules.

Most freighter companies do not allow children or pregnant women to travel. Because there are no medical facilities, anyone over 65 is usually required to produce a medical certificate of good health.

Freighter facilities

What do you get when you book a freighter voyage? You get a cabin with double or twin beds, a small writing table, and a private bathroom. You also get good company, cocktails with conversation, hearty food (you'll eat in one seating with the ship's officers), an interesting voyage, a lot of water, and the allure of days at sea. What don't you get? Organized entertainment.

The German-owned *Hatsu Crystal* carries five passengers.

Ital Contessa can carry five passengers from Europe to Asia.

You will certainly have time to relax and read books (some freighters have a small library).

The accommodation will consist of a spacious, well-equipped outside-view cabin high above the water line, with a large window rather than a porthole, comfortable lounge/sitting area, and private facilities – far larger than most standard cruise ship cabins.

While freighter travel can be less expensive than regular cruise ship travel on a per day basis ($75–$150), remember that voyages last much longer – typically 30 days or more – so the cost can be considerable. Most are sold out far in advance (often more than a year ahead), so plan ahead, and purchase trip cancellation insurance.

What to bring

What to take with you? Casual clothing (check with the freighter line, as some require a jacket and tie for dinner), all medications, cosmetics, and toiletry items, hairdryer, multi-voltage converter plug, washing powder, and other sundry items such as soap, sun protection, insect repellent, and small flashlight. There may be a small "shop" on board (for the crew) carrying bare essentials like toothpaste. Bring along your medical certificate, travel insurance details, money in cash, and some extra photos of yourself in case the ship

makes unannounced port stops and visas are required. The only gratuities needed are for the waiter and cabin steward, at about $1–$2 per day, per person.

New international security regulations mean that if you book a one-way voyage, you must have all onward travel documents with you. Check with embassies and consulates of the countries you will visit. Note that freighters visit cargo ports, so private transportation such as taxis will need to be arranged in advance.

Freighters sometimes have to cancel port calls for various reasons at short notice. Bear this in mind if you are attracted by a particular itinerary or a certain port. ❏

PASSENGER-CARRYING FREIGHTERS

These lines offer regular passenger voyages year-round:
American President Lines, Australia New Zealand Direct Lines, Bank Line, Blue Star Line, Canada Maritime, Chilean Lines, Cho Yang Shipping, Columbus Line, Egon Oldendorff, Great Lakes Shipping, Hamburg-Sud, Hanseatic Shipping Company, Hapag-Lloyd, Horn Line, Ivaran Lines, Lykes Brothers Steamship Company, Mediterranean Shipping Company, Nauru Pacific Line, Safmarine Cruises, and United Baltic Corporation.

Booking and Information

TravLtips Cruise & Freighter Association
P.O. Box 580188, Flushing, NY 11358, USA
www.travltips.com
Freighter World Cruises
180 South Lake Avenue, Suite 335, Pasadena, CA 91101, USA
www.freighterworld.com
The Cruise People
88 York Street, London W1H 1DP, England
http://members.aol.com/CruiseAZ/freighters.htm
Strand Voyages
Charing Cross Shopping Concourse, Strand, London WC2N 4HZ, England
www.seejapan.co.uk/transport/sea/cargo.html
Sydney International Travel Centre
75 King Street, Level 8, Sydney 2000, Australia
www.sydneytravel.com

Double cabin on *Hansa Flensburg* (USA to Australia).

NORTH ATLANTIC CROSSINGS

You're facing the world's most unpredictable weather, but there's still something romantic about this classic ocean voyage

Crossing the 3,000 miles (4,800km) of the North Atlantic by passenger vessel can be considered an art. I have done it myself 153 times and always enjoy it immensely. I consider crossings as rests in musical parlance, for both are described as "passages." Indeed, musicians do often "hear" rests in between notes. So if ports of call are the musical notes of a voyage, then the rests are the days at sea – temporary interludes, when physical and mental indulgence become ends in themselves.

Experienced mariners will tell you that a ship behaves like a ship only when it is doing a crossing, for that's what a real ship is built for. Yet the days when ships were built specifically for crossings are almost gone. The only one offering a regularly scheduled transatlantic service (a "crossing") is Cunard Line's *Queen Mary 2*, a 148,151-ton ship, built with a thick hull designed to hold well against the worst weather the North Atlantic has to offer. The most unpredictable weather in the world, together with fog off the Grand Banks of Newfoundland, can mean that the captain will spend torturous hours on the bridge, with little time for socializing. Captains certainly work harder on an Atlantic crossing than on regular cruising schedules.

When it is foggy, the crew of *Queen Mary 2* is often pestered by passengers wanting to know if the ship has yet approached latitude 41°46' north, longitude 50°14' west – where White Star Line's 43,326-ton *Titanic* struck an Arctic iceberg on that fateful April night in 1912.

A great tradition

There is something magical in "doing a crossing." It takes you back to the days when hordes of passengers turned up at the piers of the ports of New York, Southampton, Cherbourg, or Hamburg, accompanied by chauffeurs and steamer trunks, jewels and finery. Movie stars of the 1920s, '30s, and '40s often traveled abroad on the

Queen Mary 2 passes the Statue of Liberty in New York.

Dancing in the Queens Room, *Queen Mary 2*.

largest liners of the day, to arrive refreshed and ready to dazzle European fans.

Excitement and anticipation usually precede a crossing. First there is the hubbub and bustle of check-in, then the crossing of the threshold on the gangway before being welcomed into the calmness aboard, and finally escorted to one's accommodation.

> For reasons of time zones, five days of the six-day westbound crossings of the Queen Mary 2 are 25 hours long, but only 23 hours long on an eastbound crossing.

Once the umbilical cord of the gangway is severed, bow and stern mooring lines are cast off, and with three long blasts on the ship's deep whistle, the *QM2* is pried gently from its berth. The ship sails silently down the waterway, away from the world, as serene as a Rolls-Royce. Passengers on deck often observe motorboats trying to keep up with the giant liner as it edges away from Brooklyn's Red Hook Pier 12 towards the Statue of Liberty, the restored Ellis Island, then under the Verrazano-Narrows Bridge, and out to the open sea. Coming westbound, arriving in New York by ship is one of the world's thrilling travel experiences.

The *QM2* has year-round scheduled crossings, whereas other cruise ships crossing the Atlantic are little more than repositioning cruises – a way of moving ships that cruise the Mediterranean in summer to the Caribbean in winter, and vice versa – they offer more chances to experience the romance and adventure of a crossing, usually in spring and fall. These satisfy those wanting uninterrupted days at sea and lots of leisure time.

Most cruise ships operating repositioning crossings cross the Atlantic using the "sunny southern route" – departing from southern ports such as Ft. Lauderdale, San Juan, or Barbados, and ending the journey in Lisbon, Genoa, or Copenhagen via the Azores or the Canary Islands off the coast of northern Africa. In this way, they avoid the more difficult weather often encountered in the North Atlantic. Such crossings take longer, however: between eight and 12 days. ❏

A homely atmosphere aboard *Queen Mary 2*.

WORLD CRUISES

The idea of a trip taking in more than 70 ports may sound extravagant, but basic fares can be as low as $100 a day. However, they can sometimes be more than $3,000 a day

The ultimate classic voyage for any experienced traveler is a round-the-world cruise, defined as the complete circumnavigation of the earth in a continuous one-way voyage. Ports of call are carefully planned for their interest and diversity, and the entire voyage can last six months or longer. Galas, themed balls, special social events, top entertainers, and, typically, well-known lecturers are all part of the package. It's a great way of exchanging the northern winter for the southern sun.

A world cruise aboard a modern ship means experiencing stabilized, air-condi-

GO WEST OR GO EAST ?

Most people prefer to travel in a west-bound direction, thus gaining time instead of losing it (one hour for each 25 degrees that the ship crosses). In an eastbound direction, days get progressively shorter by one hour for each time zone crossed.

tioned comfort in luxury cabins, and extraordinary sight-seeing and excursions on shore and overland. In some ships, every passenger will get to dine with the captain at least once.

Do check brochures and itineraries carefully. Some ships spend little time in port. On the 2003 world cruise of *Aurora*, for example, there were no overnight stays, even in some of the most desirable port cities such as San Francisco, Sydney, Hong Kong, Tokyo, or Singapore.

World cruise segments

If you haven't the time or the funds for a full world cruise, it's possible to book a specific segment, flying to join the ship at one of its ports of call and disembarking at another port. In this way you can visit exotic destinations such as China, the South Pacific, the Indian Ocean, or South America while enjoying the elegance, comfort, splendid food, and good company that are associated with world cruises.

Bear in mind that you tend to

P&O's 914-cabin *Oriana* in Sydney's spectacular harbor.

ABOVE: textile shopping in Cape Town.
RIGHT: night market in Kuala Lumpur.
BELOW: shopping in London's Piccadilly.

get what you pay for. Ships rated at four stars or more, for example, will probably include shuttle buses from your ship to town centers, but ships rated three stars or less will not lay on such transport.

Ships that roam worldwide during the year offer the most experienced world cruises or segments. Most operate at about 75 percent capacity, providing much more space per person than they could normally expect.

Planning and preparation

For the operator, planning a world cruise involves daunting organization. For example, more than 700,000 main meals will be prepared in the galleys during a typical world cruise aboard the *Queen Mary 2*. A ship of its size needs two major crew changes during a three-month-long voyage. Hundreds of professional entertainers, lecturers, bands, and musicians must be booked a year in advance.

Because a modern world cruise ship has to be totally self-contained, a warehouse-full of spare parts – such as electrical, plumbing, and engineering supplies – must be ordered, loaded, and stored aboard ship prior to sailing. Once at sea, it will be impossible to pick up a replacement projector bulb, air-conditioning belt, table tennis ball, saxophone reed, or anything else the ship might run out of.

A cruise line must give advance notice of the date and time that pilots will be needed, together with requirements for tugs, docking services, and customs and immigration staff. Dockside labor and stevedoring services must be organized at each port of call, plus fuel supplies and transportation for shore excursions. It's an invigorating business. ❏

WHO RUNS WORLD CRUISES?

Many cruise lines operate world cruises. They include Crystal Cruises, Cunard Line, Fred Olsen Cruise Line, Hapag-Lloyd Cruises, Holland America Line, P&O Cruises, Princess Cruises, Regent Seven Seas Cruises, Saga Cruises, and Silversea Cruises.

The duration is usually between 80 and 130 days, calling at between 30 and 70 ports. But Hapag-Lloyd made news in 2003 when *Europa*'s world cruise lasted an astonishing 239 days.

Given the range of options, fares could work out as low as $150 a day or as high as $3,000 a day.

RIVER CRUISES

Around 1 million people a year take a river or inland waterway cruise, making this one of the industry's fastest growing sectors. And there's little chance of being seasick

Whether you want to cruise down the Nile, along the mighty Amazon or the lesser Orinoco, the stately Volga or the primal Sepik, the magnificent Rhine or the "blue" Danube, along the mystical Ayeyarwady (formerly the Irrawaddy) or the "yellow" Yangtze – to say nothing of the Don and the Dnieper, the Elbe, or Australia's Murray – there are more than 1,000 river cruise vessels to choose from.

What sort of person enjoys cruising aboard these vessels? Well, anyone who survives well without formal dinners, bingo, casinos, dis-cos, or lavish entertainment, and those who want a totally unstructured lifestyle.

The plus points

● Rivercruise vessels are built for you to enjoy the ever-changing scenery (the "river-scape"), all at eye level.
● You'll wake up in a different place each day, often in the very heart of a city or town.
● You never have to take a tender ashore – you simply step off the vessel when it ties up.
● The atmosphere on board is friendly and informal, never stuffy or pretentious.
● Cruising along one of the world's rivers is a delightful way to unwind at a slow pace.

The waterfront of Cologne, Germany, by night.

● The ride is typically silky smooth – there's no rolling like aboard many of the ocean-going cruise ships, so you won't suffer from seasickness.

● Good food and service are essential elements of a successful river cruise operation.

● All meals are provided, typically in a self-serve buffet arrangement for breakfast and lunch, with sit-down service for dinner. Additionally, basic table wines may also be included for lunch and dinner (included wines are typical of the German river cruise operators or cruise/tour packagers).

● Almost all cabins have outside views; there are virtually no interior (no view) cabins, as aboard most of the ocean-going cruise ships.

● A whole range of optional, extra-cost excursions is available, while some excursions may be included.

● You will typically sail by day, and dock at night (exceptions: Danube and Russian river cruises,

Much of Egypt can be explored during a Nile cruise.

where most vessels sail at night), so you can get a restful sleep without the noise of engines. However, bear in mind that, if your cabin is towards the aft, there may well be the soft humming of a generator, which supplies power for air-conditioning, heating, water supply, lighting and cooking.

● You can, if you wish, leave the vessel in the evening to go out to dinner, or to the cinema, theater or a concert (exceptions: Danube and Russian river cruises).

● Rivers provide a sense of continuity – difficult to achieve from a coach tour, where you may change lodgings each night, and encounter border crossings. Also, while on board, you deal in a single currency.

● The dress code is completely casual.

● There are no cars to drive, or park.

● There are no intrusive art auctions, bingo, wet T-shirt contests and the like.

The negative points

● The flow of water in almost all rivers cannot always be controlled, so there will be times when the water level is so low that even

a specially constructed rivercruise vessel, with its shallow draft, cannot travel.

● If you are tall, note that the beds aboard most rivercruise vessels are less than 6 ft (1.8 meters) long.

● Don't wear white. Rivercruise vessels are long and low, which means that their funnels are also low. Soot, created by the emissions

> *Many river vessels have a small plunge pool on the top deck, and possibly a hot tub or two. A pool is particularly welcome on the Nile when the temperature soars.*

from diesel engines and generators, can be a problem, particularly at the stern of the vessel, and on the upper (open) deck.

● Aboard some of the vessels that have an aft, open but sheltered deck area, or an open upper deck – almost all rivercruise vessels have one – smokers may be seated next to you. Few vessels distinguish between smoking and non-smoking areas outdoors, and

A Viking cruise passes Stahleck Castle on the Rhine.

staff rarely enforce no-smoking areas anyway.
● Depending on the vessel, river, the operating company, and tour operators that send passengers to the vessels, there could be passengers of several nationalities. While this can make for interesting social interaction, communication could be a problem if you don't speak the same language.

European river cruising

Cruising down one of Europe's great waterways is a soothing experience – different from sailing on an open sea, where wave motion is

Although there's little entertainment on board, younger children may enjoy certain river cruises. Vienna and Budapest are both child-friendly cities, and the Nile has distractions such as camels, felucca rides and markets.

a factor. These cruises provide a constant change of scenery, often passing through several countries, each with its own history and architecture, in a week-long journey. River vessels are always close to land and provide a chance to visit cities and areas inaccessible

to the large resort ships. A cruise along the Danube, for example, will take you through nine countries and from Germany's Black Forest to the Black Sea (Germany, Austria, Slovakia, Hungary, Croatia, Serbia, Romania, Bulgaria, Ukraine).

The Rhine–Main–Danube waterway, at 2,175 miles (3,500 km), is the longest waterway in Europe. It connects 14 countries, from Rotterdam on the North Sea to Sulina and Izmail on the Black Sea, and offers river travelers some of the most fascinating sights to be seen anywhere.

River vessels are long and low in the water, and their masts fold down in order to negotiate low bridges. Although small when compared to oceangoing cruise ships, they have a unique and friendly international atmosphere. The most modern are air-conditioned and offer the discreet luxury of a small floating hotel, with several public rooms including a dining room, observation lounge, bar, heated swimming "dip" pool (some even have a heated indoor pool), sauna, solarium, whirlpool, gymnasium, massage, hairdresser, and shop kiosk.

Although the cabins may be small, with limited closet space (take casual clothing, as informality is the order of the day), they are functional. Almost all have an outside view (facing the river), with a private bathroom, and will prove very comfortable for a one-week journey. Romantics may lament the fact that twin beds are the norm – and they can seldom be pushed together. Many cabins in the latest vessels have a personal safe, a mini-bar, a TV set, and an alarm clock/radio. The ceilings are rather low, and the beds are short.

River cruising in Europe has reached quite a sophisticated level, and you can be assured of good service and meals of a consistently good local standard. Dining is a pleasant although not a gourmet experience. The best food is that catered by Austrian, German or Swiss companies. While lunch is generally a buffet affair, dinners feature a set menu consisting of three or four courses.

Typical fares for river cruises are from $800 to over $3,000 per person for a one-week cruise, including meals, cabin with private facilities, side trips, and airport/railway transfers. If you are already in Europe, many cruises can be purchased "cruise-only" for greater flexibility.

Tip: To ensure a degree of peace and quiet, it is best to go for a cabin on a deck that does not have a promenade deck walkway outside it. Normally, cabins on the lowest deck have a

At the helm of *Volga Dream* in Russia.

four-berth configuration. It does not matter which side of the vessel you are on, as you will see a riverbank and scenery on both sides of the vessel.

Russia's rivers

Often referred to as the "Waterways of the Tsars," the country benefits from a well-developed network of rivers, lakes, and canals. Geographically, river routes for tourists are divided into three main areas: Central European Russia, Northwestern European Russia, and Asian Russia. There

THE BEST TIME TO CRUISE IN EUROPE AND ON THE NILE

There are advantages to every season in Europe. Early spring and late summer will be less crowded and can have beautiful weather. In July and August the weather is often at its most reliable, though it can be too hot for some and there will be more crowds.

It's possible to time a river cruise to coincide with certain events, such as the Rhine in Flames festival in high summer, or the paprika harvest in Hungary, or the beautiful autumn colors along the Danube's Wachau Valley. Special winter cruises operate on the Rhine and Danube to take in the Christmas markets – if you're lucky you'll get crisp, cool weather

Art in Tomb of Ramesses VI, Egypt.

and snow on the ground, but rain and slush are just as likely.

Russia tends to be hot and humid in summer, so spring and autumn are to be preferred. Take insect repellent

for travel in August and September, when midges can be a problem, and something warm to wear in the evening in spring and fall.

In Egypt the seasons are different. Nile cruises operate year-round, the peak months being January to March when it's cooler. August is really too hot for anybody except the most dedicated sun-worshipper. September is tolerable if you take things slowly, with the added advantage that there'll be hardly any crowds at the temples. Wearing shorts and a tank top might keep you cool, but they'll indicate a lack of respect if you wear them when visiting tombs and you may be hassled.

are more than 80 river cruise vessels carrying international tourists.

In the Central Basin, Moscow is the hub of river tourism, and the newly opened waterways between Moscow and St. Petersburg allow a 7-day cruise link between the present and former capitals. The best-known Russian rivers are the Don, Moskva, Neva, and Volga, but the lesser known Belaya, Dvina (and North Dvina) Irtysh, Kama, Ob (longest river in Siberia), Oka, Svir, Tura, and Vyatka connect the great system of rivers and lakes in the vast Russian hinterland.

Many Russian vessels are chartered to foreign cruise wholesalers and tour packagers, and dedicated to a specific onboard language. The vessels do vary quite a lot in quality and facilities. Some are air-conditioned and most are clean. Cruises include the services of a cruise manager and lecturers.

The Nile

A journey along the Nile is a journey through history, to more than 4,000 years before the birth of Christ, when one of the greatest civilizations in history lived along the river's banks. The scenery has changed remarkably little in more than 2,000 years. The best way

A Nile cruise is the ideal way to see Egypt.

A GOOD VIEW OF THE NILE
With a bit of cunning, you can secure a better view on a Nile cruise. As vessels head north from Aswan to Luxor, they almost always tie up on the river's left bank (except in Aswan, where they tie up on the right bank). Also, they tend to moor two or three deep. But if you ask for a starboard cabin and your vessel gets the outside position, your view across the Nile while you are in port – particularly in Luxor, where you will spend a couple of nights – will be uninterrupted. In a port cabin, all you would see would be the river bank or the vessel tied up next to you. Reverse this logic for southbound cruises.

to see it, of course, is from a river vessel.

In all, there are over 7,000 departures every year aboard 300 or so Nile cruise vessels, which offer standards of comfort, food, and service that vary between very good and extremely poor. Most have a small, shallow "plunge" pool, lounge, piano bar, and disco. A specialist lecturer in ancient Egyptian history accompanies almost all sailings, which cruise the 140 miles (220 km) between Aswân and Luxor in four or five days. Extended cruises, typically of seven or eight days, cover about 295 miles (475 km) and visit Dendera and Abydos. The longest cruises, of 10 to 12 days, cover 590 miles (950 km) and may include visits to Sohâg, El Amarna, Tuna El Gabal, and Ash–muneim, ending in Cairo.

Most Nile cruises include sightseeing excursions, accompanied by experienced guides who may reside on board, or who may meet the vessel at each call. Security in Egypt has been much improved in recent years, but the terrorist threat remains, and it's wise to be vigilant. It's also prudent to subtract two stars from any rating provided in brochures or on cruise company and tour operator websites.

China's rivers

More than 80 vessels cruise along the Yangtze, the world's third-longest river, particularly through the area known as the Three Yangtze River Gorges, a 100-mile (160-km) stretch between Nanjin Pass in the east and White King City in the west.

The Yangtze stretches 3,900 miles (6,300 km) from Shanghai through the very heartland of China. The Three Gorges include the 47-mile-long (76-km) Xiling Gorge, the 25-mile-long (40-km) Wu Gorge, and the 28-mile-long (45-km) Qutang Gorge, known locally as "Wind Box Gorge." The Lesser Three Gorges (or Three Small Gorges) are also an impressive sight, often part of the main cruise but also reached by small vessels from Wushan. If possible, take a cabin with a balcony. It is worth the extra money, and the view is better.

Standards of hygiene are generally far lower than you may be used to at home. In China, rats and rivers often go together, and

Exploring the Yangtze, the world's third longest river.

rat poison may well be found under your bed. Some vessels, such as those of Viking River Cruises, have Chinese- and western-style restaurants, a beauty salon, a small health club with sauna, and private mahjong and karaoke rooms. Fine Asian hospitality and service prevail, and cabins are kept supplied with fresh towels and hot tea.

There are several operators, but do check on the facilities, meet-and-greet service, and the newness of the vessels before booking. The best time of the year to go is May–June, and late August–October (July and early August are extremely hot and humid).

Irrawaddy River, Myanmar

Rudyard Kipling referred in his 1890 poem *Road to Mandalay* to the paddle-wheeled steamers of the Irrawaddy Flotilla Company. Even before the May 2008 cyclone devastated the area, the political situation in Myanmar (formerly Burma) deterred many tourists from taking a trip aboard the *Road to Mandalay* (Orient Express Hotels), which aims to rekindle the Kipling magic. This rivercruise vessel is normally scheduled to operate weekly

CHINA'S AMAZING DAM

The controversial $60 billion hydroelectric Sanxia (Three Gorges) Dam has created a reservoir 375 miles long (600 km), and 575 ft deep (175 meters), with an average width of 3,600 ft (1,100 meters). It has submerged 13 cities, 140 towns, 1,352 villages, 657 factories and 66 million acres of cultivated land (more than 1½ million people have been relocated). The new Three Gorges Dam locks (larger than the Panama Canal locks) are in full operation.

The dam will eventually raise the river only 150 ft (45 meters) against the backdrop of the Three Gorges, which rise majestically some 3,280 ft (1,000 meters). Cruise vessels of up to 10,000 tons will be able to sail up the Yangtze from the Pacific Ocean, and it is claimed that the dam will reduce flooding in the region.

between Mandalay and Pagan, along the Ayeyarwady (formerly Irrawaddy) River. Also, there are the four smaller vessels of Pandaw River Cruises.

River Murray, Australia

The fifth-largest river in the world, the Murray, was the lifeblood of the pioneers who lived on the driest continent on earth. Today, the river flows for more than 1,250 miles (2,760 km) across a third of Australia, its banks forming protected lagoons for an astonishing variety of bird and animal life. Paddlewheel boats such as *Murray Princess* offer most of the amenities found aboard America's *Mississippi Queen*. There are even six cabins for the physically disabled.

Barge cruising in Europe

Smaller and more intimate than river vessels and more accurately called boats, "cruise barges" ply the inland waterways and canals of Europe from spring to fall, when the weather is best. Barge cruises (usually of 3 to 13 days' duration) offer a completely informal atmosphere, and a slow pace of life, for up to a dozen passengers. They chug along slowly in the daytime, and moor early each evening, giving you time to

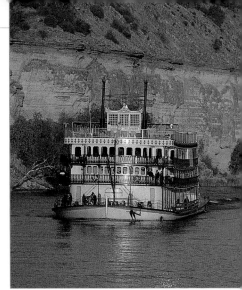
Paddling along Australia's Murray River.

pay a visit to a local village and get a restful night's sleep. The inland waterways of Europe all adhere to the CEVNI regulations (Code Européan des Voies de la Navigation Intérieur), a United Nations body with international authority and relevance.

Most cruise barges are comfortable and beautifully fitted out with rich wood paneling, full carpeting, custom-built furniture and tastefully chosen fabrics. Each has a dining room or lounge-bar. Captains take pride in their vessel, often displaying some rare memorabilia.

Locally grown fresh foods are usually purchased and prepared each day, allowing you to live well and feel like a houseguest. Most cruise barges can be chartered exclusively so you can just take your family and friends.

The waterways of France especially offer beauty, tranquility, and a diversity of interests, and barge cruising is an excellent way of exploring an unfamiliar area. Most cruises include a visit to a famous vineyard and wine cellar, as well as side trips to places of historic, architectural, or scenic interest. Shopping opportunities are limited, and evening entertainment is impromptu.

You will be accompanied by a crew

Tranquil scene on the Burgundy Canal in France.

member familiar with the surrounding countryside. You can even go hot-air ballooning over the local countryside – an expensive but memorable extra – and land to a glass of champagne and your flight certificate.

How you dine on board a barge will depend on the barge and area; dining ranges from home-style cooking to some outstanding nouvelle cuisine, with all the trimmings. Often, the barge's owner, or spouse, turns out to be the cook.

Barging on the canals often means going through a constant succession of locks. Nowhere is this more enjoyable and entertaining than in the Burgundy region of France where, between Dijon and Mâcon, for example, a barge can negotiate as many as 54 locks during a 6-day cruise. Interestingly, all lockkeepers in France are women.

Rates range from $600 to more than $3,000 per person for a 6-day cruise. I do not recommend taking children. Rates include a cabin with private facilities, all meals, good wine with lunch and dinner, all other beverages, use of bicycles, side trips, and airport or railway transfers.

Some operators provide a hotel the night before or after the cruise. Clothing is totally casual – but, at the beginning and end of the season, it's a good idea to take sweaters and rain gear.

Steamboating in the United States

The most famous of all American river cruises are those aboard the steamboats of the mighty Mississippi River. Mark Twain, a fan of such travel, at one time said: "When man can go 700 miles an hour, he'll want to go seven again."

The grand traditions of the steamboat era are maintained by the *American Queen*, and by the older, smaller *Mississippi Queen* (Majestic America Line), both powered by steam engines that drive huge wooden paddlewheels at the stern. The $27-million, 400-passenger *Mississippi Queen* was constructed in Jefferson, Indiana, where nearly 5,000 steamboats were built during the 19th century.

Steamboats have a charm and old-world graciousness as well as delightful woods (real or faux), brass, and flowing staircases.

Steamboat cruises, up and down the Mississippi and Ohio rivers, last from 2 to 12 days, and during the year there are several theme cruises, with big bands and lively entertainment. And, just before the Kentucky Derby Festival in early May, boats take part in the Great Steamboat Race, a 14-mile event up and down the Ohio River. The food is American fare, which means steak, and shrimp, Creole sauces, and fried foods. ❏

Cruising the traditional way on the Mississippi.

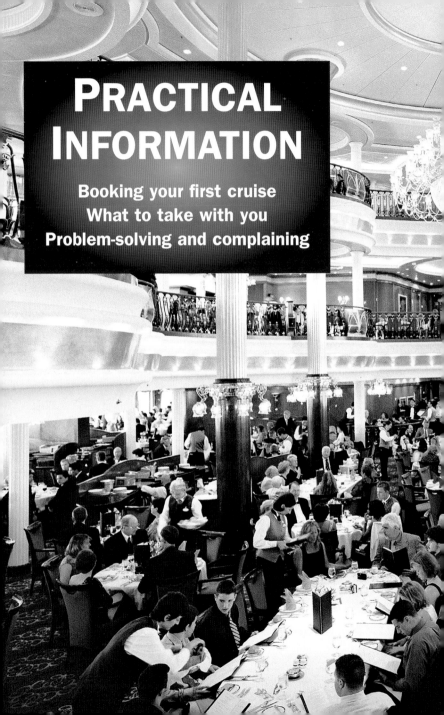

PRACTICAL INFORMATION

Booking your first cruise
What to take with you
Problem-solving and complaining

BOOKING YOUR FIRST CRUISE

Is it better to book a cruise directly with
the operator or through a travel agent?
And what hidden extras should you look
for when calculating costs?

As you digest the increasingly alluring advertising in newspapers and magazines for cruises, make sure you check exactly what's included in any offers, particularly when huge discounts tend to catch your eye. For example, make sure that all port charges, government fees, and any additional fuel surcharges are included in the price.

Perhaps because many people are new to cruising, about 80% of all cruises are still booked by travel agents. The rest are booked direct with a cruise company or tour operator, either by telephone or mail, or via the internet.

PRECEDING PAGES: dining aboard RCI's *Voyager of the Seas.*
BELOW: a cruise can enable you to meet lots of new people.

The internet

While the internet may be a good resource tool, it is not the place to book your cruise, unless you know exactly what you want. You can't ask questions, and most of the information provided by the cruise companies is strictly marketing hype. Most sites providing cruise ship reviews have something to sell or they provide automatic links to other agencies on a commission basis, and the sound-byte information can be misleading or outdated.

Many internet booking agents are unlicensed and unregulated. So, if you do decide to book a cruise with an internet-based cruise agency or wholesaler, you should confirm with the actual cruise line that the booking has been made and that final payment has been received.

The internet vs travel agents

You've found a discounted rate for your cruise on the net. That's fine. But, if a cruise line suddenly offers special discounts for your sailing, or cabin upgrades, or things go wrong with your booking, your internet booking service may sometimes turn out to be elusive or very unfriendly.

Your travel agent, however, can probably work magic in making those special discounts work for you and perhaps even providing upgrades. It's called personal service. Large travel agency groups and consortiums, such as American Express, often reserve huge blocks of cabins, and smaller independent

This is the image – but first-time cruisegoers need to remember that they get what they pay for.

agencies can access the extensive discounts, which are not available on the internet. Further, the cruise lines consider travel agents as their distribution system, and provide special discounts and value added amenities that are not provided over the internet.

Travel agents

Travel agents don't generally charge for their services, although they earn a commission from cruise lines. Consider travel agents as your business advisor, not just ticket agents. They will handle all matters relevant to your booking and should have the latest information on changes of itinerary, cruise fares, fuel surcharges, discounts, and any other related items, including insurance in case you have to cancel prior to sailing. Most travel agents are linked into cruise line computer systems and have access to most shipboard information.

The bottom line is, a good travel agent will get you the best possible price, and will get you extra things you won't be able to obtain on your own. Further, a good agency will save you a *lot* of time.

Your travel agent should find exactly the right ship for your needs and lifestyle. Some sell only a limited number of cruises and are known as "preferred suppliers," because they receive special "overrides" on top of their normal commission. They probably know their limited number of ships well, however.

If you have chosen a ship and cruise, be firm and book exactly what you want, or change your agency.

In the US, look for a CLIA (Cruise Lines International Association) affiliated agency, or one that is a member of the National Association of Cruise Oriented Agencies (NACOA). In the UK, look for a member of the Guild of Professional Cruise Agents. ACE (Association of Cruise Experts) provides in-depth agent training in the UK, as well as a full "bonding" scheme designed to protect passengers from failed cruise lines.

Questions to ask a travel agent

● Is air transportation included in the cabin rate quoted? If not, what will be the extra cost?
● What other extra costs will be involved? These can include port charges, fuel surcharge, insurance, gratuities, shore excursions, laundry, and drinks.
● Exactly what is the cruise line's cancellation policy?
● Does your agency deal with only one, or several different insurance companies?
● Will the insurance policy cover everything in case of missed or canceled flights?
● Does the cruise line offer advance booking discounts or other incentives, such as upgrades?
● Do you have preferred suppliers, or do you book any cruise on any cruise ship?
● Have you sailed aboard the ship I want to book or that you are recommending?

Indoor golf simulators are becoming popular, but you generally have to pay around $20 for 30 minutes.

- Is your agency bonded and fully insured? And, if so, by whom?
- If you book the shore excursions offered by the cruise line, will insurance coverage be provided in the cost?
- Can I occupy my cabin on the day of disembarkation until I am ready to disembark?

> *Self-service beverage stations for tea, coffee and juice are located in casual eating venues. All other beverages, including soft drinks, will cost extra.*

Reservations

Plan ahead. After choosing a ship, cruise, date, and cabin, you pay a deposit that is roughly 10 percent for long cruises, 20 percent for short cruises. The balance is normally payable 45 to 60 days before departure. For a late reservation, you pay in full when space is confirmed – when booking via the internet, for example. Note that cruise lines reserve the right to change prices in the event of tax increases, fluctuating exchange rates, fuel surcharges, or other costs beyond their control.

When you make your reservation, also make any special dietary and dining requests known: seating preference, smoking or non-smoking sections. Here are some suggestions:
- If you like to meet people, choose a large table (for six or eight).
- If you want to be more private, choose a table for two – but there are fewer of them on most modern ships.
- If you like to mix and match, choose a ship with open-seating dining, or multi-venue choices.

Extra costs

Cruise brochures boldly proclaim that "almost everything's included," but in most cases you will find this is not true. In fact, for some cruises "all-exclusive" would be a more appropriate term. In the aftermath of the September 11, 2001, terrorist attacks in the USA, many cruise lines cut their fares dramatically in order to attract business. At the same time, the cost of many onboard items went up. So allow for extra onboard costs (*see list on the opposite page*).

Your fare covers the ship as transportation, your cabin, meals, entertainment, activities, and service on board; it typically does not include alcoholic beverages, laundry, dry cleaning or valet services, shore excursions, meals ashore, gratuities, port charges, cancellation insurance, optional onboard activities such as gambling.

Expect to spend about $25 a day per person on extras, plus another $10–$12 a day per person in gratuities (unless they are included in the cruise fare). Genuine exceptions can be found in some small ships (those with fewer than 600 passengers) where just about everything is included.

Calculate the total cost of your cruise (not including any extra-cost services you might decide you want once on board) with the help of your travel agent. Here are the approximate prices per person you might expect to pay for a typical seven-day cruise aboard a well-rated mid-size or large cruise ship, based on an outside-view two-bed cabin:

Cruise fare: $1,200
Port charges: $100 (if not included)
Gratuities: $50
Total per person: **$1,350**

This is less than $200 per person per day. For this price, you wouldn't get a decent hotel room, *even without meals*, in London, Miami, New York, Tokyo, or Venice.

However, your 7-day cruise can become expensive when you start adding on a few extra touches. For example, add two flight-seeing excursions in Alaska (at about $250 each), two cappuccinos each a day ($25), a scotch and soda each a day ($35), a massage

($120), seven mineral waters ($28), 30 minutes' access to the internet for emails ($15), three other assorted excursions ($120), and gratuities $50). That's an extra $858 – without even one bottle of wine with dinner. So a couple will need to add an extra $1,596 for a 7-day cruise, plus the cruise fare, of course, and the cost of getting to and from your local airport, or ship port.

Cancellations and refunds

Do take out full cancellation insurance if it is not included, as cruises – and air transportation to/from them – must be paid in full before your cruise documentation is issued. Otherwise, if you cancel at the last minute, even for medical reasons, you could lose the whole fare. Insurance coverage can be obtained from your travel agent, and paying by credit card makes sense – you stand a good chance of getting your money back if the

TYPICAL EXTRA-COST ITEMS ABOARD LARGE RESORT SHIPS

"Alternative" dining (cover charge) . $15–$30 pp	Laundry soap . . . . $1–$1.50
Baby-sitting (per hour) $5	Massage . . . . $2-plus a minute (plus tip)
Bottled water. . . . . $2.50–$7 (per bottle)	Pottery class. $40
Cappuccino/espresso . . . . $1.75–$3	Satellite phone/fax . . . . $4.95–$15 per minute
Cartoon character bedtime "tuck-In" $20	Send/receive e-mails. . . . . . . $0.75 per minute
Wash one shirt . . . . $1.50–$3	Sodas (soft drinks) . . . . $1–$2
Dry-clean dress. . . . . $3–$7.50	Souvenir photograph (8" by 6") . . . . . $10–$12
Dry-clean jacket. . . . . $4–$8	Souvenir photograph (10" by 8"). . $20–$27.50
Golf simulator . . . . $20 (30 minutes)	Trapshooting (three or five shots) $5, $8
Group bicycling class. . . . . $10 per class	Tuxedo rental (7-day cruise). $85
Hair wash/set. . . . . $20–$40	Use of Aqua Spa (*Queen Mary 2*). . $25 per day
Haircut (men) $20	Video postcard . . . . $4.95–$6.95
Ice cream . . . . $1–$3.75	Wine/cheese tasting. . . . . $10–$15
In-cabin movies . . . . $6.95–$12.95	Wine with dinner . . . . $7–$500
Kick-boxing class . . . . $10 per class	Yoga class. . . . . $10 per class

The cruise line's insurance usually covers its own shore excursions such as this Carnival outing.

agency goes bust – or through the internet. Beware of policies sold by the cruise lines – they may well be no good if the cruise line goes out of business.

Cruise lines usually accept cancellations more than 30 days before sailing, but all charge full fare if you don't turn up on sailing day. Other cancellation fees depend on the cruise and length of trip. Many lines do not return port taxes, which are not part of the cruise fare.

> *Let the line know if you have any special celebrations during your cruise, such as a birthday, anniversary, or if you are on your honeymoon, or belated honeymoon. Get everything confirmed in writing.*

Fuel surcharges

Cruise lines publish their brochures a year ahead. If oil and other fuel costs rise in the interim, a fuel surcharge may be imposed, in addition to the quoted cruise fare. Airlines have long been adding such charges.

Air/sea packages

If your cruise fare includes air transportation (as in a one-way or round-trip air ticket), then airline arrangements usually cannot be changed without paying a premium, as cruise lines often book group space on aircraft to obtain the lowest rates.

If you do make changes, remember that, if the airline cancels your flight, the cruise line is under no obligation to help you or return your cruise fare if you don't reach the ship on time. If flying to a foreign country, allow extra time, particularly in winter, for flight delays and cancellations.

Airlines often use a "hub-and-spoke" system, which can prove frustrating. Because of changes to air schedules, cruise and air tickets may not be sent to passengers until a few days before the cruise.

In Europe, air/sea packages generally start at a major metropolitan airport; some include first-class rail travel from outlying districts. In the United States, many cruise lines include connecting flights from suburban airports convenient to the traveler. Remember that, if you fly and want to lock your check-in baggage to or within the United States, make sure you do so with a TSA (Transportation Security Administration)-approved security lock.

Most cruise lines allow you to fly out to join a ship in one port and fly home from another. An advantage is that you only have to check your baggage once at the departure airport and the baggage transfer from plane to ship is handled for you. This does not include intercontinental fly/cruises, where you must claim your baggage at the airport on arrival to clear it though customs.

Travel and medical insurance

Note that cruise lines and travel agents routinely sell travel cover policies that, on close inspection, appear to wriggle out of payment due to a litany of exclusion clauses, most of which are never explained. Examples include "pre-existing" medical conditions and "valuables" left unattended on a tour bus, even though the tour guide assures everyone that it's safe and that the driver will lock the door.

Whether you intend to travel overseas or cruise down a local river, and your present medical insurance does not cover you, you should look into extra coverage for your cruise. A "passenger protection program" may be offered by the cruise line, the charge for which will appear on your final invoice, unless you decline. It is worth every penny, and it typically covers such things as evacuation by air ambulance, high-limit baggage, baggage transfers, personal liability, and missed departure.

The best travel insurance deal

Allow time to shop around and don't accept the first travel insurance policy you are offered. Read the contract carefully and make sure you know exactly what you are covered for.

Beware of the "box ticking" approach to travel cover, which is often done quickly at the travel agent's office in lieu of providing expert advice. However, watch out for questions relating to "pre-existing medical conditions" as this little gem alone could cost you dearly. Insurers should not be allowed to apply exclusions that have not been clearly pointed out to the policyholder. Ask for a detailed explanation of all exclusions, excesses, and limitations.

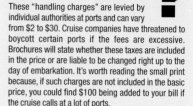

WHAT ARE PORT CHARGES

These "handling charges" are levied by individual authorities at ports and can vary from $2 to $30. Cruise companies have threatened to boycott certain ports if the fees are excessive. Brochures will state whether these taxes are included in the price or are liable to be changed right up to the day of embarkation. It's worth reading the small print because, if such charges are not included in the basic price, you could find $100 being added to your bill if the cruise calls at a lot of ports.

Check out the procedure you need to follow if you are the victim of a crime, such as your wallet or camera being stolen while on a shore excursion. If anything does happen, always obtain a police report as soon as possible. Note that many insurance policies will reimburse you only for the second-hand value of any lost or stolen item, rather than the full cost of replacement and you may be required to produce the original receipt for any such items claimed.

Watch out for exclusions for "hazardous sports." These could include things typically

On shore excursions, watch out for thieves in busy markets.

In the saddle in Jamaica – but are they insured?

offered as shore excursions aboard ships. Examples: horse riding (there goes that horse riding on the beach excursion in Jamaica) or cycling (mountain biking excursions in Alaska, Antigua or Rhodes, for example), jet skiing (most beaches), or ziplining (Hawaii). If you purchase travel cover over the internet, check the credentials of the company underwriting the scheme. It is best to deal with well-established names, and not to take what appears to be the cheapest deal offered.

Maiden voyages

If this is your first cruise, it's better not think of booking on a maiden (inaugural) voyage of a brand new ship, unless you have a great degree of tolerance and don't mind some inconvenience, or slow or nonexistent service in the dining room. Otherwise, it's best to wait until the ship has been in service for at least three months. Then again, if you book a cruise on the third or fourth voyage, and the ship's introduction is delayed, you could find yourself on the maiden voyage.

One thing is certain – on any maiden voyage Murphy's Law: "If anything can go wrong, it will" can prevail. For example:
● Service aboard new or recently refurbished ships, or on a new cruise line, is likely to be inconsistent and could be a disaster. An existing cruise line may use experienced crew from its other vessels to help "bring out" a new ship, but they may be unfamiliar with the ship's layout and won't have time to train other staff.

● Plumbing and electrical items tend to cause the most problems, particularly aboard reconstructed and refurbished vessels. Examples: toilets that don't flush or don't stop flushing; faucets incorrectly marked, where "hot" really means "cold"; and "automatic" telephones that refuse to function.
● The galley (kitchen) of a new ship if the right supplies don't turn up on time.
● Items such as menus, postcards, writing paper, or TV remote control units, door keys, towels, pillow-cases, glassware, and even toilet paper may be lost in the bowels of the ship, or simply not ordered.
● In the entertainment department, items such as spare spotlight bulbs may not be in stock. Or what if the pianos arrive damaged, or "flip" charts for the lecturers didn't show up?

Beware of groups

When you have decided your chosen ship and cruise, it's a good idea to check whether your particular cruise has any special interest groups or cruise theme (example: music festival at sea, gardening, etc). Large groups often take over public rooms, closing them to "regular" passengers.

Cruise documents

Finally, after all your choices have been made, and the line has received full payment, your cruise ticket will be sent, either as an actual paper document or online as an e-document. Make sure the ship, date, and cruise details are correctly noted. Verify any connecting flight times that seem suspiciously short. ❑

COMMON NAUTICAL TERMS: WHAT THEY MEAN

Abeam: off the side of the ship, at a right angle to its length.

Aft: near, toward, or in the rear of the ship.

Ahead: something that is ahead of the ship's bow.

Alleyway: a passageway or corridor.

Alongside: said of a ship when it is beside a pier or another vessel.

Amidships: in or toward the middle of the ship; the longitudinal center portion of the ship.

Anchor Ball: black ball hoisted above the bow to show that the vessel is anchored.

Astern: is the opposite of Ahead (i.e., something behind the ship).

Backwash: motion in the water caused by the propeller(s) moving in a reverse (astern) direction.

Bar: sandbar, usually caused by tidal or current conditions near the shore.

Beam: width of the ship between its two sides at the widest point.

Bearing: compass direction, expressed in degrees, from the ship to a particular objective or destination.

Below: anything beneath the main deck.

Berth: dock, pier, or quay. Also means bed on board ship.

Bilge: lowermost spaces of the infrastructure of a ship.

Boat Stations: allotted space for each person during lifeboat drill or any other emergency when lifeboats are lowered.

Bow: the vessel's forwardmost part.

Bridge: navigational and command control center.

Bulkhead: upright partition (wall) dividing the ship into compartments.

Bunkers: the space where fuel is stored; "bunkering" means taking on fuel.

Cable Length: a measured length equaling 100 fathoms or 600 feet.

Chart: a nautical map used for navigating.

Colors: refers to the national flag or emblem flown by the ship.

Companionway: interior stairway.

Course: direction in which the ship is headed, in degrees.

Davit: a device for raising and lowering lifeboats.

Deadlight: a ventilated porthole cover to prevent light from entering.

Dock: berth, pier, or quay.

Draft (or draught): measurement in feet from the ship's waterline to the lowest point of its keel.

Fantail: a ship's rear or overhang.

Fathom: distance equal to 6 ft.

Flagstaff: a pole at the stern flying the flag of the country of registry.

Free Port: port or place free of customs duty and regulations.

Funnel: chimney from which the ship's combustion gases are propelled into the atmosphere.

Galley: the ship's kitchen.

Gangway: the stairway or ramp linking ship and shore.

Gross Tons (gt): not the weight of a ship but the total volume measurement of all permanently enclosed spaces above and below decks, with certain exceptions, such as the bridge, radio room, galleys, washing facilities, and other specified areas. It is the basis for harbor dues. International regulations introduced in 1982 required shipowners to re-measure the GRT (formerly gross register tons) of their vessels (1 grt = 100 cubic ft of enclosed space/2.8 cubic meters).

This unit of measure was invented in England centuries ago for taxation purposes, when wine shipped from France was stored in standard-size casks, called tonneaux. Thus a ship carrying 20 casks measured 20 tons, and taxes were applied accordingly. Gross tonnage measurements may or may not include balconies.

Helm: the apparatus for steering.

House Flag: the flag denoting the company to which a ship belongs.

Hull: the frame and body of the ship exclusive of masts or superstructure.

Leeward: the side of a ship that is sheltered from the wind.

Luff: the side facing the wind.

Manifest: a list of the ship's passengers, crew, and cargo.

Nautical Mile: one-sixtieth of a degree of the Earth's circumference.

Pilot: a person licensed to navigate ships into or out of a harbor or through difficult waters, and to advise the captain on handling the ship during these procedures.

Pitch: the rise and fall of a ship's bow when the ship is under way.

Port: the left side of a ship when facing forward.

Quay: berth, dock, or pier.

Rudder: a finlike device astern and below the waterline, for steering.

Screw: a ship's propeller.

Stabilizer: a gyroscopically operated retractable "fin" extending from either or both sides of the ship below the waterline to provide stability.

Starboard: the right side of the ship when facing forward.

Stern: the aftmost part of the ship that is opposite the bow.

Tender: a smaller vessel, often a lifeboat, used to transport passengers between ship and shore when the vessel is at anchor.

Wake: the track of agitated water left behind a ship when in motion.

Waterline: the line along the side of a ship's hull corresponding to the water surface.

Windward: the side of a ship facing the direction in which the wind blows.

Yaw: the erratic deviation from the ship's set course, usually caused by a heavy sea.

DON'T LEAVE HOME WITHOUT...

Cruise ships are well stocked for most people's everyday needs, but there are certain things you should take with you

Make sure you have your passport and any visas required – in some countries, such as the People's Republic of China, or Russia, you might go ashore on organized excursions under a group visa. Pack any medication you may need in your hand luggage, keeping it in the original labeled containers, and advise family members and friends where you are going.

You already have been sent your cruise tickets and documents by the cruise line or your travel agent, or printed them out as e-documents. A typical document package might include the following items:

- Air ticket, or e-ticket boarding pass or reference code
- Cruise ticket and e-boarding pass – not all lines provide this
- Luggage tags
- Embarkation/Immigration card, to fill out before you get to the ship
- Discount coupons for the shops on board
- Bon Voyage gift selection form
- Shore excursion brochure
- Onboard credit account form
- Guide to the services on board the ship, including e-mail
- Ship's telephone and fax contact numbers

Baggage

There is generally no limit to the amount of personal baggage you can take on your cruise – most ships provide towels, soap, shampoo, and shower caps – but airlines do have weight limits. Do allow extra space for purchases on the cruise.

Tag all baggage with your name, ship, cabin number, sailing date, and port of embarkation – tags are provided with your tickets. Put your itinerary *inside* each bag to be checked in with an airline. Baggage transfers from airport to ship are generally smooth and problem-free when handled by the cruise line.

Liability for loss or damage to baggage is contained in the passenger contract (part of your ticket). Do take out insurance; the policy should extend from the date of departure until two or three days after your return home.

Thousands of passengers means a lot of baggage.

Some cruise lines offer fee-based luggage courier services that collect your luggage from your home and the next time you see your luggage, it will be in your cabin – and vice versa at the end of the cruise.

Clothing and dress codes

If you think you might not wear it, don't take it, as closet space aboard many ships is at a premium. So, unless you are on an extended cruise, keep your baggage to a minimum.

A baseball cap and shorts are fine for a daytime string quartet concert – but some people like to dress for dinner.

It's a good idea to select four or five interchangeable outfits to wear during the week, in two or three color groups and mix-and-match clothing that can be layered. Black is always a good neutral color to team with other colors.

For cruises to tropical areas, where the weather is warm to hot with high humidity, casual wear should include plenty of lightweight cottons and other natural fibers. Synthetic materials do not "breathe" as well and often retain heat. Clothes should be as opaque as possible to counteract the sun's ultraviolet rays. Take a lightweight cotton sweater or windbreaker for the evenings, when the ship's air-conditioning will seem even more powerful after a day in the sun. Pack sunglasses and a hat. Rainstorms in the tropics don't last long, but they can give you a good soaking, so take inexpensive, lightweight rainwear for excursions.

The same is true for cruises to the Mediterranean, Greek Isles, or North Africa, although there will be little or no humidity for most of the year. Certain areas may be dusty as well as dry. In these latitudes, the weather can be changeable and cool in the evenings from October to March, so take extra sweaters and a windbreaker.

INFORMATION TO COLLECT BEFORE YOU TRAVEL

Research and collect information about the destinations you will be going to, either via the internet or from travel guides, so that you will be better informed when you get there.

Collect photos of family members with you – grandparents should take photo of their grandchildren – so that you can show and compare with others you may meet on board. Grandparents' "bragging parties" may be an activity aboard some ships.

Write down addresses of

friends and relatives you may want to send postcards to.

Write down telephone and other contact details of family,

friends and neighbors in case of emergencies. At least a week before departure, tell your friends and relatives how to get in touch with you. Your cruise document package will include information about how to reach you on the ship by phone or fax.

If you are celebrating a special occasion on your cruise, such as an anniversary or birthday, your cruise document package will often include information on how to book gifts or special packages. If not, check the line's web site.

Art nouveau architecture is prominent in Ålesund, Norway.

Middle East and Far East, shorts or bare shoulders may cause offence, so cover up adequately.

Aboard ship, dress rules are relaxed by day, but in the evening what you wear should be tasteful. Men should take a blazer or sports jacket and ties for the dining room and for any "informal" occasions. Transatlantic crossings on *Queen Mary 2* are normally more elegant and require formal attire.

For formal nights (usually two out of seven), women can wear a long evening gown, elegant cocktail dress, or a smart pants suit. Gentlemen are expected to wear either a tuxedo or dark business suit and tie. These "rules" are less rigid on short and moderately priced cruises. If you are the athletic type, remember to pack sportswear and gym shoes for the gymnasium or aerobics classes.

No matter where you are going, comfortable low- or flat-heeled shoes are a must for women, except for formal nights. Light, airy walking shoes are best for walking. If you are in the Caribbean or Pan-Pacific region and you are not used to heat and humidity, your ankles may swell, so tight shoes are not recommended. Rubber soles are best for walking on the open deck of a ship.

Formal: Tuxedo, dinner jacket or dark suit and tie for men; evening gown or other appropriate formal attire for women.
Informal: Jacket and tie for men; cocktail dress, dressy pantsuit, or the like for women.
Casual (Smart/Elegant): While this is an oxymoron, it generally means long trousers (no shorts or jeans), collared and sleeved shirt (gentlemen); skirt or slacks and top for women.
Casual (Relaxed): Slacks over sweater or open shirt (no tie) for men (no beach wear or muscle shirts); a blouse with skirt, slacks, or similar comfortable attire for women. Shoes are required.

Flying to/from your cruise

Several cruise lines have "air deviation" desks that allow you to change your flights and con-

For cruises to Alaska, the North Cape, or the Norwegian fjords, pack warm comfortable clothing layers, plus a raincoat or parka for the northernmost port calls. Cruises to Alaska and the Land of the Midnight Sun are operated in summer, when temperatures are pleasant. Unless you are going to northern ports such as St. Petersburg in winter, you will not need thermal underwear. However, you will need thermal underwear, thick socks – and heavy sweaters – if you take an expedition cruise to the Antarctic Peninsula or through the Northwest Passage.

In destinations with a strong religious tradition, like Venezuela, Haiti, the Dominican Republic, Colombia, and countries in the

WHAT I.D. DO I NEED

A passport is the most practical proof of your citizenship and identification. Visas are required for some countries (allow time to obtain these). On most cruises, you will hand in your passport to the company at embarkation (it would be wise to keep a copy of the main pages with you). This helps the ship to clear customs and immigration inspection on arrival in ports of call. It will be returned before you reach the port of disembarkation.

nections, for a fee – typically between $25 and $50 per person.

Air travel today is fast and efficient. But even experienced travelers find that the stress of international travel can persist long after the flight is over; for long international flights, I recommend the flat beds in Club Class on British Airways or in Upper Class on Virgin Atlantic aircraft. Eastbound flights tend to cause more pronounced jet lag than westbound flights. Jet aircraft are generally pressurized to some 8,000 ft (2,400 meters) in altitude, causing discomfort in the ears and the stomach, and swollen feet.

Note that lithium cell batteries are no longer allowed in checked luggage when flying within the United States, or on international flights on US-based airlines. So, don't pack your lithium-cell powered camera or alarm clock in luggage to be checked.

Flying and jet lag

A few precautions should reduce the less pleasant effects of flying around the world. Plan as far in advance of your cruise as possible. Take a daytime flight, so that you can arrive at, or close to, your normal bedtime. Try to be as quiet as possible before flying, and allow for another five hours of rest after any flight that crosses more than five time zones.

Babies and small children are less affected by changes in time because of their shorter sleeping and waking cycles. Most adults need more time to adjust.

Medication

Take any medicine and other medical supplies that you need (remember to get prescription refills *before* your cruise),

plus spare eyeglasses or contact lenses. In many countries it may be difficult to find certain medicines. Others may be sold under different names. If you are taking a long cruise, ask your doctor for names of alternatives.

The ship's pharmacy will stock certain standard remedies, but do not expect to find more unusual medicines. Remember to carry a doctor's prescription for any medication (required if you are joining a ship in Dubai).

Also, be advised that if you run out of your medication and you need to get a supply aboard ship, most ships will require that you see the doctor, even if you have a prescription. There is a charge for each visit, plus the cost of any medication.

Let spouses or companions carry a supply of your medicine and medical supplies. Remember not to pack medication, or your personal medical information, in any luggage to be checked in when flying, but take it in your carry-on.

At last, a chance to sit back and relax at sea...

Sea and sand – but what about sun protection?

Sun protection

It makes sense to protect your skin from the effects of the sun. Take suncream/sunlotion with a minimum SPF 15 protection factor. Remember that once is not enough – keep reapplying it after you take a dip in the pool or hot tub, and allow for the fact that if you perspire, suncream and sunlotion will dissolve.

If you wear a tee-shirt over your swimsuit, its SPF protection factor is between 7 (white tee-shirt), and 10 (dark tee-shirt). While cotton tee-shirts allow more "breathing," remember that unbleached cotton has special pigments that can actually absorb UV rays, as opposed to polyester/other synthetic or silk tee-shirts that reflect radiation.

Clothing designated as sun-protective, including swimwear, carries a UPF number. This is similar to the SPF factor, except that the UPF number shows how much UVA and UVB is blocked. Outdoor sports clothing and swimwear manufacturers make sun-protective clothing from special microfibers that have a very tight weave to block out the sun.

Photography

Users of digital cameras should remember to pack a spare memory card unless they are carrying a laptop onto which they can trans-fer pictures. They also need the camera's AC adaptor and any converter plugs.

Film users: use low-speed film in tropical areas such as the Caribbean or South Pacific – high-speed film is easily damaged by heat. Take plenty of film with you; standard sizes are available in the ship's shop, but the selection will be limited, particularly if you use slide film. If you buy film during a port visit, try to obtain it from an air-conditioned store, and check the expiration date.

When taking photographs in ports of call, respect the wishes of local inhabitants. Ask permission to photograph someone close-up. Most will smile and tell you to go ahead. But some people are superstitious or afraid of having their picture taken or are just in an uncooperative mood. Do not press the point.

Money matters

Most ships operate in US dollars or euros, but a few use other currencies; check with your travel agent or supplier. Major credit cards and traveler's checks are accepted on board, but few lines take personal checks.

You sign for drinks and other services, as part of "cashless cruising." Some large resort ships have ATM cash machines, although a "transaction fee" is assessed. Getting cash from ATMs during shore excursions is also likely to incur a similar fee. ❑

WHEN YOU REACH YOUR SHIP...

If this is your first cruise, you need to be familiar with the embarkation procedures and with the things you must check when you eventually make it to your cabin

Y ou have arrived at the airport closest to your ship's embarkation point, and retrieved your luggage. A representative from the cruise line will ask you to place your luggage in a cluster together with those of other passengers. The next time you see your luggage should be in your cabin.

When you arrive at the port, your baggage may go through X-ray scans, and you will probably be asked for identification as you enter the embarkation building. Your photograph will be taken and loaded into the cruise line's electronic security system, together with your booking details. You then receive an encoded security card that must be used each time you board or re-board the ship.

Do not buy duty-free liquor to take on board – it will not be allowed by the cruise line and will be confiscated until the last day of the cruise.

check-in. If you are cruising from a US port and you are a non-US citizen or "resident alien," you will check in at a separate desk. You will have to deposit your passport with the check-in personnel. Ask for a receipt – it is, after all, a valuable document – and preferably keep a photocopy of the main pages.

Embarkation

Don't arrive before the embarkation time stated on your cruise documents – you won't be allowed on board. But don't leave it too late – the gangway closes 30 minutes prior to sailing time (60 minutes in any US port). On large resort ships, when you check in you'll probably be given a color-coded embarkation card, or number card. Embarking is typically done in batches – 100 people, say, at a time.

Go to the desk in the passenger terminal that displays the first letter of your surname, wait in line – having filled out all embarkation, registration, and immigration documents – and then check in. If your accommodation is designated as a "suite," there should be a separate

Cruise ships docked at Heritage Quay, St John's, Antigua.

If you are cruising from any other port in the world that is not a US port, bear in mind that each country has its own check-in requirements, setups, and procedures.

Documents in hand, you will then proceed through a security-screening device, for both your body and hand luggage, as at airports. Next, you'll walk a few paces towards the gangway. This may be a covered, airport-type gangway, or an open one. It could be flat, or you may have to walk up (or down) an incline, depending on the location of the gangway or the tide.

Aboard mid-size ships, you'll be asked to wait until general boarding starts; then you will pass through another security check. If you are sailing aboard one of the smaller ships, you'll be able to board whenever you want – there will be no lines, or very short ones.

As you approach the gangway you should be greeted by the ship's photographers, a snap-happy team ready to take your photograph, bedraggled as you may appear after having traveled for hours. If you do not want your photograph taken, say "no" firmly.

Once on the gangway, you will feel a heightened sense of anticipation. At the ship end of the gangway, you will find a decorated entrance and the comfortable feel of air-conditioning if the weather is hot.

Finding your cabin

The ship's cruise staff will welcome you aboard and ask for your cabin number. If you are sailing aboard the large resort ships of Celebrity Cruises, Cunard Line, Disney Cruise Line, Holland America Line, MSC Cruises, or Princess Cruises, you'll be escorted to your

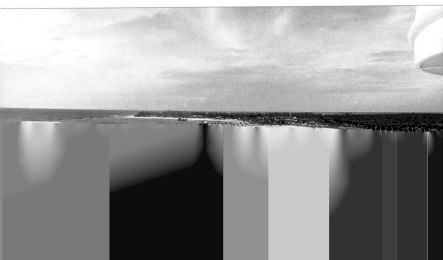

cabin by a steward. If you are staying in suite-grade accommodation, you'll be escorted by a butler or concierge.

Aboard the large resort ships of some lines, you may just be pointed in the general direction of your deck. Staff positioned on each deck stairway will keep you right. Companies with this self-service approach include Carnival Cruise Lines, Costa Cruises, Island Cruises, Norwegian Cruise Line, NCL America, Ocean Village, P&O Cruises, and Royal Caribbean International. If you are staying in one of their suite-grade cabins, however, you'll be escorted by a butler or concierge.

Things to check

The door to your cabin should be open. If it is locked, ask the steward to open it. Aboard the newest ships, simply insert your electronically coded key card. Once inside the cabin, take a good look. Is it clean? Is it tidy? Are the beds properly made? Make sure there is ice in the ice container. Check the bathroom, bathtub (if there is one), or shower. Make sure there are towels and soap. If all is clean and ship-shape, fine.

If there are problems, tell your cabin steward immediately. Or call the reception desk and explain the problem, then quietly, but firmly request that someone in a supervisory position see you to resolve it. The housekeeping in cruise ships is generally very good, but sometimes when "turnaround" time is tight, when passengers disembark in the morning and new passengers embark in the afternoon, little things get overlooked. They shouldn't, of course, but they do, just as in any large hotel ashore.

Be careful the first time you use the toilet – most of them bark like a large dog. This is because they operate on a vacuum system. So, close the lid *immediately after* you have used the toilet. Don't, under any circumstances, press the button to flush the toilet if you are still sitting on it – it will not be a life-enhancing experience.

Do note the telephone number for medical

Tempting drinks – but the cost can soon add up.

emergencies, so you know how to call for help, should any medical emergency arise.

Your luggage probably will not have arrived yet, especially on a large resort ship, so don't sit in the cabin waiting for it – it'll get there sooner or later. Put your hand luggage away somewhere, and, deck plan in hand, take a walk. The evening dress code is casual the first night on board and no one really feels like dressing up after a travel day.

> *The cost of buying drinks can very quickly add up. Aboard ships operated by Europe-based companies, mixers such as tonic for gin are usually charged separately*

Some priorities

● Check out library books as soon as possible – the most sought after will go quickly.
● Make your reservations for spa treatments as soon as possible.
● Make shore excursion reservations as soon

as possible – many of them will be limited in numbers.
● Check to make sure that any planned celebrations have been communicated to the ship by the cruise line's head office.
● Familiarize yourself with the layout of the ship. Learn which way is forward (NCL's *Norwegian Gem* and *Norwegian Pearl*, for example, have a neat carpet design that includes dolphins swimming – and their heads point the way forward), which way is aft, and how to reach your cabin from the main stairways.

This is also a good time to learn how to get from your cabin to the outside decks in an emergency – these are rare, but they happen.

The cost of thirst

You may be thirsty when you arrive in your cabin. You notice a bottle of water with a tab around its neck. You take off the tab, open the bottle and have a drink. Then you read the notice: "This bottle is provided for your convenience. If you open it, your account will be charged $4.50." Too late!

On deck, you are greeted by a smiling, happy waiter offering you a colorful, cool drink. But, put your fingers on the glass as he hands it to you and he'll also ask for your cruise card. Bang, you've just paid $6.95 for drink worth 5 cents.

The safety drill

Regulations dictate that a Passenger Lifeboat Drill must take place within 24 hours after the ship sails from the embarkation port, but typically takes place before the ship sails (you'll find your lifejacket in the cabin and directions to your assembly station will be posted on the back of the cabin door). After the drill, you can take off the lifejacket and relax. By now, your luggage probably will have arrived.

But wait....

Wait until almost the end of the cruise for bargains in the onboard shops and boutiques. Prices are often reduced on the last day. ❏

THE SHIP'S COMPANY

```
Captain
  ├─ Staff Captain
  │    ├─ Chief Officer ── Chief Engineer ── Chief Electrician    Hotel Manager or Chief Purser
  │    │     First Officer    Deputy Chief Engineer    First Electrician
  │    │     Second Officer   Second Engineer    Second Electrician
  │    │     Junior Officers  Third Engineer     Junior Electricians
  │    │                      Junior Engineers
  │    │                      Deck & Engine Staff Seamen (All Ranks)
  │    └─ Chief Radio Officer
  │         First Radio Officer
  │         Radio Officers
  └─ Principal Medical Officer
       Doctor
       Nurses
       Medical Orderlies
```

Hotel Manager or Chief Purser

- Deputy Hotel Manager (Food & Beverage)
  - Restaurant Manager
    - Maître d'Hôtel
      - Head Waiters
        - Wine Stewards
        - Restaurant Waiters
  - Executive Chef
    - Head Chefs
      - Sous-Chefs
        - Pastry Chefs
        - Butcher
        - Galley Staff
        - Storekeeper Pantrymen
  - Food Manager
    - Assistant Food Manager
  - Bar Manager
    - Assistant Bar Manager
      - Bartenders/Bar Waiters

- Cruise Director
  - Shore Excursion Manager/Deputy Cruise Director
  - Social Hostess
  - Assistant Cruise Director
    - Cruise Staff
    - Entertainment
      Headliners
      Cabaret Acts
      Bands
      Musicians
      Lecturers
      Instructors

- Purser
  - Hotel Purser
  - Purser's Staff/Concierge
    - Crew Purser
    - Printer
    - Stewards/Stewardesses
    - Concessions
      Photography
      Casino
      Hairdressing
      Shops
      Video Games
      Massage

WHAT TO DO IF...

**Things sometimes go wrong and you may
need to troubleshoot or complain. Here are
20 problems and how to deal with them**

❶ Your luggage does not arrive at the ship.
If you are part of the cruise line's air/sea package, the airline is responsible for locating your luggage and delivering it to the next port. If you arranged your own air transportation it is wholly your problem. Always have easy-to-read name and address tags both inside as well as outside your luggage. Keep track of claim documents and give the airline a detailed itinerary and list of port agents (usually included with your documents).

❷ You miss the ship.
If you miss the ship's departure (due to late or non-performing flight connections, etc), and

you are traveling on an air/sea package, the airline will arrange to get you to the ship. If you are traveling "cruise-only," however, and have arranged your own air transportation, then you are responsible for onward flights, hotel stays, and transfers. Many cruise lines now have "deviation" desks, where, for a fee, you can adjust airline flights and dates to suit personal preferences. If you arrive at the port just as your ship is pulling away, see the ship's port agent immediately.

❸ Your cabin is too small.
Almost all cruise ship cabins are too small – I am convinced that some are designed for packages rather than people. When you book a cruise, you pay for a certain category and

An interior cabin aboard Holland America's *Eurodam*.

type of cabin but have little or no control over which one you actually get. See the hotel manager as soon as possible and explain what is wrong with the cabin (noisy, too hot, etc). If the ship is full (most are nowadays), it will be difficult to change. However, the hotel manager will probably try to move you from known problem cabins, although they are not required to do so.

❹ Your cabin has no air-conditioning, it is noisy, or there are serious plumbing problems.
If there is anything wrong in your cabin, or if there is something wrong with the plumbing in your bathroom, bring it to the attention of your cabin steward immediately. If nothing gets better, complain to the hotel manager. Some cabins, for example, are located above the ship's laundry, generator, or galley (hot); others may be above the disco (noisy). If the ship is full, it may be hard to change.

❺ You have noisy cabin neighbors.
First, politely tell your neighbors that you can hear them brushing their hair as the cabin walls are so thin, and would they please not bang the drawers shut quite so strenuously at 2am. If that doesn't work, complain to the purser or hotel manager, and ask them to attend to the problem.

❻ You have small children and the brochure implied that the ship has special programs for them, but when on board you find out it is not an all-year-round program.
In this instance, either the brochure was misleading, or your travel agent did not know enough about the ship or did not bother to ask the right questions. If you have genuine cause for complaint, then see your travel agent when you get home. Most ships generally will try to accommodate your young ones – the large resort ships, those carrying more than 1,600 passengers, have more facilities – but may not be covered by their insurance for "looking after" them throughout the day, as the brochure seemed to promise. Again, check thoroughly with your travel agent before you book.

Disney Cruise Line is predictably good with children.

❼ You do not like your dining room seating.
Most "standard" market ships, particularly the large resort ships, operate two seatings for dinner – sometimes for all meals. When you book your cruise, you are asked whether you want the first or second seating. The line will make every attempt to please you. But if you want second seating and are given first seating (perhaps a large group has taken over the entire second seating, or the ship is full), there may be little the restaurant manager can do.

❽ You want a table for two and are put at a table for eight.
Again, see the restaurant manager and explain why you are not satisfied. A little gratuity should prove helpful.

❾ You cannot communicate with your dining room waiter.
The nationality and language of dining room waiters may be quite unfamiliar to you, and all they can do is smile. This could prove frustrat-

People moan about embarkation and disembarkation lines for large resort ships, but they're unavoidable.

ing for a whole cruise, especially if you need something out of the ordinary. See the restaurant manager, and tell him you want a waiter with whom you can communicate. If he does not solve the problem, see the hotel manager.

❿ The food is definitely not "gourmet" cuisine as advertised in the brochure.
If the food is not as described (for example, whole lobster in the brochure, but only cold lobster salad once during the cruise, or the "fresh squeezed" orange juice on the breakfast menu is anything but), inform the maître d' of the problem.

⓫ A large group has taken over the ship.
Sometimes, large groups have pre-booked several public rooms for meetings – seemingly every hour on the hour in the rooms you want to use. This means the individual passenger (that is you) becomes a second-class citizen. Make your displeasure known to the hotel manager immediately, tell your travel agent, and write a follow-up letter to the line when you return home.

⓬ A port of call is deleted from the itinerary.
If you only took the cruise because the ship goes to the place you have wanted to go for years, then read the fine print in the brochure before you book. A cruise line is under no obligation to perform the stated itinerary. For whatever reason – political unrest, weather, mechanical problems, no berth space, safety, etc. – the ship's captain has the ultimate say.

⓭ You are unwell aboard ship.
Do not worry. There will be a qualified doctor – who generally operates as a concession, and therefore charges – and medical facilities, including a small pharmacy. You will be well taken care of. Although there are charges for medical services rendered, almost all cruise lines offer insurance packages that include medical coverage for most eventualities. It is wise to take out this insurance when you book.

⓮ You have a problem with a crew member.
Go to the hotel manager or chief purser and explain the problem; for single women this could be a persistent cabin steward who has a master door key. No one will do anything unless you complain. Cruise ships try to hire decent staff, but, with so many crew, there are bound to be a few bad apples. Insist on a full written report of the incident, which must be entered into the ship's daily log by the staff captain (deputy captain).

⓯ You leave some personal belongings on a tour bus.
If you find you have left something on a tour bus, and you are back on board your ship, the first thing to do is advise the shore excursion manager or the reception desk. The tour oper-

ator ashore will then be contacted to ascertain whether any items have been handed in to their office.

⓰ There are too many days at sea before you reach the destination that really attracts you to the cruise.
If the destination is a long distance away from where you live, it usually makes good sense to fly to your cruise embarkation point and stay for at least a day or two before the cruise. Why? Because you will be better rested and you will have time to adjust to any time changes. You will step aboard your ship already relaxed and ready for a real vacation. Also, the last few days won't be as anticlimactic as they would be if you were heading home across, say, the Pacific or Atlantic oceans.

Carnival's "funship" nightlife – but it may not suit everyone.

⓱ The cruise line's air arrangements have you flying from Los Angeles via Timbuktu to get to your cruise ship.
Fine if your cruise ship is in Timbuktu – difficult, as it is inland. Most cruise lines with low rates also use the cheapest air routing to get you to your ship. That could mean flights from a central hub. Be warned: you get what you pay for. Ask questions before you book.

⓲ The ship's laundry ruins your clothes.
If any of your clothing is ruined or discol-

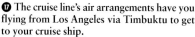
The reception desk can help solve most problems.

ored by the ship's laundry, first tell your cabin steward(ess), and then follow up by going to the purser's office and getting it registered as a proper complaint. Take a copy of the complaint with you, so you can follow up when you get home. Unfortunately, you will probably find a disclaimer on the laundry list saying something to the effect that liability is limited to about $1 per item – not a lot. So, although the laundry and dry cleaning facilities generally work well, things can occasionally go wrong just like ashore.

⓳ You have extra charges on your bill.
Check your itemized bill carefully. Then talk to the purser's office and ask them to show you the charge slips. Finally, make sure you are given a copy of your bill, after any modifications have been made.

⓴ You're unhappy with the general quality of your cruise experience.
You, or your travel agent, ultimately choose the ship and cruise. But if your ship does not meet your specific lifestyle and interests, or the ship performs less well than the brochure promises, let both your travel agent and the cruise line know as soon as possible. If your grievance is valid, many cruise lines will offer a credit, good towards a future cruise. But do be sure to read the fine print on the ticket. ❑

THE SHIPS AT A GLANCE

Authoritative ratings for more than 350 cruise ships

FINDING THE STAR PERFORMERS

**Douglas Ward explains how he evaluates
ships during a cruise, not only for facilities
but also for standards of food, service,
entertainment, staff and hospitality**

I have been evaluating and rating cruise ships and the onboard product professionally since 1980. In addition, I receive regular reports from my team of five trained assessors. The ratings are conducted with *total objectivity*, from a set of predetermined criteria and a modus operandi designed to work globally, not just regionally, across the entire spectrum of ocean-going cruise ships today, in all segments of the marketplace.

There really is no "best cruise line in the world" or "best cruise ship" – only the ship and cruise that is right for you. After all, it's the overall enjoyment of a cruise as a vacation that's really important. Therefore, different criteria are applied to ships of different sizes, styles, and market segments throughout the world. After all, people of different nationalities seek different things in their vacation.

I update and publish my findings each year in the 700-page *Berlitz Complete Guide to Cruising*, which has become a standard reference work for the cruise industry and an invaluable source of information for regular cruisegoers wanting to check out a particular ship before booking. Reviews range from 500 words to 5,500 and cover nearly 300 ships.

For the present book I have simplified these findings into a chart for easy reference. To arrive at a rating, I take account of around 400 separate items, based on personal cruises, visits and revisits to ships, as well as observations and comments from my team. These are channeled into 20 major areas, each with a possible 100 points. The maximum possible score is therefore 2,000 points, and it is on these scores that the star ratings in this book are based.

Europa, the highest-rated ship assessed in this survey.

What really counts

The ratings reflect the standards of the cruise product delivered to passengers – the dining experience, and the service and hospitality aspects of the cruise – and are less concerned with the physical attributes of the ship, though these are taken into account. Thus, although a ship may be the latest, most stunning vessel in the world in terms of design

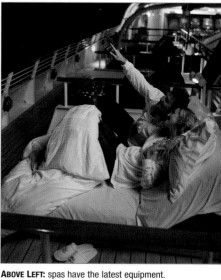

and decor, it will not receive a high rating if the food, service, staff, and hospitality fall below an acceptable standard.

The stars shown in the following chart relate directly to the overall rating. The highest number of stars awarded is five (★★★★★), and the lowest is one star. This system is universally recognized throughout the hospitality industry. A plus (+) indicates that a ship deserves just that little bit more than the number of stars attained.

ABOVE LEFT: spas have the latest equipment.
ABOVE: *SeaDream I*'s Balinese Dream Beds.

WHAT THE STAR RATINGS MEAN

★★★★★+ The best of everything, from surroundings to hospitality. In my view, only one ship currently meets this standard: Hapag-Lloyd Cruises' *Europa*.

★★★★★ You can expect a truly excellent and memorable cruise experience, with the finesse and attention to detail commensurate with the amount of money paid. Cuisine and entertainment should be creative and top-notch. Service should be attentive yet unobtrusive.

★★★★+ Perhaps the personal service and attention to detail could be slightly better, but, nonetheless, this should prove a fine all-round cruise experience in a setting that is extremely clean and comfortable, with few lines anywhere, a caring attitude from service personnel, and a good standard of entertainment that appeals to a mainstream market. The cuisine and service will be well rounded, with mostly fresh ingredients and varied menus.

★★★★ A very good quality all-round cruise, probably aboard a modern, comfortable ship with a good range of facilities and services. The food and service will be quite decent, although decidedly not "gourmet." The service will be well organized, although it may be a little robotic and impersonal at times. A lot of things may cost extra once you are on board.

★★★+ The crew should reflect a positive attitude to hospitality, and be willing to accommodate your needs, up to a point. Food and service levels in the dining room(s) should be reasonably good, although special or unusual orders might prove more difficult. There will probably be a number of extra-cost items you thought were included in the price of your cruise.

★★★ You can expect a reasonably decent, middle-of-the-road experience, with a moderate amount of space and quality in furnishings, fixtures, and fittings. The

cabins are likely to be on the small side. The food and service levels will be acceptable but not memorable. The entertainment may be weak. Unpretentious but fair value.

★★+ An average experience in terms of cabin size and facilities, in surroundings that are unpretentious. The food and its service will probably be disappointing.

★★ A ship that is probably in need of more attention to maintenance and service levels, not to mention hospitality. The food will lack taste, and staff training is likely to be minimal.

★+ Basic, with little attention to detail, from a poorly trained staff. The ship may need maintenance and facilities will be poor. But the price is probably alluringly low.

★ Bottom of the barrel, with almost nothing in terms of hospitality or finesse. The equivalent of staying in the most basic motel.

AT A GLANCE: THE WORLD'S

Check out the quality, size and suitability of a particular ship by using this list, based on the authoritative ratings created by Douglas Ward for the annual Berlitz Complete Guide to Cruising and Cruise Ships

Ship	Cruise Line	Built	Type of ship	Cabins
Adventure of the Seas	Royal Caribbean International	2001	Large Resort Ship	1,557
Aegean Pearl	Golden Star Cruises	1971	Mid-Size	395
AIDAaura	AIDA Cruises	2003	Mid-Size	633
AIDAbella	AIDA Cruises	2008	Large Resort Ship	1,025
AIDAcara	AIDA Cruises	1996	Mid-Size	593
AIDAdiva	AIDA Cruises	2007	Large Resort Ship	1,025
AIDAluna	AIDA Cruises	2009	Large Resort Ship	1,025
AIDAvita	AIDA Cruises	2002	Large Resort Ship	633
Akademik Ioffe	Quark Expeditions	1988	Boutique (Exp)	55
Akademik Sergey Vavilov	Quark Expeditions	1988	Boutique (Exp)	40
Akademik Sholaskiy	Heritage Expeditions	1982	Boutique (Exp)	22
Albatros	Phoenix Reisen	1973	Mid-Size	442
Alexandr von Humboldt II	Phoenix Reisen	1965	Mid-Size	425
Aleksey Maryshev	Oceanwide Expeditions	1990	Boutique (Exp)	22
Amadea	Phoenix Reisen	1991	Mid-Size	303
American Eagle	American Cruise Lines	2000	Boutique	27
American Glory	American Cruise Lines	2002	Boutique	27
American Spirit	American Cruise Lines	2005	Boutique	51
American Star	American Cruise Lines	2007	Boutique	51
Amsterdam	Holland America Line	2000	Large Resort Ship	690
Andrea	Elegant Cruises & Tours	1960	Boutique	57
Antarctic Dream	Antarctic Shipping	1959	Boutique (Exp)	39
Aquamarine	Louis Cruise Lines	1971	Mid-Size	525
Aranui 3	Campagnie Polynesienne de Transport Maritime	2003	Boutique	63
Arcadia	P&O Cruises	2005	Large Resort Ship	998
Arion	Classic International Cruises	1965	Small	169
Artemis	P&O Cruises	1984	Large Resort Ship	600
Astor	Transocean Tours	1987	Mid-Size	295
Astoria	Transocean Tours	1981	Mid-Size	259
Asuka II	Asuka Cruise (NYK)	1990	Mid-Size	462
Aurora	P&O Cruises	2000	Large Resort Ship	934
Azamara Journey	Azamara Cruises	2000	Mid-Size	338
Azamara Quest	Azamara Cruises	2000	Mid-Size	358
Balmoral	Fred Olsen Cruise Lines	1988	Large Resort Ship	744
Black Prince	Fred Olsen Cruise Lines	1966	Small	234
Black Watch	Fred Olsen Cruise Lines	1972	Mid-Size	421
Bleu de France	CDF Croisières de France	1982	Mid-Size	374

CRUISE SHIPS

WHAT THE CATEGORIES MEAN

Cruise line. The name of the cruise company or ship operator is provided. The cruise line and the operator may be different if the company that owns the vessel does not market and operate it (tour operators often charter cruise ships for their exclusive use – Thomson Cruises is an example).

Built. The year the ship was completed and first entered service.

Type of ship.
Large Resort Ship (1,600–6,400 passengers)
Mid-Size Ship (600–1,600 passengers)
Small Ship (200–600 passengers)
Boutique Ship (20–200 passengers)
Boutique (Expedition) Ship (50–200 passengers)
Sail-Cruise Ship (50–600 passengers)

Cabins. The number of passenger cabins (most of which have two beds).

Class. Designated as Standard, Premium, Luxury, or Exclusive, according to a general classification into which segment of the market the ship falls. This should help you choose the right size ship and cruise experience to fit your lifestyle.
Standard: the least expensive, offering the basic amenities, food and service.
Premium: more expensive than Standard, have generally better food, service, facilities, amenities, more attention to detail, and differentiation of suites (with butler service) and standard accommodation.
Luxury: more expensive than Premium or Standard, and provide more personal comfort, space, open or one-seating dining, much better food (no processed items, more menu creativity, and everything made fresh), staff and training.
Exclusive: the best in facilities, food, and service, and the finest cruise experience available, but more expensive than the other classes.

Rating. See *What the Stars Mean* on page 235. NYR indicates that the ship is not yet rated by the book. Ratings supplied courtesy of 2008 *Berlitz Complete Guide to Cruising and Cruise Ships*.

♿ A: Recommended as being most suitable for wheelchair passengers
B: A ship that is reasonably accessible for wheelchair passengers
C: A ship that is moderately accessible for wheelchair passengers
D: Not suitable for wheelchair passengers.

Suitable for	Class	Rating	♿
Families with Children	Standard	★★★★	A
Mature Couples/Singles	Standard	★★	D
Families with Children	Standard	★★★★	B
Families with Children	Standard	★★★★	B
Families with Children	Standard	★★★★	B
Families with Children	Standard	★★★★	B
Families with Children	Standard	NYR	B
Families with Children	Standard	★★★★	B
Tough Adventurous Types	Standard	★★	D
Tough Adventurous Types	Standard	★★	D
Tough Adventurous Types	Standard	★★	D
Mature Couples/Singles	Standard	★★★+	C
Explorers	Standard	★★★	C
Explorers	Standard	★★	D
Mature Couples/Singles	Standard	★★★★+	C
Mature Couples/Singles	Standard	★★	D
Mature Couples/Singles	Standard	★★	D
Mature Couples/Singles	Standard	★★	D
Mature Couples/Singles	Standard	★★	D
Mature Couples/Singles	Premium	★★★★	B
Explorers	Standard	★★	D
Explorers	Standard	★★	D
Mature Couples/Singles	Standard	★★+	D
Mature Couples/Singles	Standard	★	D
Child-Free	Standard	★★★★	B
Mature Couples/Singles	Standard	★★	D
Child-Free	Standard	★★★+	B
Mature Couples/Singles	Standard	★★★+	C
Mature Couples/Singles	Standard	★★★+	C
Mature Couples/Singles	Luxury	★★★★+	A
Families with Children	Standard	★★★★	B
Mature Couples/Singles	Premium	★★★★	C
Mature Couples/Singles	Premium	★★★★	C
Mature Couples/Singles	Standard	★★★★	C
Mature Couples/Singles	Standard	★★+	D
Mature Couples/Singles	Standard	★★★+	C
Families with Children	Standard	★★★★	B

Ship	Cruise Line	Built	Type of ship	Cabins
Blue Monarch	Elysian Cruises	1966	Small	242
Boudicca	Fred Olsen Cruise Lines	1973	Mid-Size	437
Braemar	Fred Olsen Cruise Lines	1993	Mid-Size	377
Bremen	Hapag-Lloyd Cruises	1990	Boutique (Exp)	82
Brilliance of the Seas	Royal Caribbean International	2002	Large Resort Ship	1,056
Callisto	Travel Dynamics International	1963	Boutique	17
Caribbean Princess	Princess Cruises	2004	Large Resort Ship	1,557
Carnival Conquest	Carnival Cruise Lines	2002	Large Resort Ship	1,487
Carnival Destiny	Carnival Cruise Lines	1996	Large Resort Ship	1,321
Carnival Dream	Carnival Cruise Lines	2009	Large Resort Ship	1,826
Carnival Ecstasy	Carnival Cruise Lines	1991	Large Resort Ship	1,026
Carnival Elation	Carnival Cruise Lines	1998	Large Resort Ship	1,026
Carnival Fantasy	Carnival Cruise Lines	1990	Large Resort Ship	1,028
Carnival Fascination	Carnival Cruise Lines	1994	Large Resort Ship	1,028
Carnival Freedom	Carnival Cruise Lines	2007	Large Resort Ship	1,487
Carnival Glory	Carnival Cruise Lines	2003	Large Resort Ship	1,487
Carnival Imagination	Carnival Cruise Lines	1995	Large Resort Ship	1,028
Carnival Inspiration	Carnival Cruise Lines	1996	Large Resort Ship	1,028
Carnival Legend	Carnival Cruise Lines	2002	Large Resort Ship	1,062
Carnival Liberty	Carnival Cruise Lines	2005	Large Resort Ship	1,487
Carnival Miracle	Carnival Cruise Lines	2004	Large Resort Ship	1,062
Carnival Paradise	Carnival Cruise Lines	1998	Large Resort Ship	1,026
Carnival Pride	Carnival Cruise Lines	2002	Large Resort Ship	1,062
Carnival Sensation	Carnival Cruise Lines	1993	Large Resort Ship	1,020
Carnival Spirit	Carnival Cruise Lines	2001	Large Resort Ship	1,062
Carnival Splendor	Carnival Cruise Lines	2008	Large Resort Ship	1,487
Carnival Triumph	Carnival Cruise Lines	1999	Large Resort Ship	1,379
Carnival Valor	Carnival Cruise Lines	2004	Large Resort Ship	1,487
Carnival Victory	Carnival Cruise Lines	2000	Large Resort Ship	1,379
Celebrity Century	Celebrity Cruises	1995	Large Resort Ship	875
Celebrity Constellation	Celebrity Cruises	2002	Large Resort Ship	975
Celebrity Equinox	Celebrity Cruises	2009	Large Resort Ship	1,425
Celebrity Galaxy	Celebrity Cruises	1996	Large Resort Ship	935
Celebrity Infinity	Celebrity Cruises	2001	Large Resort Ship	975
Celebrity Mercury	Celebrity Cruises	1997	Large Resort Ship	935
Celebrity Millennium	Celebrity Cruises	2000	Large Resort Ship	975
Celebrity Solstice	Celebrity Cruises	2008	Large Resort Ship	1,425
Celebrity Summit	Celebrity Cruises	2001	Large Resort Ship	975
Celebrity Xpedition	Celebrity Cruises	2001	Boutique	47
Clelia II	Travel Dynamics International	1991	Boutique	40
Clipper Adventurer	Quark Expeditions	1976	Boutique	61
Clipper Odyssey	Zegrahm Expeditions	1989	Boutique	64
Club Med 2	Club Med	1992	Small	197
C. Columbus	Hapag-Lloyd Cruises	1997	Small	205
CoCo Explorer	CoCo Explorer Cruises	1967	Boutique	56

Suitable for	Class	Rating	♿
Mature Couples/Singles	Standard	★★	D
Mature Couples/Singles	Standard	★★★+	C
Mature Couples/Singles	Standard	★★★+	C
Tough Adventurous Types	Premium	★★★+	D
Families with Children	Standard	★★★★	B
Explorers	Standard	★	D
Families with Children	Standard	★★★★	B
Families with Children	Standard	★★★+	B
Families with Children	Standard	★★★+	B
Families with Children	Standard	NYR	B
Lively Party Types	Standard	★★★	C
Lively Party Types	Standard	★★★	C
Lively Party Types	Standard	★★★	C
Lively Party Types	Standard	★★★	C
Families with Children	Standard	★★★+	B
Families with Children	Standard	★★★+	B
Lively Party Types	Standard	★★★	C
Lively Party Types	Standard	★★★	C
Families with Children	Standard	★★★+	B
Families with Children	Standard	★★★+	B
Families with Children	Standard	★★★+	B
Lively Party Types	Standard	★★★	C
Families with Children	Standard	★★★+	B
Lively Party Types	Standard	★★★	C
Families with Children	Standard	★★★+	B
Families with Children	Standard	★★★+	B
Families with Children	Standard	★★★+	B
Families with Children	Standard	★★★+	B
Families with Children	Standard	★★★+	B
Families with Children	Premium	★★★★+	B
Families with Children	Premium	★★★★+	A
Families with Children	Standard	NYR	A
Families with Children	Premium	★★★★	B
Families with Children	Premium	★★★★+	A
Families with Children	Premium	★★★★	B
Families with Children	Premium	★★★★+	A
Families with Children	Premium	NYR	A
Families with Children	Premium	★★★★+	A
Explorers	Premium	★★★★	D
Mature Couples/Singles	Standard	★★★★	D
Mature Couples/Singles	Standard	★★+	D
Explorers	Standard	★★★+	C
Relax/De-Stress Types	Standard	★★★+	D
Mature Couples/Singles	Standard	★★★+	C
Mature Couples/Singles	Standard	★	D

Standard Group: page 241 ▷

Ship	Cruise Line	Built	Type of ship	Cabins
Contessa	Majestic America Line	1986	Boutique	25
Coral	Louis Hellenic Cruises	1971	Mid-Size	378
Coral Princess	Coral Princess Cruises	1988	Boutique	27
Coral Princess	Princess Cruises	2002	Large Resort Ship	987
Corinthian	Ecoventura/Galapagos Network	1967	Boutique	45
Corinthian II	Travel Dynamics International	1991	Boutique	61
Costa Allegra	Costa Cruises	1992	Mid-Size	410
Costa Atlantica	Costa Cruises	2000	Large Resort Ship	1,056
Costa Classica	Costa Cruises	1992	Large Resort Ship	654
Costa Concordia	Costa Cruises	2006	Large Resort Ship	1,500
Costa Europa	Costa Cruises	1986	Large Resort Ship	753
Costa Fortuna	Costa Cruises	2003	Large Resort Ship	1,358
Costa Luminosa	Costa Cruises	2009	Large Resort Ship	1,130
Costa Magica	Costa Cruises	2004	Large Resort Ship	1,359
Costa Marina	Costa Cruises	1990	Mid-Size	386
Costa Mediterranea	Costa Cruises	2003	Large Resort Ship	1,056
Costa Pacifica	Costa Cruises	2009	Large Resort Ship	1,502
Costa Romantica	Costa Cruises	1993	Large Resort Ship	678
Costa Serena	Costa Cruises	2007	Large Resort Ship	1,500
Costa Victoria	Costa Cruises	1996	Large Resort Ship	964
Cristal	Louis Hellenic Cruises	1980	Mid-Size	483
Crown Princess	Princess Cruises	2006	Large Resort Ship	1,557
Crystal Serenity	Crystal Cruises	2003	Mid-Size	550
Crystal Symphony	Crystal Cruises	1995	Mid-Size	480
Dalmacia	Croatia Cruise Lines	1965	Small	156
Daphne	Travel Dynamics International	2009	Boutique	30
Dawn Princess	Princess Cruises	1997	Large Resort Ship	975
Delphin	Hansa Touristik	1975	Small	233
Delphin Voyager	Delphin Seereisen	1990	Mid-Size	325
Deutschland	Peter Deilmann Ocean Cruises	1998	Mid-Size	294
Diamond Princess	Princess Cruises	2004	Large	1,337
Discovery	Panama Marine Adventures	2004	Boutique	12
Discovery	Voyages of Discovery	1972	Mid-Size	355
Disko II	Arctic Umiaq Line	1992	Boutique	26
Disney Magic	Disney Cruise Line	1998	Large Resort Ship	875
Disney Wonder	Disney Cruise Line	1999	Large Resort Ship	875
easyCruise Life	easyCruise.com	1981	Boutique	225
Emerald Princess	Princess Cruises	2007	Large Resort Ship	1,557
Emeraude	Emeraude Classic Cruises	2003	Boutique	38
Empress	Pullmantur Cruises	1990	Large Resort Ship	800
Enchantment of the Seas	Royal Caribbean International	1997	Large Resort Ship	1,126
Eurodam	Holland America Line	2008	Large Resort Ship	958
Europa	Hapag-Lloyd Cruises	1999	Small	204
Evolution	various tour operators	2004	Boutique	17
Explorer of the Seas	Royal Caribbean International	2000	Large Resort Ship	1,557

Suitable for	Class	Rating	♿
Mature Couples/Singles	Standard	★	D
Mature Couples/Singles	Standard	★★	D
Mature Couples/Singles	Standard	★	D
Mature Couples/Singles	Standard	★★★★	B
Explorers	Standard	★	D
Explorers	Premium	★★★★	D
Mature Couples/Singles	Standard	★★+	D
Families with Children	Standard	★★★★	B
Mature Couples/Singles	Standard	★★★	B
Families with Children	Standard	★★★★	B
Mature Couples/Singles	Standard	★★★	C
Families with Children	Standard	★★★★	B
Families with Children	Standard	NYR	B
Families with Children	Standard	★★★★	B
Mature Couples/Singles	Standard	★★+	D
Families with Children	Standard	★★★★	B
Families with Children	Standard	NYR	B
Mature Couples/Singles	Standard	★★★	B
Families with Children	Standard	★★★★	B
Families with Children	Standard	★★★★+	B
Mature Couples/Singles	Standard	★★★	D
Families with Children	Standard	★★★★	A
Mature Couples/Singles	Premium	★★★★★	A
Mature Couples/Singles	Premium	★★★★★	A
Mature Couples/Singles	Standard	★	D
Mature Couples/Singles	Standard	NYR	D
Families with Children	Standard	★★★★	B
Mature Couples/Singles	Standard	★★+	D
Mature Couples/Singles	Standard	★★★	C
Mature Couples/Singles	Premium	★★★★★+	C
Families with Children	Standard	★★★★	B
Explorers	Standard	★★★	D
Explorers	Standard	★★★	C
Tough Adventurous Types	Standard	★	D
Families with Children	Standard	★★★★	B
Families with Children	Standard	★★★★	B
Lively Young Adults	Standard	★★	D
Families with Children	Standard	★★★★	B
Mature Couples/Singles	Standard	★	D
Families with Children	Standard	★★★	C
Families with Children	Standard	★★★★	B
Families with Children	Premium	★★★★	B
Mature Couples/Singles	Luxury	★★★★★+	A
Mature Couples/Singles	Standard	★	D
Families with Children	Standard	★★★★	A

CRUISE LINES BY MARKET CLASSIFICATION

◁ continued from page 239

STANDARD

Abercrombie & Kent
AIDA Cruises
American Canadian Caribbean Line
American Cruise Lines
Canodros
Carnival Cruise Lines
Classic International Cruises
Clipper Cruise Line
Costa Cruises
Cruise West
Delphin Seereisen
Disney Cruise Line
easyCruise.com
Elegant Cruises & Tours
Fred Olsen Cruise Lines
Galapagos Cruises
Golden Star Cruises
Hansa Touristik
Hapag-Lloyd Cruises *
Hurtigruten
Iberocruceros
Imperial Majesty Cruise Line
Island Cruises
Kristina Cruises
Lindblad Expeditions
Louis Cruise Lines
Louis Hellenic Cruises
MSC Cruises
Mano Cruise
Metropolitan Touring
Mitsui OSK Passenger Line
Monarch Classic Cruises
NCL America
Noble Caledonia
Norwegian Cruise Line
P&O Cruises
P&O Cruises (Australia)
Page & Moy Cruises
Phoenix Reisen
Plantours & Partner
Princess Cruises
Pullmantur Cruises
Quark Expeditions
Royal Caribbean International
Skorpios Chile
Star Cruises
Star Clippers
Star Line Cruises
Thomson Cruises
Transocean Tours
Vision Cruises
Voyages of Discovery
Zegrahm Expeditions

Ship	Cruise Line	Built	Type of ship	Cabins
Fantasea Ammari	Fantasea Cruises		Boutique	32
Finnmarken	Hurtigruten	2002	Mid-Size	273
Fram	Hurtigruten	2007	Small	135
Freedom of the Seas	Royal Caribbean International	2006	Large Resort Ship	1,817
Fuji Maru	Mitsui OSK Passenger Line	1989	Small	164
Funchal	Classic International Cruises	1961	Small	222
Galapagos Explorer II	Canodros	1990	Boutique	53
Galapagos Legend	GlobalQuest	1963	Boutique	57
Golden Princess	Princess Cruises	2001	Large Resort Ship	1,300
Grand Celebration	Iberocruceros	1987	Mid-Size	743
Grand Mistral	Iberocruceros	1999	Mid-Size	598
Grand Princess	Princess Cruises	1998	Large Resort Ship	1,300
Grand Voyager	Iberocruceros	2000	Mid-Size	420
Grande Caribe	American Canadian Caribbean Line	1997	Boutique	50
Grande Mariner	American Canadian Caribbean Line	1998	Boutique	50
Grandeur of the Seas	Royal Caribbean International	1996	Large Resort Ship	975
Grigoriy Mikheev	Oceanwide Expeditions	1990	Boutique	22
Halcyon	various tour operators	1990	Boutique	24
Hanseatic	Hapag-Lloyd Cruises	1993	Boutique (Exp)	92
Haumana	Bora Bora Cruises	1997	Boutique	19
Hebridean Princess	Hebridean International Cruises	1964	Boutique	30
Hebridean Spirit	Hebridean International Cruises	1991	Boutique	49
Holiday	Carnival Cruise Lines	1985	Mid-Size	726
Independence	American Cruise Lines	2008	Boutique	102
Independence of the Seas	Royal Caribbean International	2008	Large Resort Ship	1,800
Insignia	Oceania Cruises	1998	Mid-Size	342
Isabela II	Metropolitan Touring	1989	Boutique	21
Island Escape	Island Cruises	1982	Large Resort Ship	757
Island Princess	Princess Cruises	2003	Large Resort Ship	987
Island Sky	Noble Caledonia	1991	Boutique	61
Island Star	Island Cruises	1990	Large Resort Ship	753
Ivory	Louis Cruise Lines	1957	Small	248
Jewel of the Seas	Royal Caribbean International	2004	Large Resort Ship	1,055
Kapitan Dranitsyn	various expedition cruise operators	1980	Boutique	53
Kapitan Khlebnikov	Murmansk Shipping/Quark Expedit.	1981	Boutique	54
Kong Harald	Hurtigruten	1993	Small	227
Kristina Brahe	Kristina Cruises	1943	Boutique	57
Kristina Regina	Kristina Cruises	1960	Boutique	119
Le Diamant	CIP Cruises	1986	Boutique	99
Le Levant	CIP Cruises	1999	Boutique	45
Le Ponant	CIP Cruises	1991	Boutique	32
Legend of the Seas	Royal Caribbean International	1995	Large Resort Ship	900
Liberty of the Seas	Royal Caribbean International	2007	Large Resort Ship	1,800
Lofoten	Hurtigruten	1964	Boutique	59
Lord of the Glens	Magna Carta Cruises	1985	Boutique	27

Suitable for	Class	Rating	&#9855;
Lively Young Adults	Standard	★★	D
Mature Couples/Singles	Standard	★★+	C
Explorers	Standard	★★★	C
Families with Children	Standard	★★★★	A
Mature Couples/Singles	Standard	★★★	D
Mature Couples/Singles	Standard	★★+	D
Explorers	Standard	★★★	D
Explorers	Standard	★	D
Families w/Children	Standard	★★★★	A
Lively Party Types	Standard	★★★	C
Families w/Children	Standard	★★★+	C
Families with Children	Standard	★★★★	A
Families with Children	Standard	★★★+	B
Mature Couples/Singles	Standard	★★	D
Mature Couples/Singles	Standard	★★	D
Mature Couples/Singles	Standard	★★★★	B
Tough Adventurous Types	Standard	★★	D
Mature Couples/Singles	Standard	★★	D
Explorers	Luxury	★★★★★	D
Mature Couples/Singles	Standard	★★	D
Mature Couples/Singles	Premium	★★★★+	D
Mature Couples/Singles	Luxury	★★★★+	D
Lively Party Types	Standard	★★★	D
Mature Couples/Singles	Standard	NYR	D
Families with Children	Standard	★★★★	B
Mature Couples/Singles	Premium	★★★★+	B
Mature Couples/Singles	Standard	★	D
Families with Children	Standard	★★★	D
Families with Children	Standard	★★★★	B
Mature Couples/Singles	Premium	★★★★	D
Families with Children	Standard	★★★+	B
Mature Couples/Singles	Standard	★★	D
Mature Couples/Singles	Standard	★★★★	B
Explorers	Standard	★★★	D
Explorers	Standard	★★★	D
Mature Couples/Singles	Standard	★★	C
Mature Couples/Singles	Standard	★	D
Mature Couples/Singles	Standard	★★+	D
Mature Couples/Singles	Premium	★★★+	D
Mature Couples/Singles	Premium	★★★★	D
Mature Couples/Singles	Premium	★★★+	D
Mature Couples/Singles	Standard	★★★★	A
Families with Children	Standard	★★★★	A
Mature Couples/Singles	Standard	★	D
Mature Couples/Singles	Premium	★★★	D

CRUISE LINE INTERNET ADDRESSES

Abercrombie & Kent
www.aandktours.com

African Safari Cruises
www.africansafariclub.com

AIDA Cruises
www.aida.de

American Canadian Caribbean Line
www.accl-smallships.com

American Cruise Lines
www.americancruiselines.com

American Safari Cruises
www.amsafari.com

Antarctic Shipping
www.antarctic.cl

CDF Croisières de France
www.cdfcroisieresdefrance.fr

Captain Cook Cruises
www.captcookcrus.com.au

Carnival Cruise Lines
www.carnival.com

Celebrity Cruises/ Azamara Cruises
www.celebrity-cruises.com

Classic International Cruises
www.cic-cruises.com

Coral Princess Cruises
www.cruisingaustralia.com

Costa Crociere (Costa Cruises)
www.costacruises.com

Club Med Cruises
www.clubmed.com

Costa Cruises
www.costacruises.com

Ship	Cruise Line	Built	Type of ship	Cabins
Lycianda	Blue Lagoon Cruises	1984	Boutique	21
Lyngen	Hurtigruten	2003	Mid-Size	303
Maasdam	Holland America Line	1993	Mid-Size	632
Majesty of the Seas	Royal Caribbean International	1992	Large Resort Ship	1,190
Marco Polo	Transocean Tours	1966	Mid-Size	425
Mare Australis	Cruceros Australis	2002	Boutique	63
Marina Svetaeva	Aurora Expeditions	1989	Boutique	45
Mariner of the Seas	Royal Caribbean International	2004	Large	1,557
MegaStar Aries	Star Cruises	1992	Boutique	33
MegaStar Taurus	Star Cruises	1992	Boutique	33
Minerva	Swan Hellenic Discovery Cruises	1996	Small	178
Monarch of the Seas	Royal Caribbean International	1991	Large Resort Ship	1,192
Monet	Elegant Cruises & Tours	1970	Boutique	35
MSC Armonia	MSC Cruises	2001	Large Resort Ship	783
MSC Fantasia	MSC Cruises	2008	Large Resort Ship	1,637
MSC Lirica	MSC Cruises	2003	Large Resort Ship	780
MSC Melody	MSC Cruises	1982	Mid-Size	549
MSC Musica	MSC Cruises	2006	Large Resort Ship	1,275
MSC Opera	MSC Cruises	2004	Large Resort Ship	878
MSC Orchestra	MSC Cruises	2007	Large Resort Ship	1,275
MSC Poesia	MSC Cruises	2008	Large Resort Ship	1,275
MSC Rhapsody	MSC Cruises	1977	Mid-Size	394
MSC Sinfonia	MSC Cruises	2002	Large Resort Ship	783
MSC Splendida	MSC Cruises	2009	Large Resort Ship	1,637
Mystique Princess	Blue Lagoon Cruises	1996	Boutique	36
Nanuya Princess	Blue Lagoon Cruises	1987	Boutique	25
National Geographic Endeavour	Lindblad Expeditions	1966	Boutique	62
National Geographic Explorer	Lindblad Expeditions	1982	Boutique	81
National Geographic Islander	Lindblad Expeditions	1995	Boutique	24
National Geographic Polaris	Lindblad Expeditions	1960	Boutique	41
Nautica	Oceania Cruises	1998	Mid-Size	342
Navigator of the Seas	Royal Caribbean International	2003	Large Resort Ship	1,557
New Flamenco	Vision Cruises	1972	Mid-Size	401
Nippon Maru	Mitsui OSK Passenger Line	1990	Small	204
Noordam	Holland America Line	2006	Large Resort Ship	959
Nordkapp	Hurtigruten	1996	Small	214
Nordlys	Hurtigruten	1994	Small	213
Nordnorge	Hurtigruten	1997	Small	168
Nordstjernen	Hurtigruten	1960	Boutique	75
Norwegian Dawn	Norwegian Cruise Line	2002	Large Resort Ship	1,122
Norwegian Dream	Norwegian Cruise Line	1992	Large Resort Ship	875
Norwegian Gem	Norwegian Cruise Line	2007	Large Resort Ship	1,197
Norwegian Jade	Norwegian Cruise Line	2006	Large Resort Ship	1,233
Norwegian Jewel	Norwegian Cruise Line	2005	Large Resort Ship	1,188

Suitable for	Class	Rating	♿
Mature Couples/Singles	Standard	★	D
Mature Couples/Singles	Standard	★★+	D
Mature Couples/Singles	Premium	★★★★	B
Families with Children	Standard	★★★	C
Explorers	Standard	★★★	C
Explorers	Standard	★★	D
Explorers	Standard	★★	D
Families with Children	Standard	★★★★	A
Private Charter	Premium	★★★★	D
Private Charter	Premium	★★★★	D
Mature Couples/Singles	Standard	★★★	C
Families with Children	Standard	★★★	C
Mature Couples/Singles	Standard	★★	D
Families with Children	Standard	★★★★	B
Families with Children	Standard	★★★★	A
Families with Children	Standard	★★★★	B
Mature Couples/Singles	Standard	★★★	C
Families with Children	Standard	★★★★	B
Families with Children	Standard	★★★★	B
Families with Children	Standard	★★★★	B
Families with Children	Standard	★★★★	B
Mature Couples/Singles	Standard	★★	D
Families with Children	Standard	★★★	B
Families with Children	Standard	NYR	B
Explorers	Standard	★★	D
Explorers	Standard	★★	D
Explorers	Standard	★★	D
Explorers	Standard	★★	D
Explorers	Standard	★★★	D
Explorers	Standard	★★	D
Mature Couples/Singles	Premium	★★★★+	B
Families with Children	Standard	★★★★	A
Lively Party Types	Standard	★★+	D
Mature Couples/Singles	Standard	★★★+	C
Mature Couples/Singles	Premium	★★★★	B
Mature Couples/Singles	Standard	★★+	C
Mature Couples/Singles	Standard	★★+	C
Mature Couples/Singles	Standard	★★+	C
Mature Couples/Singles	Standard	★	D
Families with Children	Standard	★★★★	A
Lively Party Types	Standard	★★★	C
Families with Children	Standard	★★★★	B
Families with Children	Standard	★★★★	B
Families with Children	Standard	★★★★	B

CRUISE LINE INTERNET ADDRESSES

Cruceros Australis
www.crucerosaustralis.com

Cruise West
www.cruisewest.com

Crystal Cruises
www.crystalcruises.com

Cunard Line
www.cunard.com

Delphin Seereisen
www:delphin-cruises.com

Disney Cruise Line
www.disneycruise.com

easyCruise.com
www.easycruise.com

Elegant Cruises &Tours
www.elegantcruises.com

Fred Olsen Cruise Lines
www.fredolsencruises.com

Galapagos Cruises
www.galapagos-inc.com

Hansa Touristik
www.hansatourstik.com

Hapag-Lloyd Cruises
www.hlkf.com

Hebridean International Cruises
www.hebdridean.co.uk

Holland America Line
www.hollandamerica.com

Hurtigruten
www.coastalvoyage.com

Iberocruceros
www.iberojet.es

Ship	Cruise Line	Built	Type of ship	Cabins
Norwegian Majesty	Norwegian Cruise Line	1992	Mid-Size	730
Norwegian Pearl	Norwegian Cruise Line	2006	Large Resort Ship	1,197
Norwegian Spirit	Norwegian Cruise Line	1998	Large Resort Ship	983
Norwegian Star	Norwegian Cruise Line	2001	Large Resort Ship	1,122
Norwegian Sun	Norwegian Cruise Line	2001	Large Resort Ship	1,001
Ocean Dream	Pullmantur Cruises	1982	Mid-Size	511
Ocean Majesty	Monarch Classic Cruises	1966	Mid-Size	273
Ocean Nova	Quark Expeditions	1992	Boutique (Exp)	45
Ocean Princess	Princess Cruises	1999	Mid-Size	344
Ocean Village	Ocean Village	1987	Large Resort Ship	812
Ocean Village Two	Ocean Village	1990	Large Resort Ship	832
Oceana	P&O Cruises	2000	Large Resort Ship	975
Oceanic	Pullmantur Cruises	1965	Mid-Size	562
Oceanic Discoverer	Coral Princess Cruises	2005	Boutique	38
Ocean Odyssey	Indian Ocean Cruises	1965	Small	122
Oosterdam	Holland America Line	2003	Large Resort Ship	924
Oriana	P&O Cruises	1995	Large Resort Ship	914
Orient Queen	Louis Cruise Lines	1968	Mid-Size	414
Orion	Orion Expedition Cruises	2003	Boutique (Exp)	53
Orlova	Russian Owners/Quark Expeditions	1976	Boutique (Exp)	61
Pacific	Pullmantur Cruises	1972	Mid-Size	320
Pacific Dawn	P&O Cruises (Australia)	1991	Large Resort Ship	624
Pacific Explorer	Cruise West	1970	Boutique	50
Pacific Princess	Princess Cruises	1999	Mid-Size	344
Pacific Sun	P&O Cruises (Australia)	1986	Large Resort Ship	743
Pacific Venus	Venus Cruise	1998	Mid-Size	266
Paul Gauguin	Regent Seven Seas Cruises	1998	Small	165
Pearl	Pearl Seas Cruises	2008	Small	108
Polar Pioneer	Aurora Expeditions	1985	Boutique	26
Polar Star	Hurtigruten	1969	Boutique	45
Polarlys	Hurtigruten	1996	Small	220
Pride of America	NCL America	2005	Large Resort Ship	1,072
Prince Albert II	Silversea Cruises	1989	Boutique	66
Princesa Marissa	Louis Cruise Lines	1966	Mid-Size	314
Princess Danae	Classic International Cruises	1955	Mid-Size	283
Princess Daphne	Classic International Cruises	1955	Mid-Size	280
Prinsendam	Holland America Line	1998	Mid-Size	396
Professor Molchanov	Oceanwide Expeditions	1983	Boutique	29
Professor Multanovskiy	Quark Expeditions	1983	Boutique	29
Queen Mary 2	Cunard Line	2004	Large Resort Ship	1,310
Queen Victoria	Cunard Line	2007	Large Resort Ship	1,007
Radiance of the Seas	Royal Caribbean International	2001	Large Resort Ship	1,056
Regal Empress	Imperial Majesty Cruise Lines	1953	Mid-Size	457
Regatta	Oceania Cruises	1998	Mid-Size	342

Suitable for	Class	Rating	♿
Lively Party Types	Standard	★★★	D
Families with Children	Standard	★★★★	B
Families with Children	Standard	★★★★	B
Families with Children	Standard	★★★★	A
Families with Children	Standard	★★★★	B
Families with Children	Standard	★★+	D
Mature Couples/Singles	Standard	★★+	D
Tough Adventurous Types	Standard	★	D
Mature Couples/Singles	Standard	★★★★	B
Lively Party Types	Standard	★★★+	B
Lively Party Types	Standard	★★★+	B
Families with Children	Standard	★★★★	B
Families with Children	Standard	★★+	C
Mature Couples/Singles	Standard	★★★	D
Mature Couples/Singles	Standard	★★	D
Families with Children	Premium	★★★★	B
Families with Children	Standard	★★★★	B
Mature Couples/Singles	Standard	★★★	D
Explorers	Premium	★★★★+	D
Tough Adventurous Types	Standard	★★	D
Lively Young Adults	Standard	★★+	C
Families with Children	Standard	★★★	C
Mature Couples/Singles	Standard	★	D
Mature Couples/Singles	Standard	★★★★	B
Families with Children	Standard	★★★	C
Mature Couples/Singles	Standard	★★★+	C
Mature Couples/Singles	Premium	★★★★	C
Mature Couples/Singles	Standard	NYR	C
Tough Adventure Types	Standard	★★	D
Tough Adventure Types	Standard	★★	D
Mature Couples/Singles	Standard	★★	C
Families with Children	Standard	★★★+	B
Explorers	Premium	NYR	D
Mature Couples/Singles	Standard	★★	D
Mature Couples/Singles	Standard	★★★	D
Mature Couples/Singles	Standard	★★+	D
Mature Couples/Singles	Premium	★★★★+	A
Explorers	Standard	★★	D
Explorers	Standard	★★	D
Families with Children	Premium	★★★★	A
Families with Children	Premium	★★★★+ to ★★★★	B
Families with Children	Standard	★★★★	B
Lively Young Adults	Standard	★+	D
Mature Couples/Singles	Premium	★★★★+	B

Ship	Cruise Line	Built	Type of ship	Cabins
Reef Escape	Captain Cook Cruises	1987	Boutique	60
Rhapsody of the Seas	Royal Caribbean International	1997	Large Resort Ship	1,000
Richard With	Hurtigruten	1993	Small	214
Rotterdam	Holland America Line	1997	Large Resort Ship	660
Royal Clipper	Star Clippers	2000	Sail-Cruise Ship	114
Royal Iris	Mano Cruise	1971	Mid-Size	148
Royal Princess	Princess Cruises	2001	Mid-Size	355
Royal Star	African Safari Cruises	1956	Small	111
Ryndam	Holland America Line	1994	Large Resort Ship	633
Safari Explorer	American Safari Cruises	1988	Boutique	18
Safari Quest	American Safari Cruises	1992	Boutique	11
Saga Rose	Saga Cruises	1965	Mid-Size	322
Saga Ruby	Saga Cruises	1973	Mid-Size	376
Santa Cruz	Metropolitan Touring	1979	Boutique	43
Sapphire	Louis Cruise Lines	1967	Mid-Size	288
Sapphire Princess	Princess Cruises	2004	Large Resort Ship	1,337
Sea Bird	Lindblad Expeditions	1981	Boutique	36
Sea Cloud	Sea Cloud Cruises	1931	Sail-Cruise Ship	34
Sea Cloud II	Sea Cloud Cruises	2001	Sail-Cruise Ship	48
Sea Lion	Lindblad Expeditions	1982	Boutique	37
Sea Princess	Princess Cruises	1998	Large Resort Ship	1,008
Sea Voyager	Lindblad Expeditions	1982	Boutique	33
Seabourn Legend	Seabourn Cruise Line	1992	Boutique	106
Seabourn Odyssey	Seabourn Cruise Line	2009	Boutique	275
Seabourn Pride	Seabourn Cruise Line	1988	Boutique	106
Seabourn Spirit	Seabourn Cruise Line	1989	Boutique	106
SeaDream I	SeaDream Yacht Club	1984	Boutique	54
SeaDream II	SeaDream Yacht Club	1985	Boutique	54
Serenade	Louis Cruise Lines	1957	Mid-Size	300
Serenade of the Seas	Royal Caribbean International	2003	Large Resort Ship	1,050
Seven Seas Mariner	Regent Seven Seas Cruises	2001	Mid-Size	354
Seven Seas Navigator	Regent Seven Seas Cruises	1999	Small	245
Seven Seas Voyager	Regent Seven Seas Cruises	2003	Small	354
Silver Cloud	Silversea Cruises	1994	Small	148
Silver Shadow	Silversea Cruises	2000	Small	194
Silver Spirit	Silversea Cruises	2010	Small	225
Silver Whisper	Silversea Cruises	2001	Small	194
Silver Wind	Silversea Cruises	1995	Small	148
Sky Wonder	Pullmantur Cruises	1984	Large	600
Skorpios II	Skorpios Chile	1978	Boutique	55
Skorpios III	Skorpios Chile	1995	Boutique	48
Sovereign	Pullmantur Cruises	1988	Large Resort Ship	1,153
Spirit of '98	Cruise West	1984	Boutique	49
Spirit of Adventure	Saga Cruises	1980	Small	206
Spirit of Alaska	Cruise West	1980	Boutique	39
Spirit of Columbia	Cruise West	1979	Boutique	39

Suitable for	Class	Rating	♿
Mature Couples/Singles	Standard	★★	D
Families with Children	Standard	★★★★	B
Mature Couples/Singles	Standard	★★+	C
Mature Couples/Singles	Premium	★★★★	A
Relax/De-Stress Types	Standard	★★★★	D
Mature Couples/Singles	Standard	★★	D
Mature Couples/Singles	Standard	★★★★	B
Mature Couples/Singles	Standard	★★	D
Mature Couples/Singles	Premium	★★★	C
Mature Couples/Singles	Standard	★★★+	D
Mature Couples/Singles	Standard	★★★+	D
Child-Free Over-50s	Premium	★★★★	C
Child-Free Over-50s	Premium	★★★★	C
Mature Couples/Singles	Standard	★	D
Mature Couples/Singles	Standard	★★+	D
Families with Children	Standard	★★★★	B
Explorers	Standard	★+	D
Relax/De-Stress Types	Premium	★★★★★	D
Relax/De-Stress Types	Premium	★★★★★	D
Explorers	Standard	★+	D
Mature Couples/Singles	Standard	★★★★	B
Mature Couples/Singles	Standard	★	D
Mature Couples/Singles	Luxury	★★★★★	D
Mature Couples/Singles	Luxury	NYR	D
Mature Couples/Singles	Luxury	★★★★★	D
Mature Couples/Singles	Luxury	★★★★★	D
Mature Couples/Singles	Luxury	★★★★★	D
Mature Couples/Singles	Luxury	★★★★★	D
Mature Couples/Singles	Standard	★	D
Families with Children	Standard	★★★★	A
Mature Couples/Singles	Premium	★★★★+	A
Mature Couples/Singles	Luxury	★★★★+	B
Mature Couples/Singles	Luxury	★★★★+	A
Mature Couples/Singles	Luxury	★★★★+	C
Mature Couples/Singles	Luxury	★★★★★	B
Mature Couples/Singles	Luxury	NYR	
Mature Couples/Singles	Luxury	★★★★★	B
Mature Couples/Singles	Luxury	★★★★+	C
Families with Children	Standard	★★★	C
Explorers	Standard	★	D
Explorers	Standard	★★	D
Families with Children	Standard	★★★	C
Mature Couples/Singles	Standard	★★	D
Child-Free Over-50s	Premium	★★★	D
Mature Couples/Singles	Standard	★★	D
Mature Couples/Singles	Standard	★★	D

CRUISE LINE INTERNET ADDRESSES

Orion Expedition Cruises
www.orioncruises.com

P&O Cruises
www.pocruises.com

P&O Cruises (Australia)
www.pocruises.com.au

Pearl Seas Cruises
www.pearlseascruises.com

Peter Deilmann Cruises
www.deilmann-cruises.com

Phoenix Reisen
www.phoenixreisen.com

Plantours & Partner
www.plantours-partner.de

Ponant Cruises
www.ponant.com

Princess Cruises
www.princesscruises.com

Quark Expeditions
www.quark-expeditions.com

Regent Seven Seas Cruises
www.rssc.com

Royal Caribbean International
www.royalcaribbean.com

Saga Cruises
www.saga.co.uk

Sea Cloud Cruises
www.seacloud.com

Seabourn Cruise Line
www.seabourn.com

SeaDream Yacht Club
www.seadreamyachtclub.com

Ship	Cruise Line	Built	Type of ship	Cabins
Spirit of Discovery	Cruise West	1982	Boutique	43
Spirit of Endeavour	Cruise West	1980	Boutique	39
Spirit of Enderby	Heritage Expeditions	1984	Boutique (Exp)	22
Spirit of Glacier Bay	Cruise West	1984	Boutique	51
Spirit of Oceanus	Cruise West	1991	Boutique	57
Spirit of Yorktown	Clipper Cruise Line	1988	Boutique	69
Splendour of the Seas	Royal Caribbean International	1996	Large Resort Ship	902
Star Clipper	Star Clippers	1992	Boutique	85
Star Flyer	Star Clippers	1991	Boutique	85
Star Pisces	Star Cruises	1990	Large Resort Ship	776
Star Princess	Princess Cruises	2002	Large Resort Ship	1,301
Statendam	Holland America Line	1993	Large Resort Ship	633
Sun Princess	Princess Cruises	1995	Large Resort Ship	975
SuperStar Aquarius	Star Cruises	1993	Large Resort Ship	765
SuperStar Libra	Star Cruises	1988	Large Resort Ship	755
SuperStar Virgo	Star Cruises	1999	Large Resort Ship	987
The Calypso	Louis Cruise Lines	1968	Small	243
The Emerald	Louis Cruise Lines	1958	Mid-Size	500
The Iris	Mano Cruise	1982	Small	231
Thomson Celebration	Thomson Cruises	1984	Large Resort Ship	627
Thomson Destiny	Thomson Cruises	1982	Large Resort Ship	725
Thomson Spirit	Thomson Cruises	1983	Large Resort Ship	627
Tia Moana	Bora Bora Cruises	2003	Boutique	37
Tu Moana	Bora Bora Cruises	2003	Boutique	37
Trollfjord	Hurtigruten	2002	Boutique	303
Tropic Sun	Aquanaut Cruise Line	1967	Boutique	24
True North	North Star Cruises	2005	Boutique	18
Van Gogh	Van Gogh Cruises	1975	Mid-Size	253
Veendam	Holland America Line	1996	Large Resort Ship	633
Ventura	P&O Cruises	2008	Large Resort Ship	1,546
Vesteralen	Hurtigruten	1983	Small	147
Via Australis	Cruceros Australis	2005	Boutique	64
Vision Athena	Vision Cruises	1948	Mid-Size	278
Vision of the Seas	Royal Caribbean International	1998	Large Resort Ship	1,000
Vistamar	Plantours & Partner	1989	Mid-Size	152
Volendam	Holland America Line	1999	Large Resort Ship	720
Voyager of the Seas	Royal Caribbean International	1999	Large Resort Ship	1,557
Westerdam	Holland America Line	2004	Large Resort Ship	924
Wind Spirit	Windstar Cruises	1988	Sail-Cruise Ship	74
Wind Star	Windstar Cruises	1986	Sail-Cruise Ship	74
Wind Surf	Windstar Cruises	1990	Sail-Cruise Ship	156
Yamal	Quark Expeditions	1992	Boutique (Exp)	56
Zaandam	Holland America Line	2000	Mid-Size	720
Zenith	Pullmantur Cruises	1992	Mid-Size	720
Zuiderdam	Holland America Line	2002	Large Resort Ship	924

Suitable for	Class	Rating	♿
Mature Couples/Singles	Standard	★★	D
Mature Couples/Singles	Standard	★★	D
Tough Adventurous Types	Standard	★★	D
Mature Couples/Singles	Standard	★★	D
Mature Couples/Singles	Standard	★★★	D
Mature Couples/Singles	Standard	★★	D
Mature Couples/Singles	Standard	★★★★	B
Relax/De-Stress Types	Standard	★★★★	D
Relax/De-Stress Types	Standard	★★★★	D
Families with Children	Standard	★★★	D
Families with Children	Standard	★★★★	A
Mature Couples/Singles	Premium	★★★★	C
Families with Children	Standard	★★★★	B
Families with Children	Standard	★★★+	C
Families with Children	Standard	★★★+	C
Families with Children	Standard	★★★★	B
Child-Free Over-50s	Standard	★★+	D
Mature Couples/Singles	Standard	★★+	D
Mature Couples/Singles	Standard	★★	D
Families with Children	Standard	★★★+	C
Families with Children	Standard	★★★+	C
Families with Children	Standard	★★★+	C
Mature Couples/Singles	Standard	★★★	D
Mature Couples/Singles	Standard	★★★	D
Mature Couples/Singles	Standard	★★+	C
Mature Couples/Singles	Standard	★	D
Mature Couples/Singles	Standard	★★★★	D
Child-Free Over-50s	Standard	★★+	D
Mature Couples/Singles	Premium	★★★★	C
Families with Children	Standard	★★★★	B
Mature Couples/Singles	Standard	★	D
Mature Couples/Singles	Standard	★★★	D
Mature Couples/Singles	Standard	★★★	D
Families with Children	Standard	★★★★	B
Mature Couples/Singles	Standard	★★+	D
Mature Couples/Singles	Premium	★★★★	B
Families with Children	Standard	★★★★	A
Families with Children	Premium	★★★★	B
Relax/De-Stress Types	Premium	★★★+	D
Relax/De-Stress Types	Premium	★★★+	D
Relax/De-Stress Types	Premium	★★★★	D
Tough Adventurous Types	Standard	★★★	D
Families with Children	Premium	★★★★	B
Families with Children	Standard	★★★+	B
Families with Children	Premium	★★★★	B

ART & PHOTO CREDITS

INDEX